You may remember Steve Smith from my book *The Psychopath Test*. He was the young man who ended up at the Oak Ridge mental hospital—an unwilling participant in their radical experiments. They were trying to cure psychopathy by giving psychopaths massive amounts of LSD and making them strip naked and suck liquid food through straws that protruded from the walls.

It proved a bad idea. It just made them worse.

Steve just sent me a part of a memoir he's writing about his time there. I know he was there. I met him through a lawyer. He was part of a class action suit against the hospital. Obviously, I can't verify his extraordinary details below. But I know he was there.

—Jon Ronson, author of
The Men Who Stare at Goats
and *The Psychopath Test*

THE PSYCHOPATH MACHINE
A STORY OF RESISTANCE AND SURVIVAL

STEVE SMITH

◆ FriesenPress

Suite 300 - 990 Fort St
Victoria, BC, V8V 3K2
Canada

www.friesenpress.com

Copyright © 2016 by Steve Smith
First Edition — 2016

All rights reserved.

Concrete image copyright © Mayang Murni Adnin, 2001-2012

No part of this publication may be reproduced in any form, or by any means, electronic or mechanical, including photocopying, recording, or any information browsing, storage, or retrieval system, without permission in writing from FriesenPress.

ISBN
978-1-4602-8783-5 (Hardcover)
978-1-4602-8784-2 (Paperback)
978-1-4602-8785-9 (eBook)

1. BIOGRAPHY & AUTOBIOGRAPHY, PERSONAL MEMOIRS

Distributed to the trade by The Ingram Book Company

1

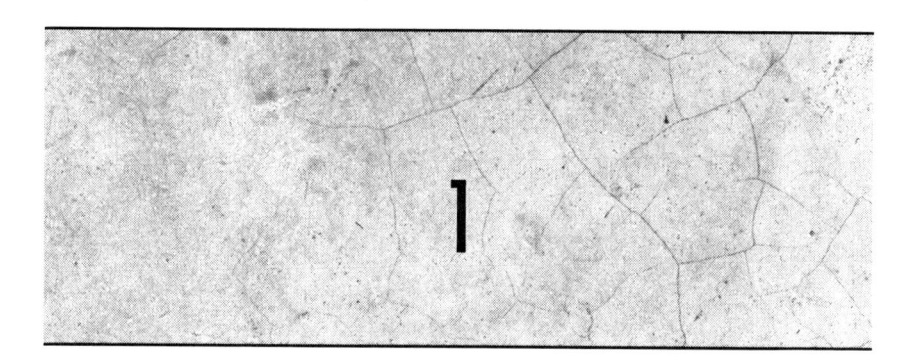

I MET PETER WOODCOCK IN 1968 WHEN I WAS EIGHTEEN YEARS OLD. HE WAS THE ONE WHO INTRODUCED me to "the Brotherhood." Peter arrived at Oak Ridge a decade before me. He knew nothing about the outside world, but he had heard about hippies. I was a hippie, so he wanted to be my friend.

At first, I didn't know why he was inside. He acted all "love and peace and flowers." Later, he told me he had murdered three children. I was surprised to hear that. He didn't look dangerous. He was a small, innocent-looking guy. No one would ever be afraid of him. If you lined up a hundred people, he would be the last person you would figure to be a child sex murderer. Already traumatized by what had happened to me, I just accepted him as part of my new existence.

When we weren't locked in our cells, Peter and I were together. He followed me around asking questions. He started combing his hair like me, walking like me, and trying to imitate the way I talked. We even tattooed ourselves with the same mark using a homemade rig and cigarette ashes. I have had it covered over, but it's still there.

The doctors and guards noticed our relationship and saw it as an opportunity for drug experiments. The experiments involved naked sessions in a padded room with no windows and liquid food sucked through straws in the wall. This went on for many days. When patients became so agitated they tried to kill each other, they were restrained with straps made of seatbelts.

I got to know Peter quite well during that time. Peter told me the details of the murders he committed. The gruesome images are still burned into my brain, although I have never repeated the details to anyone.

Before I go any further, I need to tell you how I came to be in that place. Unlike Peter, I was neither a killer nor rapist. I never hurt anyone in my life, but here is what happened a month earlier.

MY PARENTS WERE DIVORCED WHEN I was ten. My mother ran off with a tough, good-looking bartender named Bill Flowers. My brother Garry and I lived with my father in Sudbury, Ontario, but my father's life was overcome quickly by alcohol and self-destruction. Often, my brother and I were left to fend for ourselves in a house that was neglected and without food. My father's decimation took about a year. After that, we were sent to live with my mother and Bill.

We were all victims of Bill's drunken rages, enduring years of physical and emotional abuse. He committed suicide in 1987. Looking back, I think Bill was the first psychopath I ever met.

My mother lived out the declining years of her life alone with her dogs and cats. I don't blame her for anything. She was a simple woman ruled by her beauty.

In the winter of 1968, I left high school. No one seemed bothered by it. My auto mechanics teacher suspended me because he didn't like my Beatles haircut. I never went back.

An adolescent urge to wander set me on the road to the west coast. I was learning to drive, and getting a driver's license was the most important thing in my life. Sometimes I would swipe my mother's car keys and drive around the back streets in my neighborhood.

After a few brushes with the Sault Ste. Marie police and a system of justice that dealt heavy-handedly with the local counterculture, my friend Ben and I hit the road in the dead of winter—with no funds and no plans.

Our first hitch took us to Wawa, Ontario. We spent the night in the basement of a church.

The next morning was freezing cold, and hitching a ride was pure punishment, but we hitched on to White River, the "coldest spot in Canada." From there, our choices were to walk or freeze. We reached Marathon sometime in the night, desperately cold. Everything in town was closed. There was no point looking for an open restaurant. We didn't have enough money between us for a cup of coffee.

Ben and I found a small used car lot on the outskirts of town and stole a car. We arrived at the next town just before dawn and abandoned the car at a service station. As we were climbing out, the police pulled in behind us. We were caught red-handed. If we had arrived five minutes earlier or later, the course of my life would have been entirely different.

I was a child of the times, so in my shirt pocket were two hits of LSD I'd planned on taking when we reached Vancouver. The tabs were about the size of a match head. The arrest ended our trip to Vancouver, so I swallowed the tablets, and thus began my trip into hell, which was to last eight months and haunt me the rest of my life.

2

MY RECOLLECTION OF THE NEXT TWENTY-FOUR HOURS IS FUZZY, BUT SOME THINGS ARE UNFORGETTABLE.

I was placed in a black steel cell covered with lurid graffiti, handcuffed, and forced to stand in front of a doctor. The floor rolled like a wave. I told the doctor I took acid. Did he think I meant battery acid?

Before I knew what was happening, I was in a hospital emergency room where large men held me down and struggled to insert a plastic tube into my nose. I struggled and fought back.

Someone held a glass of what looked like red wine to my lips. I drank it, and within seconds, I was throwing up. I was terribly sick and more frightened than I had ever been in my life.

The next few hours are blank.

I remember standing in a courtroom full of skeletons in black robes. The judge took one glance at me, and I was bundled off to thirty days of observation at the local psychiatric hospital.

On the first day, I was confined to bed with little or no contact with anyone. The next week was uneventful. I was interviewed a few times, but I don't remember if I told anyone about the LSD. I had the impression they thought I was either faking or on a bad drug trip.

Within a few days, they returned my clothes and permitted me to wander about the hospital. I was not locked in, and I suppose I could have walked away any time.

I met a girl from another ward, and she invited me to a dance that evening. As I was leaving my ward for the rendezvous, an attendant stopped me and objected to the way I was dressed. He was quite hostile. He pushed me against the wall and pawed at my jeans, blustering something about hippies and proper dress. Then I made another big mistake.

I fought back.

In an instant, he dragged me to the floor. Reinforcements came running. Before I knew it, my pants were around my ankles, and they injected me with something painful. Then they dragged me down the hall, tossed me into an empty room, and me locked inside.

I was furious. The girl was waiting for me, and there I was, naked and locked in a little room. I pounded on the door and screamed until my lungs ached. My clinical record describes my behavior like this: "Smith tends to become resentful, hostile and uncooperative when he is not able to have his own way."

I didn't realize how dangerous an outburst of defiance could be. Never get mad in a madhouse.

The next day, I was informed I was to be sent to the Penetanguishene hospital for the criminally insane, a.k.a. Oak Ridge. I have no words to express the fear that swept over me. Oak Ridge was notorious. The place was the end of the line. You never got out of Oak Ridge.

I was in big trouble, but I was not insane!

The next day, I was dragged onto a train in handcuffs by two burly guards who made it clear that they would take no nonsense from me. They showed me a Billy club and a large syringe. We traveled in a private berth. Neither of my traveling companions shifted their gaze from me throughout the trip.

When we reached Midland, Ontario, a car was waiting for us. A short drive later, I was at the front gate of Oak Ridge. It didn't look anything like a hospital. It was a prison. Two or three layers of bars on every window. When the iron gate clanged shut behind me, I had never felt more alone and helpless. Little did I realize I would not see the outside world again for eight months.

I was struck by the size of the guards. I had never seen such a collection of oversized homo-simians. None of them said a word to me. They treated me like a slab of meat. Stripped naked, probed for concealed weapons or contraband, my head was shaved, and I was sprayed with a disinfectant that burned. Then they gave me a heavy canvas gown and locked me in a cement cell with nothing but a blanket. The door slammed shut.

No one knew I was there. I had disappeared from the face of the earth.

3

I DON'T KNOW HOW MANY DAYS PASSED. I THOUGHT I WOULD BE THERE FOR THE REST OF MY LIFE. IF there had been anything in that cell that I could have used to kill myself, I believe I would have done so.

The light was on twenty-four hours a day. I ate from paper plates. I was provided no utensils, not even a plastic spoon. My only escape was sleep. I forced myself to do that as much it as possible.

Men strolled past my cell dressed in street clothes. I thought they were doctors or hospital staff. I tried to talk to them and find out what the hell was going to happen to me. No one even looked my way. I don't know how many days that went on.

One day, the door slid open, and Dr. Elliot T. Barker entered. He was charming, soothing, smiling. He put his arm around my shoulder and addressed me by my first name. I fell for it, not knowing what this man had in store for me, the torture and degradation I was about to suffer.

"Do you know why you are here?" he asked.

"No, I do not."

He grinned and tightened his arm around my shoulder. "Why do you think you're here?"

"I don't know."

"Well, I'll tell you. You are a very sick boy. I think you are a very slick psychopath, and I want you to know there are people just like you in here who have been locked up for more than twenty years. We have a program that can help you get over your illness. If you volunteer for this treatment, it will improve your chances of release, but you must cooperate with the program."

He went on to tell me that being a psychopath was essentially an inability to communicate with others and that beneath the reinforced surface was a deep-rooted psychosis. What he proposed to do, through the use of LSD, Methedrine, and other drugs, was to bring out this "hidden psychosis" and treat it. As he put it, "To cure you, even if I must first drive you mad."

I was locked in a cold, brightly-lit cell clutching a blanket. Anything would be better than that. I agreed to cooperate.

They released me from my cell, allowed me to shower, and then gave me khaki pants and a shirt and escorted me to the "sun room." It was an unfurnished vestibule occupied by six or seven men (boys) about the same age as me. They had all been there for a week or more. Dr. Barker informed me he was locking me in with them without prior conditioning to "shake things up a bit."

I watched them for a few days without saying much. Nothing they did was rational. They seemed to be playing some kind of delusional game, talking like doctors.

When their attention shifted to me, the ringleaders forced me to concede that I was mentally ill. The pressure was intense, unrelenting. I was imprisoned in that snake pit of a hospital encircled by rapists and killers determined to convince me I was insane. My only possession in the world at that stage was my sanity, and I was not about to give it up. However, it wasn't long before I discovered that these mental patients had more resources at their command than mere peer pressure.

After a few days of silent resistance, the other patients decided I needed some drugs to "loosen me up." They recommended I be given methamphetamines—speed—a street drug. Dr. Barker signed his approval.

Dr. Barker and two attendants came in and chased me around the room until they cornered me and dragged me to the floor. I put up a good fight, but Barker managed to slip the needle into my vein.

The drug hit within seconds. Suddenly, I didn't know why I was resisting. It was liquid love.

I lived for that drug for the next year.

4

DR. BARKER'S PROGRAM WAS RUN BY THE INMATES. THE STAFF OBSERVED AND APPROVED THEIR DECI-sions. What they recommended was a systematic bombardment of drugs intended to break my resistance and to bring out my so-called "hidden psychosis." I would like to suggest that those potent drugs did not reveal something that was already there but in fact created a drug-induced psychotic state.

In his published papers, Dr. Barker describes the drugs he used and the results that he hoped to obtain, but he said nothing about the horrors suffered by the victims of his experiments.

During those drug treatments, it was standard practice to handcuff patients together with seatbelts and padlocks. It was also common for any patient resisting the injections to be choked into unconsciousness by twisting a towel around his neck. That happened to me a few times before I realized I was more likely to stay alive if I submitted to the drugs.

One time I was told I was to be an "observer," which meant I had to stay awake all night to watch the other patients sleep. To aid me in that task, they gave me as much Benzedrine as I wanted. They also gave me a log book and a pencil stub and told me to record everything that happened. As everyone slept, I wrote all night.

The hallucinations began after a few days of sleep deprivation. It started with smoke at the edge of my peripheral vision and then thousands of bugs crawling on my skin. I tried to show the bugs to other patients and the attendant who arrived with our meals. Everyone took a close look and then started laughing. Finally, two attendants came in and, without a word, put me in handcuffs and leg restraints.

I became paranoid, not the generalized anxiety that is so common in current language but the real thing, full-blown psychotic paranoia. I thought everyone just out of my range of hearing was conspiring to kill me.

I lay on a mattress on the floor with a blanket pulled over my head. I thought the two patients next to me were prying a staple out of the log book to impale my eye. I lifted a corner of my mattress. The floor was seething with bugs and worms. That was it!

I jumped up in a panic and attacked the two patients next to me. I tried to wrench my arm around one of them with the seatbelt straps locked around my wrists. I thought I could strangle him before anyone stopped me.

Later, I learned that my outburst was the result of chemical torture and sleep deprivation, otherwise known as "Defense Disrupting Therapy."

A series of drugs was forced on me, including scopolamine, a so-called truth serum. The Nazis used it as an effective means of chemical interrogation. The effects of this drug are so overwhelmingly horrifying that I am at a loss to describe them.

It was administered in three injections, about an hour apart. After the first injection, my mouth dried up completely, and my throat felt like it had constricted to the size of a pinhole. When I tried to swallow, I heard a dry, clicking sound. I couldn't even swallow water without choking. To this day, I don't drink water—ever. My resting pulse rate leapt to 160, and I had a sense of suffocation and anxiety.

After the second injection, I began to slip in and out of delirium. My sense of time and continuity were disrupted.

The third injection was followed by an eight to twelve-hour period of complete delirium.

Patients undergoing this medieval degradation were handcuffed to two other patients throughout the ordeal. It was the job of these observers to stop the subject from bashing himself into walls or to stop him from hyperventilating to death. No training was provided. The life of another patient could be in the hands of people who had been on the same drugs a few days before. Both sides of this experiment were extremely stressful.

I think I was given scopolamine three times during my stay in the sun room as well as a continuous diet of "speed" and "goofballs." In the months that followed, I slipped into a drug-soaked existence punctuated by incidents of extreme brutality.

One day, Dr. Barker came into the sun room with a small can of something. He flipped it from one hand to the other. He described it as a wonderful new invention called "mace." With no justification but a test of its effectiveness, he blasted us all to the floor. That's the kind of man he was—curious and always willing to try a little hands-on experiment.

I was in the sun room for about two weeks when Barker moved me into the regular program. At that point, I was resisting everything and fighting Dr. Barker's attempts to morph my mind with drugs so he could reshape it to suit his own idea of normalcy.

They moved me to a cell with a real bed and my own sink and toilet. Shortly thereafter, a patient-teacher came to my cell with a stack of psychological tests and insisted I do them. He was dressed in street clothes and conducted himself like hospital staff.

I'd had enough of that. I told him to take his tests and fuck off. He came back with two attendants who strangled me with a towel and injected me with something. Then they ripped off my clothes and thrust me into an empty cell.

The patient-teacher returned with the tests. "Are you ready to do this or do you need a little more prompting?" he asked with a smile.

I was so drugged I couldn't keep my eyes open. I started to do the tests, but I fell asleep facedown on the paper. I woke up with someone squeezing a nerve point on the back of my heel. I started to write again, but it was impossible to concentrate. Math questions, logic questions, "What's wrong with this picture?" questions.

I fell asleep again and came to under an ice-cold shower, locked in place by attendants holding each arm. It was torture, and I screamed.

Then they brought in their own monster. His name was George McCain. George had some physical deformities. One leg was shorter than the other. One side of his face didn't look like the other. One eye bulged out of the socket. And he had a tail—I'm not kidding! At the base of his spine, his tailbone protruded about four inches. And his dick was about a foot long. He was a grotesque human being, and he knew it. He stood in front of me licking his lips and laughing. They used him to threaten me with rape.

Back in my cell, I was dripping wet and turning blue. My choice was to do the tests or submit to torture. I did the tests. I don't remember completing the tests, but eventually, I was allowed to sleep.

The next day, a formal brainwashing program got underway. Every minute of the day was structured. The basic idea was to force patients to memorize long papers dealing with defense mechanisms and some kind of twisted logic. Then we were to write a confession of sorts like in North Korean or Chinese prisons. In fact, communist China is where Barker learned these techniques. He told me so himself.

A rule of silence was enforced. Inmates were not permitted to talk to each other outside of the groups. Any breach of the rules was met with immediate punishment. Drugs were used as punishment and injected as painfully as possible. No warnings were given. An infraction could be as simple as turning your eyes to the ceiling in a gesture of disbelief or defiance. Punishment might include having your cell stripped, leaving nothing but a blanket on the floor.

After a week of such discipline, I was a whipped animal, docile and cooperative. I followed Dr. Barker's dictates like a robot.

We were forced to perform military exercises three times a day. When the whistle blew, we dropped for push-ups.

"Put your heart into it or take the punishment!"

I never knew what the next phase was going to be. Throughout that ordeal of drugs, handcuffs, and humiliation, I gave the proper answer when asked if I was mentally ill.

I suppose I had truly been driven mad. I saw LSD used in massive doses on selected patients. There were beatings. And murders. All this occurred under direct control of the inmates. It sounds so absurd, the inmates running the asylum, but that's how it was.

In light of what I have learned since of CIA-sponsored LSD and brainwashing experiments and the part Canada played in MK-Ultra (the CIA's illegal mind control program, which ran from the 1950s to the early 1970s), my story is far from outrageous. In fact, much of what I experienced at Oak Ridge became comprehensible only after I began to fit it together with pieces of that mind control puzzle.

In that light, the following story can be seen as a successful use and redirection of a psychopathic killer.

Army clash with guerrillas killed two from Ontario
Canadian slain in Rhodesia

A Windsor man who spent seven years in an Ontario mental hospital after killing two people has been slain in action with the Rhodesian army. Lance Corporal Matthew Charles Lamb, 28, died in a clash with Black Nationalist guerrillas seeking to oust Rhodesia's white minority government. Dr. Elliott Barker, a psychiatrist who treated Lamb for several years in hospital and befriended him, said he was not recruited but traveled to Rhodesia about two years ago with the purpose of joining the army. Lamb was released in 1973 from the maximum security section of the Penetanguishene Mental Health Center, where he had been sent after the shotgun slaying of two young people walking with friends on a Windsor street. Lamb visited relatives and went to see Dr. Barker at his farm near Penetanguishene while on leave last summer. "He knew when he went back he probably would be killed," Dr. Barker said yesterday. A communiqué issued by the Rhodesian security forces yesterday said that the Canadian and eight blacks identified as guerrillas were killed in clashes during the past 48 hours. Dr. Barker said he was advised that lamb was killed on Sunday. Last month another Canadian serving with the Rhodesian forces, Trooper Michael McKeown of Dartmouth, N.S., was sentenced to a year in prison for refusing to fight. He said he was recruited in Canada. Lamb was 19 in January, 1967 when he was found not guilty by reason of insanity on a charge of murdering 20 year old Edith Chaykoski. She was in a group of young people walking toward a bus stop when a man stepped out from behind a tree and began shooting. Three other people were wounded, and one of them a 21 year old man, died later. During court proceedings in his case, Lamb made two unsuccessful attempts to escape. In 1965, when he was 16, Lamb served 14 months in penitentiary after he robbed a suburban store and exchanged shots with a policeman. After his 1967 committal to Penetanguishene, Lamb was treated by Barker, who was then head of the therapeutic unit at the hospital's maximum-security division. He was released in 1973 by order of the Ontario Cabinet, acting on a recommendation of an advisory review board. "He was given a clean bill of health," Dr. Barker said in an interview. "The advisory review board felt he was no longer dangerous. He had been sick and he was no longer sick. During his two to three years in the hospital, he was one of the patient therapists, and they looked up to him."

After he was freed, Matthew Lamb lived with Dr. Barker and his family for a year on their two hundred-acre farm near the hospital, earning his keep as a labourer.

Dr. Barker's treatment program was devised to drive young men into a drug-induced psychosis. Through fear and discipline from within the group, he created a self-sustaining system of docile mental patients. How any doctor could view this as beneficial is beyond me.

5

SOME TIME PASSED BEFORE PETER TOLD ME ABOUT THE VISITS HE GOT ONCE A MONTH. I KNEW HE HAD no family, so who could it be? With an important and secretive voice, he told me it was "the Brotherhood."

"They're a sort of religious organization."

"Bible thumpers?" I asked. "No thanks. Not for me."

He shook his head. "No, not like that. These people are powerful. They can help you. Do you want to meet them? I can arrange it."

What religious people do you know who visit a three-time child murderer every month? Peter Woodcock was one of the worst serial killers in Canada. He was Canada's Hannibal Lecter, an unredeemable and unrepentant psychopath. Were they trying to save his soul?

During his next visit, he asked them if they would invite me for a visit. The following month, they did.

Our first meeting was awkward. Four German men, all over age fifty. I stood beside Peter when they came into the visiting room. Before any of them greeted me, they each, in turn, put both hands on Peter's head and kissed him on the forehead. Then Peter introduced me. Not even a handshake, just a nod of their heads.

From that day on, I had a visit to which I could look forward. Once a month, Peter and I were alone with those four men. The inmates in that place didn't get many visitors.

I can't say much about how they behaved, what they said, or what we talked about, but I don't think there was any talk of God or Jesus. They would bring German food treats. I recall laughing the first time I heard the word "stolen." I ate them with pleasure.

Their main interest appeared to be Peter, as though he was important. None of these men would interrupt Peter when he was talking, but if Peter interrupted one of them, they would shut up right away.

They were all so much bigger than us. I always felt intimidated during those visits. I tried to be polite. It's hard to describe, but I thought they didn't want me to be nice. They were friendlier when I said something not so nice. Have you seen Pope Benedict smile? Imagine that times four in a small room with a child killer.

I think I know now why Peter was so important to them. You need to understand the depth of evil in some people. To them, Peter was an icon of evil, and I was Peter's friend, which gave me some worth by association.

During that period, the drug experiments were intense. Sometimes I would visit with the Brotherhood in a state of delirium. I wasn't not sure what was real and what was a hallucination.

DR. BARKER HAD CONTACTS AT the local high school. Some of the students were his outpatients. One day, he told me he was going to take me to the high school to talk to the students about the dangers of drugs. Wow! I was so happy. I had not seen the sky for a long time.

He took me out the heavily-barred front door. No handcuffs and no guards. I could have run away, but I didn't. Up until then, guards monitored every move I made. They made me think I was dangerous. Suddenly, I was a normal eighteen-year-old again. I thought I was important.

Barker drove his own car with me beside him. Then I found myself on a stage in the school gym with a panel of teachers and social workers. The kids asked questions, and the panel directed me to answer some of them.

I was dressed in institutional clothes, which was embarrassing, because it made me look crazy. Those kids were about the same age as me. Lots of pretty hippie chicks were in the front row.

When the event was over, I sat on the edge of the stage and talked to a group of girls. I think the panel thought I would be an example of why the students should avoid drugs. It didn't work out that way. The girls treated me like I was a rock star. For a moment, I was in heaven. Then it was back to the bars and slamming doors.

The next day, I received a visit—five girls from the high school! The following day, there were fifteen. Every day or two after that, a bunch of them would come. It was great. I can't tell you . . . just the smell of girls' hair. . . .

That went on for a few weeks. Then the staff cut it off. I still got letters from some of them though.

I WAS LOCKED UP FOR eight months. No family came to visit, and they sent no letters. What family I had would have nothing to do with me. The youngest son was in a hospital for the criminally insane. What a shame!

Fortunately for me, the laws governing committal to hospitals were changed during my stay at Oak Ridge. A review board was created to give patients an avenue of appeal.

I recall a brief interview with the review board. It was my last chance at reclaiming my life. The interview lasted less than half an hour. They decided I was not nuts and didn't belong in that snake pit. I had not killed anyone and had never hurt anyone in my life. All of my fellow inmates were killers, rapists, child molesters—monsters!

The real kind.

In truth, they had to let me go. The car theft charge had been dropped seven months earlier, and there was no legal reason to hold me. They told me I would be released as soon as arrangements could be made.

With a word, I was out of Barker's hands. It ended as suddenly as it began, but the consequences of my months as Dr. Barker's guinea pig affected the direction of my life for years to come. The only problem was, I had no place to go.

That's when the Brotherhood stepped in.

6

THE BROTHERHOOD OFFERED TO TAKE CARE OF ME, GIVE ME A PLACE TO LIVE, AND HELP ME ADJUST TO the outside. It was the only place I had to go.

I received the same clothes I had been wearing when I came in almost a year earlier. They were a little smelly. They also returned my wallet (empty) and my boots, which had holes in both heels. The last thing they gave me was a bus ticket to Toronto and the address of Karl Wieland's house. Karl was a member of the Brotherhood. A guard was nice enough to give me a ride to the Greyhound station.

I wanted to go straight to Yorkville Village, a popular hippie hangout back then, but I didn't even have money to eat, so I walked to Karl's house on Victor Street. Karl and his wife were so happy to see me. They said they didn't think I would come.

The house was big, three stories, and made of brick. They gave me a small room on the third floor. Everything in the house was German—art, furniture, and plates on the kitchen wall. It was like stepping back into 1930s Berlin. But there was nothing Christian. No crucifix or bleeding-heart Jesus, just lots of old photographs of men in uniform.

I stayed there for a few days and only came out of my room to eat. Mrs. Wieland was very nice to me. I didn't know what to do. I was kind of screwed up from the past year of drug experiments. I thought it was only a matter of time before religion came into it. I thought they would Bible- thump me eventually. But it never happened.

One day, I was alone in the house, and I started snooping around. I went to the basement and found an old leather great coat hanging on the wall. It was stiff as a board but very cool—a German officer's coat. It even had a built-in holster. I found a tin of dubbin in the kitchen. I put newspaper on the floor and spent the day working the leather with dubbin. In a few hours, it looked great again.

When Karl and his wife came home, I showed him what I had done. He was very excited and happy with me. He told me it was his coat from the war. Then he told me I could have it. It was too big, but I decided to wear it anyway.

Then he said something strange: "I have that coat because of paperclip.[1]" Then he smiled and told me it looked good on me.

I didn't have a clue what that meant, but I was happy to have the coat.

So there I was wearing a Nazi great coat. It was so big I was sort of swimming around inside, but I was a hippie, and it looked cool. Karl also gave me an iron cross on a chain. He said it went with the coat. At the time, it was known as a surfer's cross. Hippies wore them like a peace symbol.

I had no money and no job, but the Brotherhood gave me "pin money." I don't remember how much, but a cup of coffee cost ten cents at the time.

I went back to Yorkville. For those who don't know, it was the hippie hangout in Toronto. On most nights, I went go back to the Wielands' house, but sometimes I stayed out all night. They didn't seem to mind when I came and went. The only exception was Saturday evenings. They had a meeting and they didn't want me around. They would give me money to go to a movie or something.

One Saturday night, it was pouring rain, so I came back early. Three of the men who came to visit Peter were there along with their wives and a few kids my age or younger. It was the first time I had seen the other men since I had been free, but they were not happy to see me. They stopped me at the front door.

"Stay outside, boy," one of them said.

I was really pissed. By that time I thought of the place as my house. I turned around and ran down the street. I had nothing in the house I needed, so I decided I would never go back.

I went back to Yorkville and became a homeless hippie again. I just hung around for a few days, looked for a place to crash every night, and balled a few nice hippie chicks....

One day, I went into a deli wearing my great coat and iron cross around my neck, and a shit storm broke out. I had no idea what my surfer's cross meant to a holocaust survivor, not to mention the fact I was wearing most of a Nazi uniform. Some hippies wore US Army jackets, but I was wearing a Nazi great coat.

The small, old man behind the counter screamed something and grabbed the iron cross, almost cutting my head off with the chain.

"Do you know?" he screamed "Do you know?"

"What did I do?" I asked, clueless.

He showed me a tattoo on his arm. A number. Then he told me what everyone knew but I didn't.

I put the cross in the pocket of my coat. I hope that when I left the deli we were okay with each other.

---

1 Later, I learned he was referring to Operation Paperclip, the secret employment of German scientists, engineers and technicians following World War II.

One evening I was walking down Yorkville Avenue grooving with the crowd when all four Brotherhood men appeared in front of me. They all smiled their Pope Benedict smiles and told me they were so sorry they had treated me rudely. Karl said his wife cried because she had such nice plans for me, and then I ran away. They said I should return to the house with them.

Damn!

It was getting cold, so I went.

My room was exactly as I left it, right down to the socks on the floor. I was glad to have them. I was a little embarrassed when I took my shoes off.

By Saturday, everything around the house was back to normal. In the evening, they told me I could stay, but I couldn't be included, because I was not an apprentice.

"We know you are a good boy, so you can watch from the kitchen," Karl said.

The others arrived shortly after supper. First came the three Brotherhood men I knew already. They sat at the kitchen table drinking tea with Karl and Mrs. Wieland. They didn't ignore me completely, but they talked to each other in German. I could tell they didn't want to piss me off by being rude, so they included me in the conversation once in a while.

A short time later, the three men's wives arrived with three boys and two girls. The kids were all younger than me, maybe sixteen or seventeen. The boys wore suits, and the girls wore old-fashioned flower-print dresses. They went directly to the living room and didn't introduce anyone to me.

Mrs. Wieland gave me another cup of tea and said they wouldn't be long. "You can watch, but please be as quiet as a mouse."

She put her finger to her lips and winked. The wink was . . . sexy. Really theatrical. Then she smiled and went out.

From where I sat, I could lean back in my chair and see clearly into most of the living room. I was mostly interested in the teenage girls. They were both blonds, and from where I sat, they looked fine.

In the living room was a large coffee table with a couch on one side and three straight-backed chairs on the other. The three men sat on the couch facing in my direction. The two girls sat in the chairs with their back to me and an empty chair between them. The three boys stood behind the three chairs. Mr. and Mrs. Wieland and the other three wives stood behind the boys.

One of the men on the couch took out a large, old book and placed it on the table between him and the two girls. At first, I thought it was a Bible, but it didn't look right. It didn't have the right proportions; it was too square.

All three men said something in German, like a short chant. It was only a few words, but it sounded strange, like each voice was an octave above the other, sort of a guttural harmony in German.

Then everyone repeated the same word three times. I realized it was some kind of strange religious ceremony, but I had seen a lot of stranger things in the past year, and it didn't freak me out as much as it made me curious.

Two of the boys behind the seated girls took each one by the elbow and helped them to their feet. Then they helped the girls onto the table. The girls sat on either side of the book with their feet on the table and knees up, flower-print dresses covering their legs.

One of the men opened the book and put something inside it—I couldn't see what it was. Then—Holy shit!—the two boys reached forward and lifted the girls' dresses right up to their waist! From where I sat, I could only see legs and knees, but I wondered what the view was like from the couch.

The guy in the middle leaned forward so his head was between the two girls and started reading from the book. It went on for a long time with only an occasional reply from the others. It all looked well-rehearsed, as though they did it all the time.

The guy reading got more and more intense until he was almost yelling. You know in those old war movies how a Nazi officer sounds, barking orders in an ugly language? He sounded like that. Then the three boys stood erect, slammed a heel on the floor, and threw up a Nazi salute. Everyone shouted something in German, and it was over.

I thought back to the old guy in the deli. What was this all about? This little ceremony sure caught my attention. I was as curious as hell.

A few days later, Karl asked me to sit with him in the living room. He reminded me of the visits I received at Oak Ridge from those high school girls. Did I know any of their names?

I liked one of them. She came to visit every time. Some of the others came only once or twice. He asked if I would like to find her. I told him of course I did, but I had no money. He gave me a bus ticket to Midland and one hundred dollars. In 1969, that was a huge amount of money. I don't think I had ever had a hundred bucks at one time.

He smiled and told me to go have fun but to be sure to come home. "

Home." I had not had a home for a long time. I was learning to like his Pope Benedict smile.

7

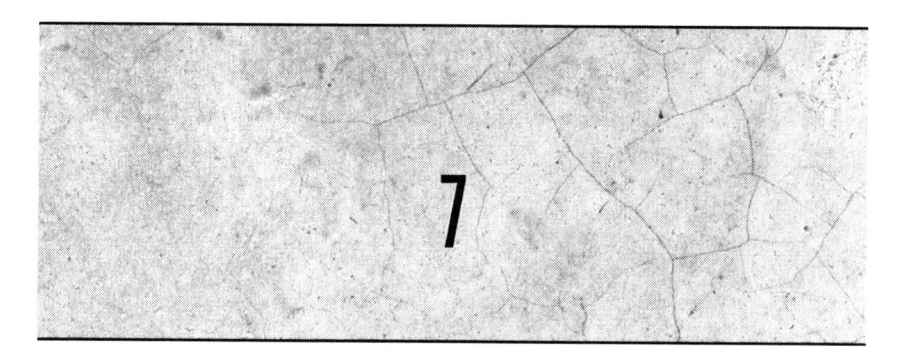

THE FIRST THING I DID WAS GO TO YORKVILLE AND BUY A BIG BAG OF GRASS, SOME PURPLE HAZE, AND windowpane (those who know . . . know). Then I took a taxi to the Greyhound depot. Looking back, I realize it was an incredibly dangerous thing to do, but I was young.

I went to the girl's high school and stood outside looking for her when the students started pouring out. Another girl I knew saw me first and rushed up to greet me. She was not the girl I was looking for, but she knew her. She gave me an address and told me to go there in the evening. I had to take a taxi again because I couldn't find the house. It was okay though because I had money in my pocket.

When I got to the house, a party was going on. Lots of kids were there. It was like everyone knew me. I felt like Timothy Leary. I had pot and acid and money, and *she* was there.

I don't know who owned the house, but it was getting kind of trashed. A girl was standing in the corner wearing nothing but plastic food wrap. The house was full of a bunch of stoned teeny boppers having fun. Remember, that was the summer of love. Everybody did everybody.

One young guy came up to me and said he was going to phone someone I knew who would want to see me. I had no idea who he was talking about.

Twenty minutes later, Dr. Barker came through the front door. Actually, he ran at me and tackled me to the floor. He was a big guy, fat and heavy, and I was pinned under him. He laughed and called my name over and over. I was scared and happy to see him at the same time. He joked around and talked to a bunch of the kids. He knew them all, and they were very friendly toward him. I had just lost my status as Timothy Leary.

He told the young guy who had phoned him that they should move the party to the farm and that it was okay to bring me along. Later, I learned it was the farm that "spree killer" Matthew Charles Lamb went to several years later.

Only one guy at the party had a car, so we had to go one carload at a time. I didn't go in the first load. I stayed behind and helped clean up the house. I also helped the girl in the plastic wrap. We had to cut it off her with scissors. She was so overheated she almost fainted a few times.

The farm was a few miles outside of Midland. It had a big, old house. I don't know how many bedrooms it had, but sleeping bags were everywhere. It was dark when I got there, so I didn't get to look around until the following morning. I can't say how many kids were there, but no adults were around, and no one seemed to be in charge. I asked whose house it was. I recall hearing someone say the owner hung himself, and now it was just a house. I don't think that was true, but it made for a cool, spooky story. It was good enough for me. I was the guy with the bag of pot, so lots of people hung around with me.

As daylight dawned, I realized it would be more accurate to call the place a ranch. At least six horses were stabled in an enormous barn. One guy there knew a lot about them. He showed me how to put on a saddle and bridle. One mare would hold her breath when I tightened the straps and then let it out when I tried to mount her, and the saddle would roll over and dump me off. That's where I learned horses have a sense of humour.

I liked it there, and I wanted to stay. Although no one was in charge, there was always work to do, such as digging fence posts, and someone to show me how to do it. The skills I picked up there still come in handy today. I have fond memories of the farm. Two girls there liked me, and that was okay at the time. I stayed there all winter.

DIFFERENT PEOPLE CAME AND WENT, but a core group of hippies was always there. The strange thing was the food. There was always lots to eat, and the fridge always had milk, ice cream, veggies, big jars of peanut butter, and jam. I never bought food, and I still had some money after being there for months.

One day, someone handed me a letter addressed to me—just my name, no stamp or address. It was from Karl. He asked me to come home. He said he had a job for me. He also said that if I had any special friends, I could bring them, too. If he had not invited my friends, I would not have left the farm, which means I would have been there when Matt Lamb arrived with the other musketeers, Paul, Doug Billings, and Michael Mason.

There was just one problem: money. I didn't have enough for three bus tickets. So we hitchhiked. It was easy with two cute, young girls.

We made it back to Toronto that same day. We went directly to the house on Victor Street. Karl and Mrs. Wieland were happy to see me, but there were never any hugs. Unlike us hippies, they behaved in a polite but formal way. I don't recall the Wielands ever touching me, not even in Oak Ridge, not even a handshake.

They served us home-baked pastries and tea. Then we went off to my room. As always, it was exactly how I left it. Mrs. Wieland didn't ask anything, just assumed we would sleep in the same room, even though we were all still teenagers. We didn't think she was odd—we thought she was cool.

The next morning, Karl told me we needed an apartment and jobs. I agreed. I needed money, and I didn't think he was going to give me any more. I told him I wanted to live in Yorkville.

Karl arranged an apartment at 24 Hazelton Ave., just off Yorkville. Anyone who knows the area knows that today it's the most expensive real estate in Toronto. Even then it was a choice location. I had a paid-for, two-bedroom apartment and two girlfriends. Back then I thought it was normal.

I had to take the job as well. Karl's friend owned a picture-framing business. He had a bunch of retail stores in shopping malls and a factory where the work was done. The owner told me he had known Karl most of his life, and if I was Karl's friend, then I was his friend, too. He was a Jew.

I went to work in the factory and learned how to frame pictures. The job was fun. The only problem was it took more than an hour to get to and from the factory by subway and then bus.

Soon, my apartment on Hazelton became a crash pad for lots of hippies. Funny, in those days, we didn't think of ourselves as homeless. Being homeless was illegal. We were careful at night. We had to show a rent receipt and some money if the cops stopped us. You could get sent to jail for being homeless. Then, when they let you out after about a week, you were still homeless, so you could get busted again on the front steps of the jail.

Karl paid the rent, so I didn't get a receipt. I was picked up one evening and disappeared for a week. When I was released, I went to Karl's house and told him what had happened. He said he couldn't give me a receipt for the apartment, but he wrote a fake one and said I could use it for anyone in the apartment.

People came and went, and I went to work every day. I was very good at picture framing. I did lots of creative work. I learned fast.

The owner introduced me to Hugh Whitney Morrison. He was over seventy then. Every few days, he and his wife brought in a piece of art for me to frame. Real art, not prints. Some of it was priceless.

They invited me to their house in Rosedale. It was a mansion. Their art collection was amazing, like a museum. I told them I liked to paint and that I was trying something called linocut printing. They asked if they could come to my place to see what I was doing.

I had to throw the hippie crashers out and clean the place up. The two girls from Midland stayed.

When the Morrisons came, they looked at my art, and I sold them a piece I had just finished. They were very friendly to the girls, and the girls were impressed by my new friends.

THE PSYCHOPATH MACHINE

The Morrisons invited us all to dinner at the celebrity club, a.k.a. the Blake House. Hugh said it was a fancy club and asked me to dress up a bit. I said I didn't have a suit or anything like that.

"Well, let's go shopping," he said. "You don't need to wear a suit."

Funny how details of old events stick with you. The clothing boutique was named "Take 5." It was right on Yorkville Ave. I wound up with a brown corduroy vest suit and a purple satin shirt with big, puffy sleeves and a huge collar, "Carnaby Street fashion."

For the first time in my life, things were going my way. I was a 1960s fashion plate, I had a posh apartment, a job, two girlfriends . . . Wow!

I was on top of the world—briefly.

I asked what the girls should wear. They were always dressed nicely anyway. Girls didn't wear pants much then. They were still feminine, and they wore dresses mostly. And miniskirts, some not much wider than a belt. Climbing a flight of stairs behind them was always a treat. Hugh said it didn't matter, that they looked nice as they were.

That evening, the Morrisons came to the Hazelton apartment to pick us up in a Lincoln limousine, no less. I had never seen the inside of something like that. It even had a bar. It was like a movie.

The driver opened the door for the girls and me. Hugh and his wife were in the back seat. They offered us a drink, but we declined. I didn't drink at all back then. It wasn't cool for hippies.

The club was really fancy. It was located in an old building not far from Yorkville. A doorman dressed in a funny suit met us at the door. I tried to act sophisticated but I was totally intimidated. I had a girl on both arms, and I was dressed okay, but I felt like I stuck out like a bug on an ice cream cone. I thought the best thing to do was keep quiet. Then no one would know.

The place had several dining rooms, all with dark wood walls and heavy furniture. We were shown to our table. We passed through two rooms to get there. Quite a few people were there. Most of the tables were full. Everyone was either old or close to our age. It looked like a collection of grandparents and grandchildren. The children were all girls. Not really children but teenyboppers.

There was too much silverware! Four or five knives, forks, and spoons and folded white napkins. Oddly, I think it was the silverware that did it. My face must have turned red, and my eyes got a little wet. I kept my hands in my lap and looked at the floor.

Hugh saw how disturbed I was, and I'm sure he knew why. Although he was a cultured and educated man, he was no snob.

"Don't let it bother you," he said. "Just start with the outside fork and work your way in. If you want to eat a fuckin' olive with your dessert fork, go ahead."

Everyone laughed, and that set me at ease.

That night, I ate food with names I could not pronounce, like "Vichyssoise."

STEVE SMITH

"It's just potato soup," Hugh said.

We drank wine with the meal. We had to. I had no tolerance for alcohol, and it went right to my head. The same thing happened to the girls. I never thought about it, but we were all under the legal drinking age at the time.

After dinner, crème brûlée flamed at the table. I had never experienced anything like this, and I was still reeling from Oak Ridge.

Then it was time for the men—and me—to move to another room to smoke and drink. The women stayed at the table.

I'm sure you have all seen that room somewhere—big leather chairs, cigar smoke, and old men, perfect for serious conversation. After Hugh gave me a lecture about scotch, I had to drink some.

Two other men and Hugh sat across from me. He introduced them by first name. Both were German with heavy accents.

Hugh's light-hearted conversation changed suddenly. He leaned forward in his chair.

"Do you like this?"

"Yes," I replied. "The food was great." I was a little drunk.

"Not the food," he said, "the lifestyle. We have a sort of employment agency," he continued. "We find house workers for clients all over the world. They want exceptional people, and we help find them. We know you are an exceptional boy, and if you want to, you can help us."

"Well, yes, of course I will," I replied. "Do I have to quit my job?"

"No, but you will likely find it boring."

With that, dinner was over. On the way back to the room where the girls were, I looked into one of the other dining rooms and saw Karl with his wife and the two girls who had sat on the coffee table. I passed by quickly, but I'm sure he saw me.

Hugh drove us home. When we got there, I went straight to the bathroom and puked. All that good food wasted.

I couldn't drink.

8

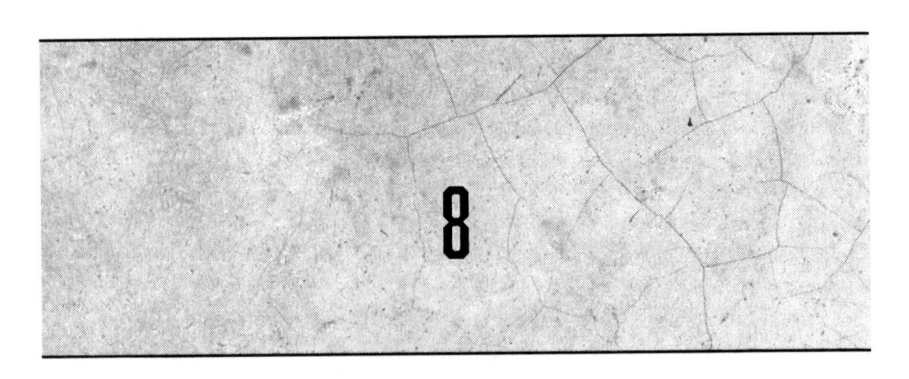

NOTHING MUCH HAPPENED FOR A FEW MONTHS. I KEPT WORKING AT THE PICTURE FRAME FACTORY. THE owner was friendly toward me. He showed me lots of things about fine art treatment, even some restoration work. You know what they use to fix spots on old priceless paintings? Crayons.

The owner had one bad habit: He liked speed and coke. He gave me lots of both and kept me working long hours. Some days I would stay until late night pumping out framed posters. One night I stayed past the last bus, so I had to stay in the warehouse overnight. It wasn't so bad. I worked most of the night.

Speed and coke were not cool in those days. They didn't reach "cool" status until the 1980s. They were hard drugs, junkie stuff. Hippies did not mess with such things. From my Oak Ridge experience, I knew what tweaking looked like. I knew my boss was addicted to both.

At Oak Ridge, I had also acquired a liking for speed. Before Oak Ridge, the thought of sticking a needle into my arm was repulsive. But I remembered the rush when Dr. Barker slipped in the needle. Just once, and I was hooked. That's all there was to it.

It didn't take long for my boss to take things to a whole new level. I never questioned him. He was the boss. I also never bought any drugs from him. He gave them away.

At home, I kept my little bag of crystal meth secret, along with the glass syringe. Speed brings you down fast. It will make a mess of you quicker than any other drug. At the same time, it will make you think you are on top of the world. I was on top of the world. Rich people were being nice to me.

For a while.

It was bound to happen. One day, Mrs. Morrison brought an old watercolour for me to frame. I guess by then I didn't look quite right.

She asked if I was okay.

Then I screwed up big time. When I started working on the painting, I blew it off with compressed air. I used too much pressure and I blew the painting to pieces, right in front of Mrs. Morrison and destroyed it.

Mrs. Morrison was not happy with me. She rightfully scolded me. I barked back at her. I called her a snake. As soon as the words were out of my mouth, I regretted it. What an idiot. I was a stoned junkie fool!

She turned and walked out, and my life changed again.

I blew Mrs. Morrison's watercolour to pieces, I blew my relationship with the Morrison's to pieces, and I threw my job away. My boss didn't fire me. He didn't even give me too much shit about it. I just lost confidence and was too embarrassed to go back to work.

NONE OF THE PEOPLE AT twenty-four Hazelton knew I was shooting speed. I kept it to myself.

Speed is hard to write about. Hard to think about. Speed is not a plant; it doesn't come from anything natural. It's a chemical agent made with poisons. Every ingredient will poison you if you take it on its own. Everyone who destroys his or her life with speed knows this to begin with. And yet you still see them jonesing down the street anyway. Why? Why do they do it? More importantly, why did I do it? How did I reach a point where I was living in the back of an abandoned vehicle using a refill from a ball-point pen for a fix?

Sticking a needle in your arm does not come naturally. It's a technical thing. It requires precision and practice. It's also painful for an amateur. My boss gave me my first fit. A nice glass syringe. He showed me how to flag it to make sure it was in a vein. I also copied what Barker did to me on the sun room floor, knowing euphoria would overcome the pain.

This chemical, in all its varieties, does something to your brain the first time you do it. If only the natural state of humanity was like meth euphoria. Is that how Adam and Eve existed in the garden? There would be no war, no strife or pain. We would love each other all the time. And we would be more intelligent and focused all the time. I got hooked on the feeling from the start, but there is a dark side.

Addiction to speed is not the same as heroin. When you don't have it, you don't go through the withdrawal you do with opiates. You just feel like there is no colour in anything. The inside of your skull feels like ashes. Everything feels wrong.

A WEEK WENT BY, AND I didn't go home much. Then one night I went home, and the place was empty. No one was even crashing on the floor. All of the clothes were gone. Even the few things I owned were gone.

I found a note in the bathroom. It was from the girls. It said, "Karl has a job for both of us in England. We waited for you, but we have to go now. Peace."

Two days later, there was an eviction notice on the apartment door. I ignored it. Then the landlord came and put me out, and I was homeless again.

I went to Karl's place. I had not been there since I got a job, but he was still paying the rent. The front door was locked. It had never been locked before. I knocked for a while, but there was no answer. I went around to the back, but that door was locked, too. I climbed the fire escape to the third floor where my room was. Everything was closed and locked.

In those days, there was no place for homeless youth, just the Salvation Army, which had a place where drunks could stay the night. I was not going there. I had a good stash of speed, so things didn't seem so bad.

I spent the first night in a phone booth. It was cold. Wind blew through the space beneath the bottom of the door. I didn't have my great coat anymore. It had disappeared along with everything else.

I went back to Karl's house late the next evening. I thought I would just look to see if there were lights on in the house. I didn't know if I would knock on his door or not. By then I knew I had no friends.

The house was dark. Somehow, that made me feel better. It meant they weren't avoiding me or hiding. They had just gone somewhere, that's all.

I didn't want to go far from the house, just in case they returned, so I walked around the neighborhood for a few hours. Walking in circles is okay when you are high on meth. I had to hide every time I saw headlights. Could be a cop.

A nearby church had a backyard overgrown with weeds and full of old cars and junk. I found a place to hide in the back of an old van. Both front doors and the windshield were gone, but inside was better than the night before in the phone booth. I had nothing but the clothes I was wearing. It wasn't enough to keep warm. Meth doesn't keep you warm like alcohol for a drunk who falls asleep in a snowbank.

I spent three nights in the van. During the day, I sat on Karl's doorstep or walked the streets. I had no money. I don't think I ate anything during that time.

On the fourth night, a short time after I snuck back into the van, a flashlight shone in my face, and a voice commanded me to get out.

Handcuffs. Police station. Mug shot. A few punches in the stomach and slaps on the head. Then back into a cell.

They charged me with attempted car theft. It was Friday night, so I had to stay in the police cell until Monday morning. My appearance before a judge lasted less than sixty seconds. I was remanded to the Don jail for one week.

In the 1960s, the Don jail was truly a medieval dungeon. The cells were less than three feet wide. Just enough room for a steel cot and a piss bucket. The ceiling was about fifteen feet high, so I felt like I was locked in a slot. And it was brutal. The guards looked for any excuse to beat me up. I had learned how to deal with that sort of thing in Oak Ridge. Call them sir or officer. Always be subservient. Never complain.

One night, a prisoner a few cells from me committed suicide. I don't know what he used, but he slashed both arms from elbow to wrist. Some said he pulled a paint chip off the wall and cut himself with it. His blood was all over the floor in front of his cell.

The guards opened all the cell doors at the same time every morning. Prisoners set out their piss bucket to be dumped. The morning after the suicide, everyone had to walk around the blood. They wanted us to see it.

I got through the week, and on the day before court, a lawyer interviewed me. There was no such thing as legal aid back then, only a duty council appointed by the court. He told me to plead "not guilty" to vehicle theft, and he would take care of the rest.

The hearing took only a few minutes. The duty counsel spoke only one sentence to the judge: "Your honour, there was no motor in the vehicle this young man is accused of attempting to steal."

The police had not found the bag of meth or the syringe. It was lost in the back of the van. They did not charge me with being homeless either, so my case was dismissed, and I walked out. At least I had eaten something over the past week, so I could still walk the streets, but I was homeless all the same.

Today, every city has homeless people. You see them sleeping in doorways and back streets. We pass by, and if we think about it at all, we are just glad we're not them. There is something liberating about not having a home. You can stand on any street corner. It makes no difference what direction you walk. Still, I found myself walking past Karl's house again. I didn't knock though.

I went back to the van to see if I could find my bag of speed. It was gone. Then it struck me. All those things they said about me were true. I was worthless. I didn't want it to be that way, but everything I did went wrong.

I have to say, in those days I believed in God. I didn't have any religion, but I thought God was watching over us. I thought I heard "Go home" inside my head. But I had no home.

I decided to break a window in the back of the church and climb inside. Then I smashed open the donation box and took the money. Yes, I stole from a church. There was about twenty-five dollars, mostly in change. It was another turning point.

Take the money and buy speed or go home.

I went to the Greyhound station and bought a ticket to Sault St. Marie. For better or worse, I was going home.

It turned out to be for the worst.

9

THE BUS RIDE TO THE SAULT WAS LONG, DARK, AND WARM. A GREYHOUND SEEMED LUXURIOUS COMPARED to my recent circumstances. I settled into my seat and thought about the last time I had been home.

My mother lived with her boyfriend Bill Flowers in a one-bedroom apartment above a sporting goods store. It was the same place Garry and I had lived since I was ten and he was twelve. I don't have good memories of those years.

I know Garry was molested by Joe, the owner of the sporting goods store. Garry grew up gay and died of AIDS in 1998. I suppose the molestation is where it started. This store owner was also the coach of the Sault Greyhounds hockey club.

It was a small apartment with two adults, two kids, a big dog, and a white rabbit named "Buck."

And Bill. Bill was a bartender. He worked at the Royal Hotel a few blocks away. Bill liked to say he was also the bouncer, but he didn't get paid for it. I'm sure he enjoyed punching out drunks and throwing them into the street.

When I was ten, my father sent us to live with my mother. "Tell Bill I don't like you," he said. And that's exactly what I did the first time we met. Bill looked straight at me with a cruel eye and said, "I don't give a fuck!"

But it was home, and that's where I was going.

Looking out the window at the sameness of the scenery, a window seat on a Greyhound creates a sort of time machine of the mind. Country and western songwriters know this. I was going home, but why? Well, I guess it's part of the English language. Home is a concept we need to have. A hometown. A home run. Home is where the heart is. Home is good. Every dog needs a home.

I hoped things had changed. The Greyhound station had not. Neither had the streets. I didn't like that town. I never did. I suspected the town did not like me either. I didn't know how true that was until I became an adult. Then I understood that everyone—teachers, parents, neighbours—labeled me because of my mother's lifestyle. I could see they didn't want their children hanging around me. I didn't understand at all. I hadn't done anything bad. I received good marks in school. I wasn't a bully. I was probably the smallest kid in my class.

I walked to my mother's apartment and stood outside for a while looking up at the window. It was early evening. I had come all that way. I had no place else to go, so I knocked.

Bill opened the door. He looked shocked for only a second. Then he stepped into the hallway, closed the door behind him, and came at me like a prison guard. He grabbed me by the neck and lifted me right off the floor, slamming my head into the wall so hard I thought my skull cracked.

"Get the fuck out of here," he hissed. "You come around here again, and I'll kill you."

He pushed me toward the stairs and would have thrown me down had I not broken loose and ran.

So much for the voice in my head saying, "Go home." I'm sure my mom's dog and rabbit still had a home.

Once again, I found myself standing on a street corner and it didn't matter what direction I went. I took a few steps down Albert Street and then turned and went the other way. I stopped and went a few steps down Gore Street, stopped again, and then sat down on the sidewalk and started to cry. I couldn't remember the last time I had allowed myself to cry. I had had lots of reasons, but I was always in a place that would not allow it.

In those days, you could not just sit on a sidewalk. Sidewalks were for walking. A normal person always had someplace to go and did not sit where people walked. A few people looked at me as they drove past. In a few minutes, the police would surely drive by, and if they saw me, they would put me in jail. I got up and walked without any idea where to go. I had no money. I had spent the last of what I stole from the church on French fries at the bus depot.

I found myself at the Sault locks and power plant. The locks are where big ships pass from Lake Superior to Lake Huron. It was my favourfavourite place when I was a kid.

The power plant generated the town's electricity, using the drop in elevation between the two lakes to send falling water through turbines. The road to the locks passed over what we called the "tail race." It's where water comes out from the turbines. The water looks like it's boiling because of the pressure coming up from the outflow pipes. It's the scariest water I have ever seen.

I stood on the bridge for a long time looking into that boiling cauldron. I wanted to jump in, but I knew it was very cold water, and that's what stopped me. I can't stand cold water. That was the place where Bill ended his life fifteen years later. In the end, it must have been worse for him than it was for me, because he jumped.

I knew the area well. There were plenty of places to hide around the locks. My favourfavourite place was an old building full of rusty machinery.

THE PSYCHOPATH MACHINE   33

On the second floor was a pile of rope used to hold the big ships as they passed through the locks. The rope was about four inches thick and smelled of oil. I burrowed a hole in the pile. It was my bed on my first night home.

It was a long night. I didn't sleep much. It wasn't the cold so much as the oily smell that kept me awake. I left at the first light of dawn, stiff and thirsty. There was no place to find water, so I headed back downtown.

At the entrance to the locks was a historic house. One of my classmates from elementary school lived there. A few years earlier, he had been caught making obscene phone calls to my mother. It was such a strange affair. I was still living at home then. My mother would sunbathe on the roof behind the apartment. You could see her from the sidewalk in her leopard skin bathing suit. No doubt she was very beautiful back then.

Then, every day around the same time, the phone would ring. There would be heavy breathing and some obscene words on the line. She had the phone tapped, and the police identified the caller quickly.

The kid was thirteen or fourteen years old, so the police just made him apologize. That was it. His family was important in the Sault. I don't know what they did, but it was why they got to live in that historic stone house.

As I walked past his house, I thought I had never done anything as bad as that, and look what had happened to me. It was another lesson on how unfair the world is. My world anyway.

I continued walking downtown. Then it struck me what I would do. I was angry, and I decided to take a big chance.

I already told you about the sporting goods store below my mother's apartment. Let me go back about five years. I was thirteen, and my brother was fifteen.

One day, I got home from school early. As I came through the apartment door, Joe, the owner of the store downstairs, came rushing out of our bedroom. He passed me without a word and rushed down the stairs. At first, I thought he was snooping around our apartment. Then I saw Garry in the bed looking shocked and upset.

"That guy's a homo, you know," he said. "Watch out for him."

As time went on, it became clear that Garry was also a homosexual. I didn't know anything about such things. I liked girls, but for the next few years I was afraid I would become a homosexual, too.

One day, I was home alone, and the toilet plugged up and overflowed. Water was all over the floor. I was mopping it up when I heard a loud knock at the door. It was Joe from downstairs.

I opened the door, and he tried to come in. I blocked him and told him the toilet overflowed and that it was okay because I was cleaning it up. He said water was overflowing downstairs. Then he reached out and put his hand on my shirtless chest.

I was a skinny kid—I doubt if I weighed a hundred pounds—but I shoved him backward, and he almost fell down the stairs. He took off. I never told anyone about that moment. Until now.

I decided to go back there and confront him. I was going to blackmail him.

10

I HAD NO PLAN. I DIDN'T KNOW HOW TO BLACKMAIL SOMEONE OTHER THAN WHAT I HAD SEEN IN MOVIES. But desperation and anger gave me courage. I knew Joe was the reason my brother was a homosexual. And because Garry was gay, other kids thought I must be, too.

I walked in the front door of his shop and went straight to him. He smiled and looked pleased to see me.

"I haven't seen you around for a while," he said. "Are you visiting your mother?"

"You made my brother into a homo," I replied, ignoring his question. "I want twenty-five dollars, or I'll tell the police."

He laughed. "The police won't believe you, and they'll probably lock you up, you little prick." Then he smiled again. "Come on back here," he said, and then he went into the back room.

I followed him, thinking about whacking him on the head with something. Once I was back there, the bastard pulled out his dick.

"Suck this," he said, "and I'll give you twenty-five dollars."

I could have killed him at that moment. I was boiling. Seething. Furious. But helpless. I had made it through the past few years and didn't turn gay. I was not going to change now.

"Fuck you!" I said. "I'm going to the police anyway."

I turned and walked toward the door.

"Wait a second," he said. "Maybe I can do something." He looked worried. "If you need money so badly, maybe you can do something for me. I'm not homosexual, you know. I actually prefer girls. There's a restaurant downtown where all the hippies hang out. Go there and find some girls for me and I'll give you the twenty-five bucks."

"How can I do that?" I asked. "I don't think hippie chicks are going to like you. You're an old Wop."

"Wop?" He laughed. "Don't use that word. We own this town, you know. Those hippie girls, they like money? Tell them you know how they can make lots of money doing what they like to do anyway."

He handed me ten dollars. "Go have breakfast at the Four Winds and see what happens."

I knew the Four Winds Motel. It was right downtown. It had an all-night restaurant and a bar in the basement. I had never been in the bar, because I was underage, but I knew the restaurant.

Joe told me he knew someone who lived in the motel. He gave me his name and room number.

"Tell him Joe sent you," he said. Yes, he really said exactly that, like in a gangster movie.

I was nearly starving. The last thing I had eaten was French fries at the bus depot the day before. Or had it been two days before?

Bacon, eggs, hash browns, toast, and a bottomless cup of coffee. Sometimes all it takes is food in your stomach to change everything. I felt good. I thought things would be okay, even though I still didn't know where I would sleep that night.

I hung out in the restaurant for as long as I could without looking like I lived there. I had a little money, so I walked around town for a while. Later, I went back and ordered a hamburger and fries.

A guy came in and sat at the counter right across from me. He was a fashion plate hippie. Older than me, maybe twenty-five, dressed in fashionable clothes. He looked like rich a guy. I watched him from the corner of my eye as I took a bite of my burger. Finally, he turned toward me on his stool.

"You're Steve, right?"

I almost choked. I swallowed before answering. "Yeah. Who are you?"

He leaned forward. "Joe sent me," he said and then burst out laughing.

The waitress turned and smiled and then went back to the dishes.

The guy slid into my booth. "I'm Dave," he said. "I'm from Toronto, too."

"What makes you think I'm from Toronto?" I asked. "This is my hometown."

"Yes," he said, "but you haven't been here for a while. Joe called and said you're okay. I need some help right now, and you can do it—or not. It's up to you."

"Okay," I said. "I need to do something. What do you want?"

Dave glanced around. "We can't talk here. I have a room I rent by the month. Let's go."

"No way," I said. "Joe's a fag, you're a fag, and I'm not fag. I'm not going to your room."

He laughed again, loudly. "No, man, I'm not a fag. Listen, if you like chicks, come with me. I'll show you something."

We went to the far end of the motel. Second floor. He opened the door, and the cutest blonde hippie chick greeted us. She was wearing the shortest possible mini-skirt and a see-through top that would not be allowed in public. Dave was not gay. Good.

"Come on in," she said.

Dave stepped behind her, put a hand on each shoulder, and pushed her forward.

"This is Debbie," he said. "She's everyone's girl."

He said it like he was selling a used car or something.

"Debbie is the best joint roller in the world," he continued, then laughed again. "Look here." Dave lifted a towel from the desk, revealing a pile of perfectly-rolled joints and a pile of grass.

He lit one up, took a deep haul, and passed it to me. "Best weed this town has ever seen. It's Panama Red, imported direct from Central America for your pleasure. I have an unlimited supply. You'll be surprised where I get it, too. A friend of yours in Toronto sends as much as I can sell."

"A friend of mine? I don't know anyone with that kind of connection. Who?"

"We'll talk about it later," Dave said. "I have work to do. I'll be back in a few hours. Stay here, relax, and enjoy yourself."

He grabbed a handful of joints and stuffed them in his pocket. Then he slapped Debbie on the ass and breezed out the door.

Debbie sat on the bed, crossed her legs, and passed the joint.

"Dave's a great guy, you know."

"Well, yes, I guess he is, but I just met him," I replied.

"Are you going to work with us?"

I shrugged. "I don't know. I don't know what I'm going to do."

"Well, if you do, you're going to have a great time and make lots of money, too. We have the best drugs in town. Mostly, we have the only drugs in town. No hard stuff, you know, just grass and acid. Look here."

She got up the bed, showing me a nice panty flash, went to the window, and picked up a box of wooden matches. She opened it and showed me the contents. Acid. LSD. Lots of it. Two kinds: windowpane and blue barrels.

"You want to try some?" she asked.

"Yes, of course," I said. "But do you think Dave would mind if I took a shower? I had a bad night last night, and I think I smell like a diesel engine."

"Sure, go ahead," she said. "You can have some clothes, too. You guys are about the same size. Dave won't mind. I told you he's a very cool guy."

I spent a long time in the shower. I was a dirty hippie, but I didn't want to be. They say you don't miss your water until it's gone. Unlimited hot water is a luxury you will miss in two days. I was thoroughly steamed and wrinkled before I gave it up. I was hoping Debbie would join me, but she didn't.

I opened the bathroom door and looked into the room. It was empty. Debbie was gone. She had left clean clothes for me laid out neatly on the bed and a note that said, "I have to go to work, see you in the Winds."

The clothes were nice. Nothing fancy. Bell-bottom jeans, white poet's shirt, and a black leather vest. They were a little big, but they looked okay. My shoes were a wreck, but I didn't see a replacement.

I left my stuff in the room. When I closed the door behind me, I wondered if I would ever get it back.

All I had left of Joe's ten bucks was pocket change. It was enough for toast and coffee, so I went back to the Winds.

I was sitting at the counter looking up at the menu board on the wall when I heard a voice right behind me, close to my ear.

"What would you like?"

I turned and saw Debbie in a waitress uniform, pen and bill pad in hand.

"Oh, you work here? I didn't think I would see you again."

"Why not?" she asked, pouting. "We're friends now. You're with the Brotherhood."

I was a little confused. "Brotherhood" was a strange word to hear from her. I didn't say anything about it though, just, "Thanks for the clothes."

"Groovy," she said. "You look like Jim Morrison." She laughed. "That's two Morrisons now."

I was even more confused. Was she thinking about Hugh Morrison? I let it pass.

"So, what will you have?" she asked.

"Oh, just toast and coffee, I guess. I don't have much bread, you know. I have to be careful."

I was wearing her boyfriend's clothes. I didn't want her to know I only had fifty cents to my name. I think she knew my situation anyway.

She leaned in closer. "When I'm working, the food is free. I just make a fake bill, and you act like you pay me. The cook is my friend, so it's okay. Order whatever you want."

I nodded. "Cool. I'll do it, you know. I'll order the most expensive thing on the menu."

She smiled. "Go ahead. I recommend the hot turkey sandwich. It'll fill you up."

So I did, and I was filled up. It was only my second day "home," and things were looking up.

When I was done eating, Debbie came to the table and gave me the bill. She had drawn a little flower on it. There was no price. She told me to go to the front counter and act like I was paying. No one was looking anyway. I was thinking I wouldn't go hungry in my hometown.

"You should go find Dave," she said. "He's probably downtown in front of the library. I'll be working 'til midnight."

It was a short walk. Dave was there leaning against the building smoking a cigarette. I saw him first, so I stopped and watched for a minute. Two younger kids walked up to him, and I saw the deal go down. He was selling single joints. It was a cool way to do it right out in the open. He kept them in his cigarette pack. It looked like they were bumming a cigarette. He didn't see me until I was right in front of him.

He laughed. "You look like that Doors guy."

"I know," I said, laughing with him. "I've heard that already. Jim Morrison."

He didn't say anything about the clothes being his. I was glad.

"I just got a free dinner at the Winds," I told him. "Debbie has it worked out pretty good."

"Yes," Dave said. "We got all the free stuff we need in this town. It's easy. Here." He handed me two packs of cigarettes. "These are free, too. I'll show you later how to get them. Let's take a walk, and I'll explain a few things."

11

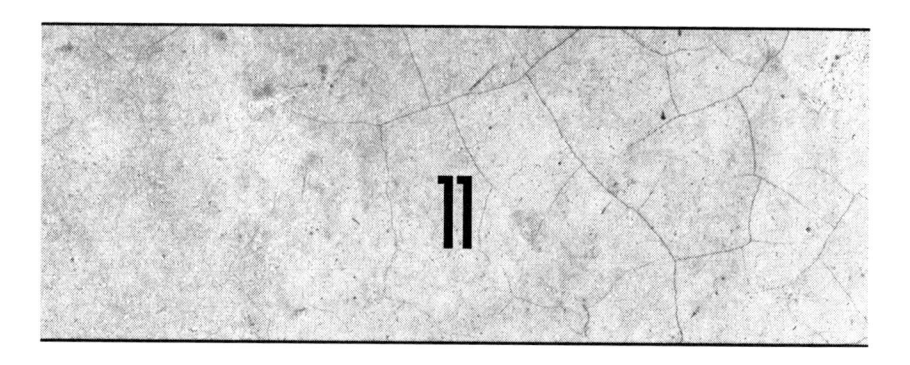

WE HEADED DOWN QUEEN STREET, THE MAIN DRAG IN MY TOWN.

"You need to watch out for greasers," Dave told me. "There's lots of them around here, and they don't like me. I got into a fight with a few of them a while ago. I fucked one of them up pretty good, so they leave me alone for now. They act tough, but they're chicken shit. It's the wops mostly. They have this gang called WEMA. Stands for 'west end mafia association.' Just punk assholes."

He leaned in close. "I got two secret weapons. Well, one's not a secret anymore, since I fucked up their best man. Here, watch."

He took two steps forward and did a scissor kick, leading with his left foot. His right foot hit a street sign that must have been over seven feet high. He hit it hard, too, rang it like a bell. I had never seen anything like it. Impressive.

Dave held out the toe of his shoe. "Push on it."

The fashion was called Romano's. Ridiculously long and pointed. I pressed my thumb on his toe. It was hard as rock. Like a pointed hammer.

"Wow, that's cool," I said.

Without thinking, I glanced down at my own worn-out shoes.

Dave laughed. "Yeah, man, you need some shoes. I don't know if I can get them for free, but let's go try something."

We continued walking up Queen Street, past the Sault Memorial Gardens.

"You'll get to know this place," Dave said. "I have a key to the back door."

The Gardens was the town hockey arena. Sault Ste. Marie was a hockey town. I didn't like hockey—or the Sault Greyhounds!

"What do you do in the Gardens?" I asked. "I'm not big on hockey, you know. I tried it when I was around thirteen. I can't skate for shit, and I don't like getting beat up over a round piece of rubber."

"No," Dave said. "No hockey. Don't worry. The only time I'm in the building, no hockey is happening. Only owners and wops. You'll find out."

We arrived at a men's clothing and shoe store.

"This place is owned by wops," Dave said. "Let's see what we can squeeze out of them."

I looked at shoes while Dave went to the counter and talked to the old man. I knew what I wanted—the same shoes as Dave, oxblood Romanos.

The old guy came over. "You like the new style? These are good shoes. Made in Italy. These shoes will outlast the fashion. What size are you?"

I glanced across the store, and Dave nodded and smiled. I turned back to the old man.

"Size eight."

He went to the back and returned with the box. He shoved it into my hands and walked away. Didn't even ask if I want to try them on.

Dave walked over. "Let's go."

By then, I wasn't going to question anything Dave did. The guy was fucking magic.

Outside the store, I burst out laughing. "How did you do that, man? What did you tell him?"

Dave's face went serious. It was the first time I saw him not laughing or acting light-hearted.

"This may be your hometown, but you don't know shit about it," he said. "Joe's family runs this town. They don't own Algoma Steel, but they run the union that keeps the place operating. Joe is the front man. His father is the boss of this town. Notice every business on the street is Italian. You'll find out later. First, let's go fix your shoes."

Then he laughed again in his normal way.

Directly across the street was a Sears store. My mother worked there for a while. When I was twelve, I got my first skateboard there. When I was fourteen, I got a Beltone electric guitar and amp. Dave went in and bought a box of plaster of Paris and we headed back to the Four Winds.

Back in his room, he put newspaper on the floor and mixed up the plaster. "It dries fast," he said. "We need to be quick."

He rolled a newspaper into a funnel and poured the mixture into the toe of my new shoes.

"There," he said. "Put your feet in and wait for it to harden. Make sure it doesn't go between your toes or we'll have to cut the shoes off you."

In a few minutes, it was done. My shoes were deadly and as comfortable as could be.

"There you go," Dave said. "Now you've got a secret weapon. I'll show you how to put a greaser on the ground rolling around in pain. And, just in case. . ."

He reached under the bed and dropped a pistol into my hand.

I had nothing against guns. I grew up with them. My only good childhood memories were hunting with my father. But this pistol was out of place. I didn't want to be involved in anything that might need a gun. Kicking someone in the balls with pointy shoes was one thing, but I had just gotten out of a nuthouse. I didn't want a gun. I handed it back.

"I hope you don't need it," I said.

"I don't need it," he replied, "but I like it. I can take care of myself, but I'm not going to get taken out by wop punks."

"So, Dave," I asked, "what's going on here? You're a cool guy. You fed me, gave me clothes and a pair of shoes, and almost set me up with your girlfriend. You sell single joints. I sold grass and acid, too. I know you can't make much money with single joints. If you want me to do something, I'll stick around, but I don't want to go to jail for nothing, and I'm not packing a gun."

"I'm not asking you to carry it around," Dave said. "I just want you to know I have it. I'm not sure about some of the people who pay me. One day, they may decide to off me, and I want an even chance. Don't let it freak you out."

Dave could tell I was still hesitant. "Look," he said, "you're not new to this. People in Toronto who know you also know me. I'm American, as you may have guessed. I'm from Frisco. My family is rich, but if I go back, I'll get drafted. I need to stay in Canada, and this is how I make money to stay."

I was stunned. It was like someone was spying on me. "Am I being set up for something?" I asked.

"Not set up, 'helped up' is more like it," Dave answered. "I guess you have two choices. You can stay and help me, or you can hitchhike back to Toronto. I'll show you how we do this, and then you can decide."

"Okay," I said, realizing I didn't have much of a choice. "But I want to know who you know in Toronto who knows me."

"Sure," Dave said. "His name is Hugh. He's an art collector—and a spy. He collects girls, too. Do you remember him?"

All I could think to say was, "It's a small world, eh? I'll stay here."

"Good," he said, "but one more thing: no speed. We don't do hard drugs."

Damn. This guy knew all about me. More than a few strange things. Luck, coincidence, karma. I didn't know what was up with my new friend. Since I had gotten out of Oak Ridge, strangers had been offering more help than I got from anyone in my life, even from my family. What was Dave up to? He wasn't a big time pot dealer. He gave me enough reasons to like him, but I still didn't trust him completely. I hoped he wasn't a hit man for the mafia. I had no choice but to go along and see what happened. At least I knew I could eat, courtesy of Debbie.

"Okay," Dave said. "Let's take a walk, and I'll show you the main attractions. You came in on a Greyhound, so that's where we'll start."

The bus depot was just two blocks down Wellington Street. To get from there to downtown, we pretty much had to pass by Dave's joint-dealing corner. The depot was open twenty-four hours. Busses came in from northern Ontario, Toronto, and the US.

"Early evening is usually the best time," Dave said. He laughed. "It's like fishing. Every day, kids run away from home. The Sault Saint Marie bus depot is a hub because of its location. Soon as they turn sixteen, they want to go join the hippies. Sometimes you see draft dodgers. Sometimes Indian kids from up North. They're the really dumb ones. Easy. Most of them wind up in Yorkville. Just stand around and wait for chicks to get off the bus. You'll see. They look confused. Just walk up to them, smile, and look like the cool hippie you are. Tell them the Winds just up the street is the main hangout. Don't offer to show them. Just tell them where it is. And tell them if they want some grass, there's a guy in front of the library who sells joints. He's cool. That's why I stand on the corner. I can usually pick them out on my own. I don't want to talk to them first. If they come to me, it looks like they're bumming a cigarette. If they want to buy a joint, I'll know they have some money. You'd be surprised how many kids land here without a dime in their pocket. Like you. If they stop to talk to me, I tell them they should go to the Winds if they want to meet the local hippies. If I think they don't have money, I tell them the waitress is my friend. She'll give them free coffee and not kick them out. Debbie's job is to make friends with them and later tell them how they can make some money and meet cool people."

"So," I said, "you're a pimp." I said it with a smile. A pimp wasn't a respectable occupation.

Dave laughed. "Sort of, but these girls aren't hookers. Not yet anyway. Call us matchmakers. Or an employment agency."

That sounded familiar. This was all connected, but I didn't know how. I thought about asking Dave if he knew Karl Wieland, but maybe it was better to hold that until I had a better idea about who knew who.

"Okay," Dave said, "you understand how it works?"

I nodded. "Sure. You don't want me so scare them off by hitting on them in the bus depot."

"That's right," he said. "You don't look like a scary guy anyway, but some of these runaways are jumpy."

We continued down Queen Street.

"How're your shoes?" Dave asked.

"Great," I said. "My old ones were wrecking my feet."

"Want to learn how to kick a basketball jock on top of his head?" Dave asked.

"I don't know if I can do it like you," I replied, "but I'll give it a shot."

"Well, this is how French men fight," Dave said as he jumped in the air and kicked a street sign. "The wops and Americans don't like it at all. They think it's dirty fighting."

Dave said American frat rats would often cross the "ditch" and pick fights with local hippies. "I hate those assholes," he said as he kicked another street sign. "Wait 'til we find a place with a soft landing. You'll probably fall on your ass a few times before you get it. Don't want to crack your skull on the sidewalk."

We were nearing the Memorial Gardens. It would be accurate to say it was the center of culture in the Sault. I don't recall anything but hockey happening there, although it would have been a good venue for concerts o of entertainment.

"I don't like hockey either, but sometimes I have to act like I d "I make my living from these jocks and jokers. I'm going to show yc own office in there." He laughed. "But first I want to show you this."

We stopped outside the building next door. It was a four or five story brick apartment building, large by Sault Ste. Marie standards. I had passed the building a thousand times but never paid much attention to it.

"Right here," Dave said, pointing at an alcove with a steel door. He stepped in and pulled the door open. It looked like a door that would be locked, but it swung open, revealing a long flight of stairs.

"Wow," I exclaimed. "I didn't know this was here. What is it?"

"A bomb shelter," Dave said. "Joe told me about it. The place is well stocked with everything, too. Come on, take a look."

He started down the stairs. Halfway down was a landing, a long hallway that must have run the length of the building. Then another set of stairs went further down. At the bottom was a big steel door with a double handle. Dave pulled it open, flicked on a light, and stepped aside.

"Take a look," he said. "Groovy or what?"

The first thing I saw was a fifty-caliber World War Two tripod-mounted machine gun.

"Oh wow!" I exclaimed. "Holy fuck, man, do you think it works?"

"I'm sure it does," Dave said. "But I didn't see any ammunition. Why would it be here if it didn't work? I guess its good I didn't find any ammo. Too tempting to see if it will fire."

Rows of bunkbeds lined both walls. Another room had toilets, sinks, and walls full of green, military-style boxes. It looked like it was stocked with everything you would need to survive a Soviet attack.

"If you ever need a place to hide out, here it is," Dave said. The door locks from inside. You'd need a tank to get through it. Joe told me there was room in here for his friends and family. I guess the rest of the people in the Sault can just get fried. Okay, let's go. I still have to show you my office."

The Sault Memorial Gardens opened a few days after I was born. It's long gone now. It was an average hockey arena except for one odd feature. The front of the building was dominated by a big tower that looked like a lighthouse. Whenever a hockey game was happening, the tower would light up red, casting an eerie glow on the entire street front. I never did like it. I thought it was sort of spooky, like a red light on a whorehouse.

Dave and I walked to the rear parking lot. He showed me a door in a recess much like the entrance to the bomb shelter.

"My office," Dave said, taking a key from his pocket. "This is where you take our precious cargo."

He unlocked the door and led me inside. "There's nothing to it," he said. "By the time they come to this door, they already know what's going on. Debbie explains what we have to offer, and they will come with you. You don't need to tell them anything and you're not tricking anyone. Usually, it's two girls at a time, but sometimes we bring as many as we can find for big parties. The girls are the entertainment. Debbie is good at explaining the details. I'm not around when she does the recruiting, but she's good at it. Nine out of ten will agree to ball some rich guy or hockey player for money." He laughed. "But they don't think they're hookers.

"Like I'm not a pimp," I added. "I'm an employment agent."

"It's true," he said. "The thing is, you will hardly ever see any of these girls again. When the party ends, they always get some kind of deal with someone. Anyway, don't fall in love. You can't keep any of them."

We walked down a hallway that went all the way around the building. We passed several doors with nameplates and various posters. I didn't pay much attention. It was all hockey. We came to a door marked "Utility Room."

"Your office," he said. He used the same key to open the door and then handed it to me. "Don't lose it, and don't copy it."

It had been a long time since I had a key to anything. It made me feel important.

Dave opened the door. The room was long and narrow, full of pipes and wiring. At the far end was a locked door.

"I haven't been past that door," Dave said, "but I know it goes to the shower in one of the dressing rooms. My business ends right here in this room. That door only opens from the other side."

He pointed to some wire baskets on the floor. "Here's what you need to do. You tell them to take off all their clothes, everything. Even socks. You put them all into these baskets and take them out the door we came in. Put the baskets outside the door, and then you lock it and leave. That's it. You may be tempted, but don't touch them. Just go. This is serious. Don't hang around. We do this two, sometimes three times a week, and we all make good dough. Are you into it?"

I didn't need to think about it. "You bet I am," I replied. "When do I start?"

"You already have," Dave said. "Tomorrow or the next day. Not sure yet. I'm just waiting for the phone call. It's like pizza delivery." He laughed. "You need to deliver them while they're hot."

We left the utility room. I locked the door and pocketed the key.

"Speaking of pizza," Dave said, "free pizza is another bonus. You know Clato's place on Gore Street? Just tell them you work for Joe and you don't pay. I don't think Clato likes it, but just walk out. He won't do anything."

"Are you sure?" I asked. "I don't want to get chased down over a slice of pizza."

Dave laughed. "Oh, yes. He's one of the wops into this up to his eyeballs."

Dave pointed down the hall. "There's more perks. Come this way, and I'll show you how to get more free stuff."

We walked to the main entrance where there was a boarded-up concession stand and several cigarette machines.

"Take that mat and drag it in front of this machine," Dave said.

I did as he asked. He grabbed one side of the machine and told me to grab the other.

"Okay," he said, "we're going to pull it forward and lay it down on the floor. But be careful, it's heavy."

As we laid it flat on the floor, I heard coins crashing around inside.

"Now, grab the legs and help me tip it completely upside down."

As we did, I heard the coins fall to the top of the machine.

"Okay, now we tip it back upright."

As the machine came upright, all of the money poured out of the slot—quarters, dimes, and half dollars—crashing onto the mat I had placed on the floor. Coins were mostly silver back then. They made a nice sound. There was lots of change. The mat kept it from rolling all over the place.

"Why on Earth do you want to steal a bunch of change?" I asked, surprised.

"Don't want the coins," Dave replied. "Now we put the change back into the machine and buy back all of the cigarettes. Cool or what? Everything is free," Dave boasted, filling his pockets with cigarettes.

I saw cars driving past the front windows. I was worried someone would see us. I stuffed five or six packs into my pockets.

"Let's get out of here," I said.

We headed back to the Winds. I didn't say much on the way back. I didn't like stealing things. The cigarettes felt heavy in my pocket. Dave was a cool dude, but I didn't want to get locked up again. He already knew too much about me. At the moment though, I couldn't even feed myself. I'd be sleeping on a greasy pile of rope again that night. I couldn't back out now.

"So, where do I get to stay?" I asked.

"You get a room at the Winds, same as me," Dave said. He took a wad of money out of his pocket and peeled off two twenties. "You're in," he said as he handed them to me.

I had no idea how much money he had in his pocket, but I had never seen anything like that. Dave had told me his parents were rich. Did he get money from them or from being a pimp?

In those days, renting a motel room was different. There were no credit cards, and you didn't need ID, only money up front.

We went into the office. It was empty. Dave pounded on the desk bell. An old guy came out scratching his head and looking like he had just woken up.

"Hi, man, how ya doing?" he asked when he saw Dave. He sounded a bit drunk.

THE PSYCHOPATH MACHINE

Dave put a hand on my shoulder. "This is a friend of mine. He's okay."

Dave turned and opened the door. "Come to my room when you're fixed up," he said on his way out.

The old guy turned the desk book toward me. "It's eight bucks a night or thirty-two a week."

"I'll take it for a week," I said.

"Okay, sign here."

He dropped a key on the table, turned, and walked out. He didn't even ask for money.

This was nuts. Even if I had money, it looked like there was no place I could spend it. Everything was free. Or stolen.

I made my way to the room. The Four Winds was a standard motel, but it felt like five-star luxury to me. I took off my new shoes and sat on the bed admiring them.

What a day! I had woken up intending to commit a serious crime, blackmail. I wound up stealing cigarettes instead. Somehow, it felt worse.

12

I WOKE UP THE NEXT MORNING WITH THE SUN SHINING THROUGH THE WINDOW. I DIDN'T KNOW IF I HAD missed something important the night before. It was like being late on my first day at work. Oh, well. If I had blown it, it would be nothing new. It was the way it had been for years. Start positive, and then I did something dumb.

I figured I might as well have one more shower before I hit the street. Who knew when I'd get another? Then I realized this room was mine for a week! But I hadn't paid yet. I decided to take a shower first and then pay.

I think every bathroom in the modern world has a vent fan. Not in those days. The room steamed up nicely. Water dripped down the walls.

I had long hair back then and got soap in my eye. I heard a sound, blinked one eye open, and there was Debbie standing in front of me with nothing on but a smile.

"Can I join you?" she asked, having already done so. I had no time to reply.

She looked me straight in the eye. "You need a new name, man. No one uses their real name, you know."

"Okay," I said, not really surprised by her demand or the situation. "Do you have any ideas?"

"You sort of look like that Doors guy. I like him."

"Jim Morrison," I said. "You told me that already."

"Yeah, him," she said. "But you're skinny, so I'll call you Slim Jim, okay?"

"Okay with me," I said. "I had an uncle named Jim."

Debbie turned around and leaned into me. I won't spend a lot of time on a few parts but skip them like a stone. Those who lived in the 1960s and 1970s will be happy to be reminded of how it was. Free love and all. Sex was just another way of saying hello. No fear.

Later over breakfast at the Winds, Debbie told me about the waitress serving us. "She acts nice, but I know she doesn't like me."

"Why do you say that?" I asked. "She was all polite and smiles when we ordered."

"She's over thirty," Debbie said. "You can't trust them. She doesn't understand hippies or our movement. And she doesn't like it that I give the cook a BJ once in a while." She laughed.

"Okay," I said as I stared at her with a big grin.

"I want to show you something cool," Debbie said.

"You're always showing me something cool," I replied. "Every hour!"

"Let's go," she said. "It's not far from here."

We walked four or five blocks before she spoke again. "You ever hear of the Diggers?" she asked. "They came from Toronto with lots of money. Last year they bought a big house on Albert Street. It's open to all the hippies, local and just passing through. Right here," she said, pointing at a house on the other side of the street.

I was a little worried about the location. My mother's apartment was only two blocks away. I thought about Bill. If he saw me, I was sure he would kick my ass or even kill me like he had threatened to do.

As we crossed the road, I told Debbie about the situation.

"Don't worry about it, Slim Jim," she said. "We have some tough friends. If you want, I can get someone to break his leg for you."

Coming from her, it was a real surprise. Debbie was a true "peace and love" hippie, just as sweet as could be. I believed she could do it though.

The front door of the house was open. We walked into a living room full of long hairs and freaks. Everyone knew Debbie, and she knew everyone in the room.

"This is Slim Jim," Debbie said to no one in particular.

Her words were met with a chorus of "Hey, man," "Groovy," and "Where you from, man?"

"I'm from right here," I replied, "but I don't think I'll be staying around."

Debbie showed me around the main floor and the backyard. It was a big yard with fruit trees and at least six tents set up.

A long hair walked past me and handed me a fat joint. "Here, man, smoke this for me," he said. "Not allowed to smoke in the house."

I turned to Debbie. "What's up with this place? It's too cool. Who lives here?"

"I don't know as much as Dave," Debbie said, "but there are four or five bedrooms upstairs. That's where the girls we collect stay."

"Oh," I said. "I'm collecting girls. That's nice. So, who pays the rent?"

"Well, Dave told me there are two groups who set this up," Debbie replied. "One is called the Diggers. They're from Frisco. The other is from Toronto. They're called the Brotherhood. The Diggers are hippies, but I think the money comes from the Brotherhood."

Debbie looked at me. "I've got a plan. Come over here and I'll show you."

A falling-apart garage was at the end of the yard. Debbie opened the door. Inside was a VW micro bus, the kind with windows all around. It looked almost new. A 1967, I think.

"It's mine" Debbie said. "I'm going to this big outdoor music festival in New York State. A place called Woodstock. Everyone will be there. Do you want to come with us? I have four other people so far. We can take turns driving."

"Sure I do," I replied. "When do we leave?"

"It's not until August," Debbie said. "We have to save money, so let's get busy."

At that moment, I realized that returning to the Sault might turn out to be okay, even though going home had been a disaster. I would never call Sault Ste. Marie my home again. The house on Albert Street became my new hangout, a few blocks from what should have been home.

A plan was taking shape. I could make some money working for Dave and then take off with Debbie in her van. I hoped Debbie wasn't Dave's old lady. He was an okay guy, but there was something dangerous about him. At that time, I didn't have much understanding of who was dangerous and who was not.

"I have some things to do before I go to work," Debbie said. "You can hang out here, but you should go to the bus depot at around four. The buses from Toronto and the west start coming in around then."

I hung out with the hippies, smoked pot, played some guitar in the backyard, and ate peanut butter sandwiches.

The kitchen was a busy place. There was an endless supply of bread and peanut butter. I asked a guy if I should pay something.

"No, man," he said. "There's always food around. You don't need to pay. The Diggers bring it."

I wandered back to the Winds later in the afternoon and went to the front desk. It was a different guy from the night before. I told him I had rented a room for a week but hadn't paid yet.

"Okay," he said, "it's twenty-five bucks."

I didn't mention that the other guy had told me it was thirty-two.

As I headed for the bus depot, I saw Dave standing on his corner. I walked toward him.

"Don't stop, Slim," he said, "just keep going."

He smiled, and I kept walking.

The bus depot was a small building with only enough seating for a dozen people. It had a decent snack bar with counter stools. I ordered a coffee and watched the people come and go.

The place was quiet for a while, a few old men smoking and talking. Then two buses arrived at the same time. I acted like I was waiting to meet someone. I scanned every face. Ignored the old people and the fat people. Just looked for young, pretty girls. It was sort of fun. The same as the house on Hazelton in Toronto. Find girls, send them to someone else, and get paid for it.

Three girls stepped onto the platform. They looked a little lost. Just what I was looking for.

Now, consider this: I had just been released from a hospital for the criminally insane. My best friend there and my fellow patients were child killers. Monsters, all of them. I had been screwed over by mad doctors for almost a year. They had made me crazy with bizarre drugs and physical torture. All that to say, it didn't occur to me there might be something wrong with what I was doing. I have no excuse or explanation, only that I was young and didn't know any better. I had no evil intent. I only wanted to make friends and have a place to live.

The three girls looked in all directions. One looked straight up. It's odd how tourists or people new in town look up.

I wasn't shy. Never have been. I walked straight up to them with a smile on my face. "You chicks looking for the hangout?"

All three of them smiled. "Yeah, man," one of them said. "Where's the main stem?"

I told them I had to stay there to meet someone, but there was a restaurant just up the road called the Winds. "Ask for Debbie," I said. "She works there. She'll introduce you to everyone."

I turned and walked toward the next bus as if I was looking for someone, and then I turned back.

"If you want some grass, there's a friend of mine up the block," I whispered. "He'll be leaning against the library building. You'll see him."

They giggled and headed for the door, the smell of patchouli oil wafting behind them. Such different times we live in today. People simply trusted each other then.

Over the next four hours, I repeated the same casual encounter with five or six other girls. Two of them were native girls from some northern reservation. They may have been over sixteen, but I can't be sure. They said they were headed for Toronto. I convinced them they should stay in the Sault for a while, that there were some cool people there.

As they headed out the door to the Winds, I thought about the local native school. I wondered if it was still open. When I was in public school, the Indian bus would pass by, and girls would throw notes out the window. I was maybe eleven years old. One girl I saw every few days threw a note that said, "HELP ME."

She was cute. I had a crush on her. I would time my walk to school hoping to see her face fly past. I tried several times to throw a note back into the school bus window, but I never managed to do it.

Then one day her face didn't fly past, and I never saw her again. I didn't even know her name. If she's alive, she would be close to seventy years old by now.

Later in the evening, the depot emptied out. I saw the woman behind the snack bar look at me a few times. I didn't want to draw any attention, so I wandered out and walked back up to the Winds.

It was packed with hippies. All of the booths were full. That meant all of the jukeboxes were on. Not many remember the musical instrument called a jukebox. Stereo speakers in a deco box at each table. One song for a dime, three for a quarter. As long as someone kept feeding it, the place was rocking.

I spotted Dave and Debbie in the back booth. She had her uniform on, so she was working. I slid into the booth opposite Dave.

"Well, that was an interesting day at work," I said.

Dave smiled. "Easy work, man."

"I talked to five chicks today," Debbie said. "Two are into it."

"Nicely done, Slim," Dave said. He pulled out his wad of cash and handed me another forty bucks.

"Is this the going price of a pimp?" I asked.

Dave frowned. "You've got to stop using that word, man. We're offering an employment opportunity, and we get paid for it. You have to understand; these are some very rich establishment types we work for. They can set you up nicely, or they can fuck you up big time, so stay cool."

I leaned back in the booth. Dave's character was changing as I got to know him. That hard edge would flash and then disappear, but it was there. In Oak Ridge, I was packed in tightly with killers and psychopaths. I could sense danger in my newfound friends, but what could I do?

"Sorry," I said. "I'd rather be an employment agent anyway. So, what do I do now?"

"Nothing," he replied. "Just wait 'til I get a phone call. Tonight, we party. I've got some good acid."

We hung out in the restaurant drinking coffee until midnight. When Debbie got off work, we headed to Dave's room with a crowd of invited hippies. Ten or more packed into his room.

Someone had a bottle of whisky they passed around. We drank from the bottle, acting like movie cowboys or tough guys. Every time the bottle came my way, I pretended to glug down a big swallow, but I only got my lips wet. I knew I couldn't drink like that. I didn't want to embarrass myself.

Then Dave went from person to person, put a hit of acid on their tongue, and made the sign of the cross like a priest. "Have a nice trip, brothers and sisters," he said. "Here are the keys to the universe."

Then he walked out.

Let's talk about acid. LSD—Lysergic acid diethylamide. It's a well-established fact that LSD was introduced to the counterculture in California in the mid-1960s. Apparently, it was a massive experiment in social engineering. LSD was one of many drugs and chemicals used in the so-called MK-Ultra mind control experiments. In those days, all LSD was under the control of the CIA. My first experience with LSD landed me in Oak Ridge, where I was given more LSD as treatment. I can't help but apply the same logic to an accident where you break a leg and go to the hospital, only to have the other leg broken as well so you would have a matching pair.

I don't really know what to say about LSD now, except that I would never do it again.

It was indeed the key to the universe: all encompassing, a complete loss of self-awareness, and a profound connection to the infinite, total immersion in the nature of everything. It came on fast. Less than ten minutes after the windowpane dissolved on my tongue, I began to dissolve and merge with the others in that tiny but infinitely large room. There were perhaps eight people in tune with each other's thoughts without saying a word. Disassociation from the physical world for two or three hours, then a gradual reuniting of my atomic structure with my sense of self.

Just before dawn, the experience was reduced to something more like "Lucy in the sky with diamonds," as the Beatles told us. Newspaper taxis and flowers that grew so incredibly high. We were able to pick ourselves up and go outside. A glow of energy surrounded everything. I saw electricity flow along the wires from pole to pole.

We hid in the bushes, laughing as the odd car prowled the road. They looked like living beasts. Not scary, but you never know.

At dawn, we went to the river to see the sunrise. I had a profound revelation about the sun, about what it really is. I don't remember it now, but the sun hasn't feel the same to me since.

We sat quietly on the riverbank, sad because the world was not as colourful as before. Our eyes are not designed to see all the colours.

Everyone hugged, said goodbye, and went their separate ways. I went back to my room and slept for most of the day with ashes in my brain.

13

I WOKE UP TO DEBBIE JUMPING UP AND DOWN ON MY BED.

"Wake up, Slim Jim, you've got work to do and you're missing a beautiful day."

My head felt as thick as a brick. I heard a loud *pop* in my ears, and then I was wide awake, energized. I reached up, grabbed Debbie by the shoulders, and rolled her under me, laughing as I pulled off her uniform.

"I have to go to work," she protested. "I'm already late. Okay, okay. You have ten minutes, Slim."

I didn't need ten minutes. There's something about a girl in a waitress uniform!

Debbie headed off to work. I waited a while, got dressed, and then went to the restaurant.

It was four o'clock in the afternoon, but I ordered breakfast anyway. I acted like I didn't know her.

"Bacon and eggs," I said.

Debbie stuck her tongue out at me. "Would you like a sausage with that?"

When I finished eating, she came back. "Dave wants to see you. He's in his room."

As I walked out, I thought it could be the end of this trip. Maybe Dave had found out about my past and was going to tell me to get on a bus to Toronto. I wasn't secure about this situation at all. From homelessness to this in a few days. It was too good to last.

It was a hot day. Dave's door was open. I saw him talking on the phone, so I waited outside. He spotted me and motioned me to come in.

"It's organized, Joe," he said into the phone. "Don't worry. We have three."

He hung up and smiled at me. "Okay, Slim, it's on for tonight. Pick them up at the house at nine."

"Does Debbie live there?" I asked. "At the house?"

"She's there most of the time, but she doesn't live there. She lives at home in her parents' house. She keeps everything together with the girls. None of them stay long, A week at most. They get some kind of job offer right here or they continue to wherever they were going."

"What kind of job offer can they get?" I asked.

Dave smiled. "Depends how enthusiastic they are. Some go to the US. Some even go to England."

"England," I said. "Wow, I wouldn't mind going to England. How do I apply?"

"It's not the kind of work you'd like," Dave said. "Besides, you're too old."

That was odd. It was the first time someone had told me I was too old for anything.

Dave gave me that serious look again. "This is a big deal in England. A lot of big shots are waiting for our party supplies. Nothing we do is illegal. Everyone gets what they want, but I've heard stories about things not working out so well with some girls. Anyway, we just do our part and keep everyone happy."

"Okay," I replied. "I like being able to sleep in 'til four o'clock and not get fired."

"No one ever gets fired," Dave said. "Just be there on time."

"I'll be there "I said.

I had a few hours before I had to be at the house, so I wandered around town. I walked past the Royal Hotel on the other side of the street. That was where Bill worked. I thought about taking Debbie up on her offer to break Bill's leg. The son of a bitch deserved it, but I didn't have the guts.

I walked past the town's only movie theater. My mother worked there for a while. I remembered the night she came home spitting mad. It was Halloween, and all of the employees were in costumes. She was dressed as a cat.

"That jerk manager wouldn't keep his hands off me," she said. "I had to slap him in the face to stop him. I quit and walked out." She started to cry.

My mother cried a lot. I think she used crying to make people around her feel guilty over things she caused herself. I can look back at her life with more compassion now than I had then.

Her mother, my grandmother, was taken from the streets of Dublin when she was a child and sold to a farmer in Quebec. They were called "home children." The man's wife died, and the farmer, Gorman, took my grandmother as his wife. I don't think they ever got married. She was no more than fifteen.

I remember Gorman well. When I was a child, I was afraid of him. He was a stern, angry-looking man. I'm sure he abused my mother from a young age. I think my mother always got involved with bad, useless, and violent men because of Gorman. Yes, I am a descendant of slavery, but we don't talk about it. And I don't expect any compensation, just a little recognition.

I decided to take a walk past my old high school. I had gone there for less than a year. I was kicked out because my hair was too long. I'm still pissed about it fifty years later.

Nothing had changed. School was out for the day, but the doors were open. I went inside and walked around the hallways. It was the smell of the place I noticed, like stale bananas in a lunch box. It made me sick, so I got out fast.

It was getting close to the time to go pick up the girls. I wandered over to the house. As usual, it was full of hippies. There were pot smokers in the backyard and Steppenwolf on the record player. I sat on a beat-up, overstuffed couch and waited.

Two girls came bouncing down the stairs, both typical hippie chicks with long dresses, long hair, and lots of beads around their necks. One had a leather headband holding down a mass of curly, red hair. The other was short and a little chunky but a cute as can be. They came straight to me.

"You're the guy we met at the bus depot," one of them said.

"It's my hangout," I replied. "I meet lots of chicks there. So, you talked to Debbie, and you're cool with the plan?"

"We're cool," the one with the red hair said. "I don't mind a party with rich guys."

"I've never met any of them," I said. "I think some are hockey players, but I guess they're rich." I stood up. "Let's get going. Better to be early than late."

We took the side streets. I linked elbows with a girl on each side, singing, "We're off to see the wizard."

I didn't even ask their names.

When we got to the Gardens, I noticed several big, expensive cars in the parking lot. I took the key from my pocket and opened the door to my "office."

I followed Dave's instructions exactly. The girls knew what was expected. I didn't have to say anything. They took off their clothes, flirting and smiling, and dropped them into the basket one item at a time. They posed and danced around half-naked and then completely naked.

"Can I keep my beads?" one asked. It was all she had.

I laughed. "I guess so. I don't think they'll get in the way."

They were both nice to look at. Girls in those times were . . . how to say it? Hairier!

I was tempted to hang around for a while, but I knew I had better follow instructions.

"Have fun," I said, and then I went out and locked the door behind me.

For a moment, it felt wrong. I knew what it was like to be locked into a small room. I had just locked them in like prisoners. But they were into it, I told myself. They had volunteered. I turned and left.

I went straight back to the Winds and fell asleep.

14

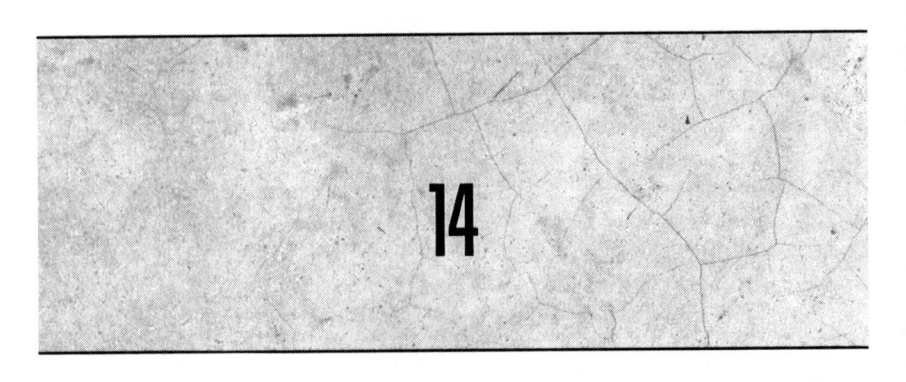

IT WENT ON LIKE THAT FOR SEVERAL WEEKS. MY TASK WAS SO SIMPLE. I NEVER QUESTIONED IT AT ALL.
Everyone was happy, and the party never ended. I would hang around the bus depot during the day, fishing. It was July. So many kids were on the road. It was like an entire generation was on the move. People were always looking for hitchhiking partners or just changing partners.

On most evenings, we would sit for hours in the Winds restaurant or hang around the house with the hippies, making music and smoking pot. I saw a few of the girls I had taken to the Gardens. There was no order not to touch them outside of my work, so I made the most of it.

One girl told me there was no sex involved when she went to the parties at the Gardens. She just served food and drinks naked. Got slapped on the ass by some old men, and that was it.

"It was weird," she said. "Some of them didn't even look at me. I thought they were homos."

I completed my task three times in total. That last time, there were four girls. I hadn't seen any of them before. It was July 20th, the middle of the afternoon. Debbie and I, a hippie guy, and his old lady, were sitting in Dave's room. Dave was in his corner doing his thing.

We were all laughing over something when the door burst open and four cops crashed into the room. One of them went directly to the window and picked up the matchbox where Dave's acid was stashed. The cop knew it was there.

"All right, you're all under arrest!" one pig bellowed.

"It's not my room," I protested.

They put us all in handcuffs.

As they marched us to the police cars, I said the dumbest thing: "Can I go lock my room first?"

"Oh," a cop said, "you live in this motel?"

"Yes," I said reluctantly. I should have just kept my mouth shut, but I had no drugs in my room, so I thought I would be okay.

One cop took me to my room. He told me to stand outside facing the wall. I heard him throwing things around inside my room, opening drawers and slamming them shut. He came out with two packs of cigarettes.

"Are these yours?" he demanded.

"Yes," I said, terrified because the cigarettes were stolen. Both packs were unopened. I did not smoke much in those days.

The cop put them in his pocket. I was relived, because I thought he was just going to steal them.

They drove us to the station in separate cars, took off the handcuffs, and sat us on a wooden bench. We were too scared to say a word to each other.

They took Debbie into a separate room first. When she came out, she gave me a helpless look and then walked out the front door. I never saw her again.

The hippies were next, leaving me alone on the bench. They were in there for at least half an hour. When they came out, they didn't even look in my direction, just walked out the door.

Then the cops took me into the windowless room.

"Who owns the LSD?"

"LSD?" I asked, acting shocked. "I don't know anything about LSD."

"Look," one cop said, "your friend was arrested for selling narcotics. You were in his room. Did you know there was drugs in the room?"

"No," I replied. "Of course not."

"Fine," the cop said, smiling. "These are your cigarettes." He pointed at them on the table. "You are being charged with possession of stolen cigarettes."

"I didn't steal them," I protested.

The cop showed me the government tax seal on the box. "You may not know this," he said, "but we can prove where these came from. You also may not understand that stealing cigarettes is a federal offence."

They took me to the lock-up and stuffed me into a cell. It's easy to remember the date. I could hear the radio playing in the office down the hall. Mamas and Papas, "California Dreaming." The song was interrupted to tell the world a man had just set foot on the moon. I thought I would like to trade places with him. I might as well have been on the moon.

The police lock-up was basically a steel box with bars on the front. In those days, they didn't need to provide a mattress or even a blanket.

It's hard to sleep on a steel bench. At least I had half a roll of toilet paper to use as a pillow. No food. Not even water. It was a long night. I didn't sleep much. As I lay there, I thought about what it would be like for the guy walking on the moon. What did Earth look like from there?

The next morning, they took me to the courthouse. The duty council talked to me for a few minutes.

"You should get this over with quickly," he said. "Plead guilty, and you will most likely get a fine. If you insist on a trial, they will find you guilty anyway.

And for wasting the court's time, they will give you a jail sentence. You're lucky they only charged you with possession of stolen goods under fifty dollars," he added as he walked away.

I never intended to plead "not guilty" anyway. I was guilty! It was a relief to know I would only get a fine. I just hoped I could pay it.

Three other cases were in the prisoner's box with me. Two of them were men who had taken a newspaper from a box without paying. The evidence was astonishing to me. The police actually emptied the coin box and then watched and waited, checking the box each time someone picked up a paper. Both received a twenty-five dollar fine.

The other case was "attempting to commit an act of gross indecency." An undercover cop had hung around a public washroom to entrap homosexuals by pretending he was one of them. Being gay was illegal then. The word "gay" had not been re-defined yet. It meant "happy." I'm sure the poor guy was not. He got a three-month suspended sentence. I guess it was punishment enough to stop him from being a sunny guy.

Then it was my turn. The charge was read. The judge asked how I pleaded.

"Guilty, your honor."

"Three months in provincial custody," he said and then banged his gavel and left the courtroom.

I didn't understand what had just happened. "How much is the fine?" I asked the bailiff.

"No fine," he said. "You're going to prison." By "prison," he meant Burwash Correctional Centre.

It was then that I realized I wasn't going to Woodstock with Debbie.

15

I WAITED ABOUT A WEEK IN THE SAULT COUNTY JAIL FOR A "CHAIN." THAT'S WHAT THEY CALLED A busload of prisoners coming from all over northern Ontario.

It was a long, bumpy ride chained to the seat hand and foot. The initiation into this prison was nothing like Toronto's Don jail. The guards didn't push me around. They called us by our first names. The worst part was the mandatory haircut—all of it shaved off. It was like being an army recruit.

They gave us two sets of fresh clothes, work clothes and dress clothes. They also gave us a personal grooming kit and a Kit-Kat chocolate bar. Imagine that!

I was assigned to a dorm with about twenty beds. The other inmates called us "whiffles," referring to our army-style haircuts.

It was late afternoon by the time I got settled into my new accommodations. Most of the inmates were young, in their teens or early twenties. Burwash was a provincial as opposed to federal prison. Everyone had a sentence of less than two years. In some cases, two years less a day. Officially, it wasn't a prison; it was a "reformatory."

Early the next morning, I was interviewed by a "classification officer." He was very friendly. He called me "Steven."

"Okay, Steven," he said, "you're not here for long, but let's see if we can teach you something to help you when you leave. This institution is a working farm. We are self-sufficient. We get some funding from the province, but we grow all of our food, and we have several industries."

He handed me a single sheet of paper with a list of places I could choose to work. "Do you see anything you would like to do?"

I glanced at the list and then dropped it on his desk. "I don't want to be here," I said. "I have better things to do."

"Well, okay," he said, "I can understand that. But you are here, and while you're here, you have to either work or go to school."

He looked at my file. "It says here you weigh only a hundred and twenty-five pounds. Is that correct?"

"I guess so," I replied belligerently. "It's your file."

"Tell you what, lad," he said. "You need to gain some weight and get healthy, so I'm going to assign you to the quarry. That will put some meat on your bones."

A guard took me straight to my new job. A large, noisy rock-crushing machine with a wooden ramp going to the top and a dump truck collecting the crushed gravel at the bottom. About a dozen inmates with nine-pound hammers were breaking boulders into coconut-sized rocks. It was my task to put the rocks in a wheelbarrow, push them up the ramp, and dump them into a hopper on top of the crusher. The wheelbarrow had a leather harness from the handles that went over my shoulders to help lift the weight. That was how the gravel road to Burwash was cut through the wilderness—by the inmates.

At first, the crusher scared the hell out of me. It was noisy, and there was nothing between me and the crushing steel wheels. If I lost my balance and fell into the hopper, my sentence would be over—permanently. No safety equipment at all, not even work gloves.

I worked in the quarry for the first month. The first day left me with blistered hands and wobbly knees. It didn't take long for my hands to toughen up and my back to get strong. Sometimes I would break rocks, and sometimes I would haul them to the crusher.

Breaking rocks with a hammer was sort of fun. There was a sense of accomplishment making big ones into little ones. I had to be careful, because there was no safety equipment. I learned to squint my eyes almost shut when the hammer struck to avoid blinding myself.

One thing about Burwash was good: the food. Everything was farm fresh. The bread was baked on site, and the facility's chickens laid the eggs. A lot of them.

I had a huge appetite from working. I would eat a whole loaf of bread with scrambled eggs or a stack of pancakes a foot high with maple syrup and butter. Soon, I noticed I was gaining weight. I felt stronger than I ever had in my life. With time off for good behavior, I was looking at two months. It didn't seem so bad.

Burwash had all sorts of industrial programs. All an inmate had to do was ask. One of them was an upholstery shop where guards and their friends could have furniture recovered. Burwash also had an auto body shop, a machine shop, and a farm with horses and cows. I think we drank raw milk the entire time.

I asked to be moved to the farm. The same day I asked, I was transferred. Rows and rows of beans needed tending. What can I say? Prison is prison. We were locked in, and no one wanted to be there. I'm sure I didn't think this way back then, but Burwash was doing something that might work.

Around halfway through my sentence, the warden called me to his office. He informed me that I was wanted in the Sault as a witness.

Two police officers came for me the next morning. They informed me that I had to testify in a drug trial. I wasn't charged with anything. All I had to do was get on the stand and tell the court the same thing I had told the police when I was arrested. It was Dave's trial. I wondered why it had taken so long when my case was over in one day.

Here's what happened that horrible day.

I decided I would take the rap for Dave. I was already locked up. LSD was still a controlled substance. It wasn't yet classified a narcotic. I thought I would get a little more time in Burwash. Maybe it would even be concurrent with what I had left on my sentence. Besides, Dave was my friend. He had helped me, so I thought I should help him.

When they took me into the courtroom, I saw Dave sitting at the table with a lawyer. He wasn't in custody, which was a good sign. I smiled at him and nodded. He looked right past me.

They called me to the witness box. I swore to tell the truth, but when they asked me if I knew the LSD was in Dave's room, I lied.

"Yes," I said. "I knew it was there, because I put it there. It was mine, and Dave didn't know about it."

After a moment of silence, Dave's lawyer stood up and asked for a ten-minute recess.

They left the room together. I was left standing in the witness box.

When they returned, Dave's lawyer said, "Your honor, my client would like to change his plea to guilty."

I didn't understand what had just happened.

"Very well," the judge said. "I will impose a six-month suspended sentence." Then he turned to me. "And you, Mr. Smith, have committed perjury in my court. I am sentencing you to an additional two years less one day to be served concurrently with your present sentence. Court adjourned."

The bailiff came and put me in handcuffs.

"What? What did I do?" I asked.

"You go back to Burwash with two years," the bailiff said.

I didn't even get a trial. I don't know if I got any justice that day. I don't even know if what the judge did was legal. There was no opportunity to defend myself. I wasn't even allowed to enter a plea. The judge imposed the sentence, and that was that.

I didn't have to wait in the county jail for a chain. The same cops who drove me to the Sault drove me back to Burwash the next day.

I sat on my bunk in the dorm. Three days earlier, my sentence was almost over. Now I had nearly two more years to go. That meant I would turn twenty-one in prison. What was it I did? I didn't think it was enough to deserve that. But then, no one in prison ever did anything. Just ask them. They're all innocent.

They wanted me to turn bad. They expected me to be bad, so, God damn it, I would be bad. Fuck it! I'd finish this sentence, get a gun, and rob banks.

I was angry for a long time.

16

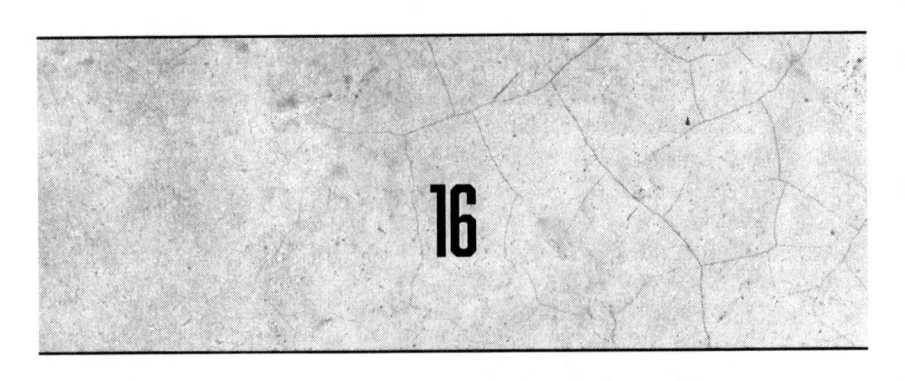

MY WORK IN THE FIELDS CONTINUED. HARD WORK WAS WHAT I WANTED, THE HARDER THE BETTER. THIS bad shit had happened to me because I was weak. I needed to be tough to get along.

I took up boxing and martial arts training. In spite of weighing less than 130 pounds, I discovered I had lightning-fast reflexes.

I got into trouble from a few inmates, because I worked too hard. It made them look like slackers.

One day, an Indian kid tried to stab me, but I was faster than him and took his shank away easily. I didn't hurt him. I could have, and I thought I should have, but I had never injured anyone in my life. I just put him on the ground and let him know he had better not get up and try again.

Time passed as it does in prison. Days went by in the blink of an eye, but the sentence seemed slow and endless. Autumn harvest came and went. My birthday came and went. I didn't tell anyone.

Every morning was mail call. It was the cruelest thing. Everyone lined up while a guard with a handful of letters called out names. I never got a letter, but I had to line up anyway, just to be humiliated, I guess.

The farm work ended when the corn was picked. All harvesting was done by hand. Bushel baskets carried one at a time from the fields. When the first frost came, it was time for another job.

The classification officer said I should go to school and get my grade twelve. "You'll never get a good job without it."

"I don't want a good job," I said. "I want a hard job."

He sent me to "Camp Bison." It was a short drive from the main Burwash building in an old military-type truck. Bison was a logging camp. It was primitive and cold. Bison would not have been out of place in Siberia.

The work day started before dawn. We ate as big a breakfast as we could. It would be a long day.

Our work began with a one-hour walk through the bush to reach the worksite. The first thing we did was gather firewood to make a big bonfire and boil water for tea. Then we got at it with bucksaws, a whippletree, and horses.

The kind of logging we did could only be done when the ground was frozen. None of us knew anything about logging. We were city kids for the most part. The guards were loggers though; they showed us what to do. With a little practice, it was easy to drop a tree exactly where we wanted it. But not always. We cut off the branches with an axe, and then the horses pulled the logs out. They were skidded onto a big, unstable, and dangerous pile.

The only safety equipment was decent boots and gloves. There were a lot of accidents. Something went wrong almost every day. I never found out what happened to the boys who got hurt.

One morning, this kid from Toronto took one of the horses up a hillside to get some dry firewood. He tied a chain around a dead, standing tree, hooked it to the whippletree, and pulled it down. The top of the tree struck the horse, causing it to take off at a gallop. The kid was dragged under the tree. We saw the horse running down the hill toward us. No sign of the kid.

Someone managed to get hold of the horse and stop it. We found the kid halfway under the log with a short branch piercing his chin and sticking out his mouth. He had been dragged all the way down the hill like a fish with a hook in his mouth. I don't know if he survived. They told us he was okay, but I never saw him again.

I made it through winter without major injury. I did crack myself on the forehead with the back of an axe. It was dramatic but not serious. I walked back to camp with blood streaming down my face and dripping off my chin. It got me a few days off work.

When the ground began to thaw and the horses could no longer pull logs, it was time to quit.

On my last day, I saw one of the horse drivers beating his horse with a chunk of wood. He had it by the reins and was hitting it on the head. I went nuts. I ran at him full speed and drove my fist into his face. He went down like a sack of shit. Out cold, twitching.

It scared the hell out of me. I thought I killed him. I put in for a transfer that day. Burwash never forced inmates to work at a job they didn't want to do.

I looked at all the educational options and decided to take an electricity course. It was all indoor classroom work, wiring and theory. Soon, I realized I didn't have the basic math skills to learn anything, so I enrolled in the high school equivalency course. Until then, I didn't even know I had a thirst for knowledge.

History, geography, mathematics, science. I devoured all of it. I read books, anything I could get my hands on. I didn't know what a good book was and what trash was. I would just pick a book at random from the library cart. Sometimes a cowboy story, Louis L'Amour. Sometimes Ayn Rand or a classic like *Quo Vadis*. I devoured every Steinbeck. I even read a book called *Urban Planning*. Boring, but I read it cover to cover. Books were a great escape from prison.

I finished high school in three or four months. They had a fake, contrived graduation ceremony. I got to wear a black robe and square hat while we clapped for each other, but I was proud of the diploma. Now I had some good math and geometry skills, so I asked for the machine shop course. It was the best and the worst decision I ever made.

17

AS A WORKING FARM, BURWASH HAD A LOT OF MACHINERY IN CONSTANT NEED OF REPAIR. THE MACHINE shop kept the place functioning. It had machine lathes, milling machines, surface grinders, cut-off saws, everything. The equipment was old but good. The instructor was old, too. He was German—the best machinists always are.

We became friends, and after the course was complete, he wanted me to stay on in the shop. Something always needed replacement or repair. I discovered I had a real talent for that sort of work.

He told me some people could never be a machinist, because they had what he called "poison fingers." He said if you handled a piece of cold, rolled steel and the next day there were rusty fingerprints on it, you had poison fingers. It was something to do with the salt content and moisture on a person's hands.

Some days there was no work, so we would sit in his office talking. On one of those days he asked about my father. I told him he fought in the war and was wounded in Holland.

"You're German," I said. "Maybe you fought against him."

He smiled. "No, no, I never fired a gun in the war. I was a machinist. I worked on Hitler's rocket program. I'm sorry about your father, but I'm proud of the part I played."

He stood up and walked around his desk. "There are many things about the war you don't know," he said, putting his hand on my shoulder. "I know you think you won the war and defeated Germany, but the war didn't end the way they told you in school."

"I never heard anything about it in school," I said. "I must have skipped that history lesson."

"I'll tell you what happened if you want to know the truth," he said. "If we had just a few more months we would have won. We had the bomb. I was working on the rocket that would have delivered it to England. We only needed a little more time."

He shook his head. "Hitler made so many mistakes. Close to the end, he disappeared. Everything was in chaos. We were without a leader. Hitler abandoned us and fled the country. I don't know where he went, but the Americans and Russians didn't stop him. I think he's still alive," he said with a smile.

"I took off my uniform and went from house to house hiding from the occupying forces. I was in Berlin. One of my colleagues told me I should surrender to the Americans. 'If the Russians get you, they will shoot you right away,' my friend said. I was so scared. I couldn't speak English at all.

"I found an American garrison, put my hands in the air, and walked toward them. I expected to die there and then, but I was tired of hiding. There was no food, no water, and my lovely city was in ruins. There was nothing left for me to do. I showed them my papers. They took them and then tied my hands together with a piece of wire.

"I know what it's like to be a prisoner, my young friend. Maybe that's why I work here now. You may not think you're lucky, because you are a prisoner, but it was much worse back then."

He shook his head in remembrance. "In time, I was interviewed by an American officer and a translator. I was told I was not wanted as a war criminal. I could choose to leave Germany and go to Canada or America. There was nothing left for me in Germany.

"The officer handed me a file with my picture on it held in place by a blue paperclip. 'Don't lose this,' he said. 'It is the start of your new life in Canada.' That's how the war ended for me," he said with a smile. "Thank God I never killed anyone."

I wish I could remember that old machinist's name. It was almost fifty years ago, but he had a tremendous impact on me. We talked of many things, "shoes and ships and sealing wax, cabbages and kings." I'm sure I learned how to think from him, not *what* to think like others tried to impose.

One day, I told him about Peter Woodcock and the Brotherhood. I asked if he knew anything about Karl Wieland and that strange German ceremony I had witnessed.

"Many Nazis from the Third Reich came to Canada," he said. "They didn't give up their beliefs, and many were helped by the Canadian government. I, myself, was allowed to leave Germany only because I was useful. Those things are better for you to forget about though," he said. "You should not tell anyone about that."

I wanted to know about his war experience. I told him that my father had lied about his age and enlisted when he was seventeen. He had two weeks of basic training, and then he was put on a ship and landed in Holland. My father always seemed embarrassed by the fact he only saw a few days of combat. He was wounded and taken prisoner by the Germans.

The only war story my father told me was how the Germans sent him out to pick up their wounded. The fighting was intense, and his captors had no time to evacuate prisoners from the battlefield. He was within range of snipers, but in spite of his shrapnel wound, he grabbed a gun from a dead soldier and ran for it.

That was the end of the war for my father. He made it to his own line and was evacuated to a hospital.

My mentor, prison guard, and friend almost cried when I told him the story. "War is what happens when money gets confused," he said.

"I don't understand," I replied.

"Young man," he said, "war is always about money, not territory. We need to stop falling for the same tricks."

I didn't fully understand what he meant until recently.

IN TIME, I BECAME THE second instructor for the machine shop course. Sometimes the old guard would not show up at all. He trusted me to do what was needed.

One day, he gave me a key to the shop.

"For God's sake, young man, don't tell anyone."

As far as I know, I'm the only prisoner at Burwash who ever had a key to anything.

I got on with the necessary tasks: fixing broken gears, making chicken catchers, and such.

Often, there was nothing much to do. I had all this great equipment, and I wanted to test my skills, so I did what any prisoner in my situation would do. I designed and manufactured a gun!

I had no bullets, but I was pretty sure I had the bore for a .22 caliber correct. It would be fully automatic if I had the extractor right. I worked on it for months. The thing was a real work of art. The slide was perfect. I even managed to Parkerize it. I wished I could show it to someone, but I had to keep it secret. I wasn't good at keeping secrets, and I'm still not, but I kept it hidden in the shop.

Until that fateful day.

18

ONE AFTERNOON JUST BEFORE QUITTING TIME, TWO GUARDS CAME TO THE SHOP AND TOLD ME SOMEONE wanted to interview me. I never got visits, so I had no idea who it could be.

They took me to the sick bay. I thought it was strange as they sat me in a heavy wooden chair and handcuffed my wrists to the chair's arms. Then I got really scared.

"What's going on?" I asked.

Two men in suits and white lab coats came in. "We want to ask you a few questions," one of them said as he stepped behind me and took hold of my right arm. "But first, a little prick."

He stuck a needle in my arm. The affect was instant. I knew what it was. Scopolamine! And I was gone.

"The Devil's Breath," "the Zombie drug," "the scariest drug in the world." These are some of the terms used to describe scopolamine. It has been called the most dangerous drug in the world, and for good reason. In powdered form, it can be placed on a piece of paper and blown into an unsuspecting person's face right in the middle of a busy public street. Within seconds, that person becomes your zombie. You can lead the person to an ATM, and he will empty his bank account for you. You can even take them home, and they will help you pack up all of their belongings for you.

Those are the lucky ones.

Others are taken and gang raped for days. Still others wake up in a hotel bathtub filled with ice and find one of their kidneys missing.

No memory of anything

I have no memory of what took place in Burwash sick bay. I have no idea how long I was interrogated, by whom, or why.

I have found an almost universal experience of those intoxicated with scopolamine. They see demons. Real hallucinations, not just visual distortions like LSD. It is always bad, very bad.

I told you about Oak Ridge and Dr. Barker experimenting on patients with scopolamine. I knew what it was, and I knew it had something to do with Oak Ridge.

When I came to my senses, I didn't know if it was days or hours later. I was on a hospital bed with leather straps around my wrists and ankles. I struggled to free myself and started screaming.

"What the fuck? What the fuck?"

A guard came in and told me to calm down. "You had a fainting spell," he said. "We strapped you onto the bed to make sure you didn't hurt yourself."

He untied me and handed me a glass of orange juice.

"Well, you look okay now," he said. "You can take the rest of the day off. Go back to your bunk."

I left the sick bay and walked back to the dorm feeling a little shaky and weak. I put my hand in my pocket and felt for the shop key. It was still there.

That's when I made my decision.

I went to the machine shop. It was closed and locked. I went inside and took my gun from its hiding place. It was nothing more than a useless piece of metal without a bullet, but it comforted me somehow.

You must understand, my sentence was almost over. In three or four months, I would be free. I never told anyone why I did it, and no one ever asked. They just shook their heads, bewildered.

That evening, just before dark I kicked the screen from a window and ran for the bush. I escaped from Burwash for no apparent reason. And I had a gun in my waistband. The last I saw of the place was the astonished faces of inmates in the common room. I wonder if any inmates who saw me run ratted me out. I doubt it. I was a "go boy," and they thought it was heroic. That was the name for what I did, "go boy." I don't think the guards even knew I was missing until the evening count.

It wasn't a well-planned escape. I had no plan at all aside from just running into the bush. I ran as fast as I could to the treeline, expecting someone to chase me. I ran through thick underbrush, branches cutting my face, barely avoided poking my eye out. Heart pounding, fear and anger driving me, I ran until I collapsed under a tree.

The effects of the scopolamine were still with me. Mouth so dry I couldn't swallow. I had no water. I lay there face-down in the dirt and fell asleep.

19

I WOKE UP IN A CLOUD OF BLACK FLIES. IT WAS ALMOST DARK, AND THEY WERE EATING ME ALIVE.
Anyone who knows the bush in Northern Ontario knows black flies can drive a moose crazy. I had to get up and move.

I pulled the collar of my shirt over my head to try to keep them off my face. It didn't work! I just kept stumbling forward.

I came to a river and almost fell into the fast-flowing water. By then it was dark, and the water was too wide to cross.

I thought I read somewhere that Indians used pine sap to keep insects off them. It was mostly pine trees around me, so I had no trouble finding sap dripping down a trunk. I got a good handful and smeared it all over my face and hair. It felt awful. And it didn't work. It turned me into human flypaper.

Sleep was out of the question. Just enough moonlight to keep moving forward. The lack of light wasn't my biggest problem though. My eyes were swelling shut from bug bites.

I thought I saw other eyes watching from the dark. More than one pair. There were wolves in this forest. I could have wind up a pile of bones, never found. My life was in danger. It wasn't just an idea; it was an imminent reality.

Even though I didn't really believe in God, I prayed anyway. Why was my life such a nightmare? I just wanted to be good, but I didn't know how.

I kept moving, and then a strange thing happened. I don't have adequate words to define it. Everything slowed down, like in a slow-motion film. A sense of peace and oneness with nature overcame me. I became calm when I understood that this was what happened when you died in the forest. I was part of nature, and there was no good or bad. If wolves came and ate me, it would be good for them. I honestly couldn't think of anyone but me who would think it was bad.

I kept moving, following the river. For some reason, I thought I would be safe on the other side. It was too dark to see across, but I kept testing the riverbank for a crossing.

I couldn't swim. Even today, if I get water in my face, I panic. I had a greater fear of water than I did of wolves. I stayed on my side of the river. I could see

I was on some sort of overgrown path. The black flies weren't as bad. A bit of wind came from the river.

I reached a clearing with a manmade structure. I circled it from the edge of the trees. No lights, and no sound. I drew closer and saw it had been abandoned a long time ago. Half of the roof had fallen in. It had no door or windows.

I went inside and looked around as best I could, finding only dark corners. It was only a one-room wooden structure. Against the wall was a metal frame bed with no mattress, just springs.

I sat down and picked at the pine sap in my hair. I tried to pull out bits of wood and some bugs that were still alive. If I had had something sharp, it would have been better to just cut it all off.

How long ago had it been since I had gone "go boy?" I didn't know. I thought it was a long time, but I guessed it was only hours. How far had I come?

I didn't think they would be coming after me until daybreak. Still, I kept an eye out for flashlights in the forest and the sound of dogs, like in the movies. Did they really do that?

I guess I slept for a while, but mostly I waited for daylight. I raised my head, blinked, and it was morning. The shack was bright with sunlight.

I put my hand to my face, and it stuck like glue. That stuff was horrible! I had to get it off me.

I went to the riverbank and found a shallow spot. My reflection in the water looked like a wild man.

Inside my head, I knew who I was though. My thoughts were of self-preservation. I wanted someone to take me by the hand and lead me out of this situation. But no one would try to reason with someone who looked like I did. I was the reason police did target practice with pistols. To them, it was the circumstances that counted, not what was in my heart. I was sure they would shoot me on sight.

I took off all of my clothes, lowered myself into the water, and tried scrubbing myself with sand to get the sap off. No good. It just made me cold.

I went back to the shack to see if there was anything I could use. I didn't find much, just some rusty bits of metal and an old box of nails. Then I found it. One .22LR shell on the floor almost fallen between the planks.

I picked it up and chambered it in my gun. It fit perfectly.

I heard the words, "Leave it," inside my head. The voice was not my own. It could have been the last vestige of my conscience. It might have been God.

I put the gun on the floor and stared at it for a while. One round. What should I do with it? Would the gun even work? The best thing I could do was shoot myself in the head. But what if it only half worked? Things were bad enough. I didn't want to just wound myself.

I picked the gun up, pointed it at the floor, and pulled the trigger. A bang is very loud when you expect a click, just as a click can be very loud when you expect a bang.

It went bang all right. Pieces of wood flew into the air.

My first thought was that I had just given myself away. Surely they had heard the shot and would be coming for me.

I sprinted back into the forest. I ran for at least half an hour. It was easier because I had a trail to follow. I didn't know if I was running toward or away from the posse. Trails always lead to something though. If I kept following it, I thought I should come to a road eventually. Then what?

I had a vague notion of making it to Sudbury. I heard there was a biker bar. If I could find it, maybe they would help me. I didn't even know what direction Sudbury was. Besides, how could I walk around a city dressed in prison clothes?

I didn't have a plan at all. I only wanted to get away from whatever plan they had for me. That's all there was. I wasn't going to let anyone inject me with anything ever again. They didn't own me. I was hungry, dirty, and tired, but I was free. At that moment, no one could force nightmare drugs on me.

I kept walking, thinking about the great breakfasts I had eaten at Burwash. By evening, hunger was too much to bear. I started looking for anything I could eat. I turned some rocks over, but I couldn't bring myself to eat any of the things under them.

I was sure there were fish in the river, just below the surface, but I had no way to catch one. Then, in a shallow spot, I saw some crayfish. They are like little lobsters, easy to catch. Just split the shell open and suck out the inside. It was something anyway.

I spent that night under a tree. It was cold, and my clothes were wet, and the blackflies came back.

By morning, my face was all puffy. I didn't care about the flies in my face anymore. I was just worried my eyes would swell up so much I wouldn't be able to see at all.

I thought it must be the third day. I wasn't sure. I wished I had a cup of coffee.

Suddenly, there it was, a road and a bridge and a cottage that was neither abandoned nor broken down.

I crept up to it, looked in the windows, and then tried the door. It It was locked. I tried one of the windows, and it opened.

I climbed in and looked around. It was furnished and clean. It was someone's summer cottage with no sign of anyone being there recently.

I opened the kitchen cabinet door. My God! It was full of canned food. I didn't take time to plan a menu. I found an opener and started eating things from the can.

I choked and dropped the can when I heard a car on the gravel road. It went past. It wasn't a safe place. I had no idea how busy the road might be or where it went.

I gathered some canned food and put it in a pillowcase. Better to follow the river, I thought.

Behind the cottage I saw a small aluminum boat turned upside down. I dragged it to the riverbank and looked around for a paddle. Nothing. I found a piece of plywood I thought would work. I jumped in and shoved off into the fast-flowing water.

The boat moved with the current under the bridge. I didn't have much control of it. Then up ahead I saw white water. I heard it getting louder as I approached. The boat started hitting rocks on the bottom. It was totally out of control and moving fast. I could see that the rapids were more than the boat could handle. I was about to capsize, leaving me another way to die from my stupidity. They would find me floating facedown somewhere.

I paddled for my life with the piece of plywood. All that hard work in Burwash paid off. I made it close enough to shore that I could jump to safety. But the boat was lost. I watched it go down river, hit the rapids, and flip over and over until it sank. The bag of food went with it.

Then I realized I didn't have my gun. I had left it in the cabin in the forest. I had to go back and get it. I can't tell you why because I don't know. I just had some sort of unbreakable connection to the thing, as useless as it was.

It was another spark point in the web of life. If I had left it, everything likely would have been different.

20

I DECIDED THAT WHATEVER THE RISK, I'D STAY THE NIGHT IN THE COTTAGE. I COULDN'T TAKE ANOTHER night under a tree.

I found scissors in the bathroom and cut off as much pine-soaked hair as I could. I couldn't get it off my face and arms. My face hurt too much to scrub it. Soap didn't work anyway. I didn't recognize myself in the mirror.

I looked like I was in black face. I laughed at the mirror and sang an old Al Jolson song. "Mammy, how I love ya, how I love ya, my dear old mammy."

It felt good to laugh. Why not? I was as free as a . . . I didn't know. Could I ever be free again? What did "free" even mean? Janice said, "Freedom's just another word for nothing left to lose." I stared at myself in the mirror and wondered how things had come to this. How bad was I, really?

I thought about all the things I had done wrong. When I was around eight years old, I stole a ball from the Sears toy department. I got caught right away. I never stole another thing until the car, and I wound up in Oak Ridge for that. But then I broke into a church and stole money from the poor box. I didn't know what to think of that. I was poor. Did I have to ask for money from the poor box? I thought God would get it, but the court would not. If they pinned that one on me, I was sure it would be worse than stealing cigarettes or trying to blackmail an old homosexual.

What about the things I was doing at that moment? How bad a person did they make me? I was an escaped convict and I was running with a gun. I had broken into someone's cottage and made a mess. I smashed their fishing boat, too. I didn't expect to gain anything from this mess. It was bound to end badly.

I ate some canned food and then looked through their book collection. I picked one. It was by a Persian poet named Omar Khayyam. I wondered who owned this cottage, if they read this sort of thing. The words calmed me. I was sure the owners wouldn't be too pissed off at me.

There were oil lamps, but I didn't want to risk lighting one when it got dark. The bed looked comfortable, all white sheets and feather blankets, but I slept on the floor. I was too dirty.

I was startled awake in the morning by the sound of a car in the driveway. I was trapped.

I heard the front door open, followed by a woman's voice.

"Oh my, someone broke in."

I was going to hide under the bed, but I knew it was useless.

The couple came into the bedroom and saw me crouching on the floor. They were old by my standard then, maybe in their fifties.

I had learned from my father at an early age never to point a gun at anyone, even if it wasn't loaded. No one should ever see the hole in the business end of a gun unless they were cleaning it. At that moment, I forgot the rules.

I jumped to my feet and pointed the gun with both hands like a cop. "Don't move!"

They froze like statues. A small squeak and a gasp were the only sounds. We stood that way for an endless time. I didn't know what to do next.

I gestured with the gun and told them to go into the other room. The three of us were scared to death. I must have looked like a madman. They didn't know what I knew. I knew the gun wasn't loaded. I also knew I would not hurt them, not even if the man attacked and tried to kill me.

I ordered them to sit on the couch. They moved together like they were attached to the barrel of the gun. Wherever I pointed, they went. The man moved the book I was reading and sat down. His wife remained standing until he pulled her down beside him.

Another long silence. I was trying to think clearly, make a plan.

"Did you escape from Burwash?" the man asked in a low voice.

I nodded. "Yes, I had to."

"What do you want from us?"

"I don't want anything," I replied. "I only needed some food."

"Are you going to kill us?" the woman asked in a shaky voice.

It was more than I could take. I felt the flood coming from my feet to my head. It was over. I was defeated. I couldn't see clearly. My eyes filled with tears as I sat on the floor and handed my gun to the man.

"I don't want to do this anymore," I said. "I want to go home."

That's what I wanted to do, but I knew I never could. I asked if they would drive me back to Burwash.

"I don't think that's the way to do this," he said. "I can take you to the police in Sudbury. It's not far."

I agreed, and we went to their car. Before we got in, he looked me straight in the eye.

"You're sure? You can run into the bush if you want."

I just nodded my head and looked at the ground.

It took less than half an hour to reach town. I didn't know how close I was. He kept asking questions all the way. He was trying to keep me calm, I guess.

He asked about the Omar Khayyam book. He said I must be an intelligent young man if I liked that book. He asked why I was in Burwash. I don't think he believed my story. I don't blame him.

I actually thought he was helping me until we stopped in front of the police station. He told his wife to go in and tell them I was outside. As soon as she was gone, he leaped over the front seat and landed on top of me. I pushed the door open and struggled outside. Again, he jumped on top of me and pinned me to the ground.

I didn't try to get away. I understood he was going to be a hero for capturing an armed, escaped convict. It was fine; he deserved it.

The police arrived in seconds. The street was filled with yelling and screaming. I heard the commands, "Drop it!" and "Drop the gun!"

"It's him!" the man on top of me shouted. "I got him. I got his gun."

He had the gun in his hand and was acting as though he had just ripped it from my hands. That was the official narrative published in the Sudbury newspaper. "Man Captures Escaped Convict: 55-year-old man disarms young gunman."

I read the news clipping more than a year later. It claimed the homemade zip gun was loaded. I'm the only one who knew it was a spent shell stuck in the chamber. I was disappointed that they called it a zip gun. It was my creation—and my downfall. That's all there was. No explanation why all of this had happened right in front of the police station.

I didn't get to surrender. They dragged me into the station and threw me into a cell.

A few hours later, some paramedics came in and examined me. They cleaned up the pine sap with towels soaked in kerosene. It hurt like hell. I think they enjoyed it, but I didn't resist or complain.

The trial was swift. I expected to be charged with escaping custody, breaking and entering, and theft, but I didn't expect the kidnapping charge. It was read out in court, and I pleaded guilty to everything. I had no defense, nothing I could say.

Altogether, I received an odd sentence: nine years, nine months, and nine days. I thought there was something symbolic about the total. It's possible there was. Years later, I found out the man who "captured" me was master of the Sudbury Grand Lodge.

I can tell you this. I have not committed another crime since then—aside from smoking a joint once in a while or doing a line of coke back in the 1980s when it was cool. I respect the rule of law, as flawed as it is. But it was too late. The deed was done, and I had to pay the price.

LIFE FELL INTO A ROUTINE at the county jail where I was held awaiting transfer to the big house. Lights on at five thirty. A bucket of soapy water and a scrub brush was passed from cell to cell. The first thing we did in the morning was scrub our already spotless cell.

The morning after I was sentenced, I kept my head under the blanket and refused to do any scrubbing. Why should I? What more could they do?

The guard showed me. He pulled the blanket off and dumped the dirty water, scrub brush and all, onto my head.

You know that saying, "He just snapped?" That's what I did. I actually heard a snap inside my head like a breaking bone.

I swung at the guard and hit the steel bucket. Then I heard the snap of real bones breaking. My bones. I swung again, unable to see past the water in my face. That time I hit the cement wall. I felt the knuckle bones move into a place they should not be.

Other guards came running. They put me into some sort of leather harness, like horse tack. My hands were strapped tightly to a belt around my waist. They did the same thing around my ankles and then clipped them to my waist, knees bent backward, hogtied.

I don't know how long I remained like that. I had snapped, and nothing mattered.

Eventually, someone came and put a rough cast on my broken hand.

I stayed hogtied for the night. The next morning, they came in and put me into a proper straightjacket, like the ones you may have seen in the movies. They actually exist.

They had to force my right hand with the cast through the extra-long sleeve. I suppose it hurt like hell, but I didn't care. I was somewhere else. I remember not being able to scratch my nose. I thought it would drive me crazy.

Then they injected me with something that left me barely conscious. It was a long drive to a familiar front gate. Oak Ridge!

When I left the first time, they said I would be back. They were right. I had to be crazy.

Four attendants placed me on a wooden cart with two big wheels like wagon wheels. It was an antique, like some sort of medieval hay wagon. They bumped me up the front stairs and back into the torture chamber. This time, I thought it would be ten years. But I didn't care. I was . . . elsewhere.

21

EVERYONE HAS A PLACE IN THE CORNER OF HIS OR HER MIND WHERE HE OR SHE CAN GO WHEN REALITY becomes too much to bear. In war, they call it the thousand-mile stare. I was put in a cell, the straightjacket taken off, and the door slammed unnecessarily hard.

I was content to stare at the water in the toilet bowl. Water is beautiful no matter where it is. I pulled off some gauze from the cast and went fishing. I knew there were no fish, but I was going fishing anyway. It felt good. I hoped no one would ever open the cell door again. I was content to fish. But I was in Oak Ridge. Contentment was not allowed.

Someone noticed the unraveling cast. They came in, took it off, and took my fishing gear away. Didn't want a hanging, you know. So I had to be content looking at my smashed hand, counting the colours of blue and purple.

What I thought was a baloney sandwich was shoved under the door on a paper plate along with a paper cup of tea or coffee, I couldn't tell which. I couldn't remember the last time I had eaten. I wasn't really hungry, but I ate it anyway. What I wanted was the paper plate.

I ripped it up into little fish shapes and dropped them into the toilet. It was a challenge to make them with one hand.

A guard came and told me to put the plate under the door. I just kept working on the fish.

"Put it under the door, you little shit, or I'll break your other arm."

I believed he would, so I surrendered what was left of it.

He ordered me to flush the toilet. I did, but it didn't refill. No more water.

The first time I was there, I was not crazy; I was railroaded. The second time I was a nutcase, no doubt about it. It was better that way. You didn't want to be in a place like that if you weren't nuts. You would be provided more drugs to make you nuts.

I endured three or four days without any contact other than food shoved under the door. No water either. Nothing to drink, no flushing the toilet. My right hand looked bad. The bones were out of place. I wondered if I would ever be able to use it again.

Then, like déjà vu, the door opened, and Dr. Barker walked in, all friendly and smiling. "Nice to see you Steven. I thought we would see you again."

I wasn't so pleased to see him. I didn't say anything. Just gave him a fierce stare. I thought he stank of white shirt and stale sweat.

"I guess you're wondering what happens now."

"I know what happens," I replied. "I sit in this cell forever."

He laughed like I had just made a joke. "No, you go back into the program. You have a significant sentence to serve. The court sent you here for a thirty-day assessment. We will decide if you stay here or go to Kingston Penitentiary."

Well, this is a rock and a hard place, I thought. Kingston Penitentiary was the "big house." I was scared to death of going there. I knew it would be worse than the Don jail, and it would go on forever.

"Just leave me in this cell," I said. "I don't need to go anywhere."

"No," Barker said. "We put a lot of effort into training you, and you will have to participate in the program."

He tapped on the door for the guard to open it. As he was leaving, he turned back. "Oh, we better get that hand fixed up first."

Nothing happened quickly in Oak Ridge. Except punishment.

It was late in the evening when two attendants and a nurse came to my cell. They had everything necessary to make a new cast. Except painkillers.

The nurse gave me a rolled-up facecloth to bite while they repositioned two of my knuckle bones. I didn't make a sound. I would not give them the satisfaction of hearing me scream. It was difficult.

"If you use the cast as a weapon, we'll amputate your hand," one of the guards said when they were done. And then they were gone.

That was what it was like to be at the mercy of primitive thugs. I knew they were immoral, brutal people. They thought I was the dangerous one, and they knew they could get away with anything. From then on, anything I did, everything that happened around me, was totally and forever out of my hands.

As hopeless as it is, I was not going to cooperate. I didn't think they wanted me dead or they would have made it easy for me to make it so. Nothing short of death mattered then anyway. They could hurt me any way they wanted. If they didn't kill me, then fuck them. I hoped my hatred of that place and those people would keep me strong.

The next morning, they came for me. They gave me new clothes, not the usual untearable canvas gown worn by most prisoners but normal street clothes. The pants were five sizes too big, but they actually trusted me with a belt to hold them up.

They took me to "H" ward, the "training" ward. I knew it from the first time around. It was the indoctrination ward for new arrivals. I didn't want to go through that particular nightmare again, but I said nothing.

Barker was in the office at the front of the ward. I don't know why I use the word "ward." It was a cell block. He went on for a while in his smiling, friendly way.

"Well, Steven, we have you for thirty days. We may as well make use of what we taught you. I'm sure you will remember what you learned in the training ward. You are now a teacher," he said, as though bestowing a PhD on me. "You will help teach new patients the rules and expectations."

I didn't say anything. Just looked at him mildly with no expression. I had learned one thing when I was the student in the program: Don't look harshly at anyone. No emotions. Stay neutral no matter the provocation.

The first thing they wanted me to do was staple papers together. The papers were pure communist Chinese-style indoctrination. So I went to work collating and stapling. The only silent protest I could make was to mix the papers up and then staple all four corners together.

Another "patient-teacher" came to pick up my stack of work and noticed my error. He walked out, came back with two attendants, and helped drag me out of the room and into a cell.

They came back a few minutes later with a nurse and a syringe.

"You're not going to like this," one attendant said. "This is apomorphine. Every time you cause trouble, you will get this."

As soon as they injected me, I started to puke. I didn't stop puking for four or five hours. I thought my stomach would come out of my mouth.

Scopolamine is bad, but apomorphine is pure evil. Useful in treatment or not, at least scopolamine has a psychoactive element. They could claim that scopolamine was an experimental drug that might have some benefit to hopeless mental patients. They could make no such claim about apomorphine. It makes you sick like you have never been sick. The only purpose is punishment. I would have preferred a beating with an iron bar.

The slightest sound or light set me off on a puking and retching bout. I don't know how long it went on. I do know I never want to experience it again.

Okay, enough about apomorphine. It makes me sick just thinking about it.

I still hated them all, even more so now, but I wouldn't show my feelings. I would do what they told me, like a robot.

The next day, they sent me back to the same task. Despite a horrible hangover, I was careful to be sure the papers were positioned perfectly and stapled in exactly the right place.

Whatever fate awaited me in Kingston Pen was less painful to contemplate than life in Oak Ridge. At least I had a release date. I just needed to concentrate on staying alive, avoid their drugs, and not do anything they could use to certify me.

No more fishing in the toilet.

I already knew the content of the brainwashing papers. I had had to memorize most of them the first time around. I was put into a group of newcomers, all wearing the thick gowns that made them look like mental patients. I was wearing street clothes. I knew they didn't understand I was also a prisoner.

Two other patients I knew came into the room with an armload of stapled papers: Matt Lamb and Doug Billings.

Doug was a quiet, polite young man. I don't know what he did to get himself into Oak Ridge. He always said "please" and "thank you." If he had to make someone do a task, he would be pleasant about it.

Lamb, on the other hand, was awe-inspiring. Lamb had shot-gunned four people at a bus stop for no particular reason. Lamb was articulate, handsome, and charming. He was a natural leader. Given the opportunity, I'm sure he could have had a successful and productive life. But here he was, the leader of the pack. All crazies.

Lamb introduced himself, Doug, and me to the group. I could see they were a sullen, angry bunch of recently screwed crazies. They all looked dangerous. They didn't know we were patients.

Lamb handed the pile of papers to me. "Pass these out, please."

A simple request. A simple task. As soon as I responded, I knew I had joined the other side. I was helping my enemy. I was becoming one of them.

22

AT FIRST I WASN'T COMFORTABLE BEING ON THE OTHER SIDE OF THE BRAINWASHING AND SELF-CONFES- sion program. Years later when I read about the Milgram experiments at Stanford University, I was embarrassed by my behavior.

If you're not familiar with it, here is how the Milgram experiments went. A test subject was placed in a room with an electric device on a table in front of him. He was told by a man with a clipboard and white lab coat that a person was in the next room attached to a wire. The other person would be given an electric shock if he gave the wrong answer to a question. The subject was told to push the button to administer the shock.

Despite being able to hear the screams of the supposed victim, the subject would almost always deliver the shock when told to do so by the man in the white lab coat. The conclusion was, most people would follow instructions from an authority figure even if it meant torturing an unseen victim, and even when they could hear the screams. I regret to admit it, but I did exactly what this experiment predicted.

Now it was Matt Lamb, Doug Billings, Michael Mason, and me in charge of the ward. The first four cells at the front of the ward were for us "teachers." We had pictures on the wall, a real bed, a bookshelf, and personal clothes in our cells. Michael Mason even gave me a wristwatch.

"Makes you look more professional," he told me.

It was our job to force new patients to memorize and then discuss the contents of those papers. After each round of memorization, the patients went to their cell for half an hour. They had to write an example for each type of manipulation they had just studied.

Of course there was a lot of resistance, just like me the first time around. The abused had become the abuser. I was no longer a patient. I was part of the staff. I was "helping" those unfortunate criminals. All I needed was the slightest show of resistance, and I could call in the drug squad. I could stand over them in my street clothes while directing their daily exercise. The only way one would be able to prevent him or herself from falling for this was to know what I know now. I didn't know then, but it's no excuse.

Every evening after lock-up, the teachers would meet with staff. Sometimes Barker would attend. The meeting was in the nurses' station at the front of the ward. It was nothing more than another concrete and brick room, but that's what they called it.

Everyone sat in a circle on heavy wooden chairs. Michael Mason usually led the group. He was amazingly professional. Each patient had a file. We would review and add comments to each of them. We would discuss each case and make recommendations for treatment. If we determined one patient or another might present a threat, we could have him put in cuffs as a preventative measure. The cuffs were made from seatbelt material and grommets. The previous time, I was the one in the cuffs. Now I was directing others to the same.

As I relate this, I am disgusted with myself. Today, we know how and why this happens. No one is immune to it given the right circumstances. I experienced both sides. But I still think I should have put up more resistance.

Michael Mason was a mystery to me. The first time around, I thought he was a doctor or social worker or something. Mason has actually co-authored several professional papers with Barker—never mentioning that he was a patient in Oak Ridge.

I don't know what his crime was. I do know he went on to help Barker as one of the founding members of the Canadian Society for the Prevention of Cruelty to Children, or "Empathetic Parenting," as it is called today. Mason wrote a chilling introduction called "Snug as an alcoholic in a brewery," something about how easy it is to crush a child's skull.

As the leader of the teaching ward, Mason's fantasy and delusions were fulfilled. Sometimes we talked late into the night about each patient, Mason taking notes on a clipboard and posing with pen to lip.

Matt Lamb was next in order. I will never be able to associate the Matt Lamb I knew with the psychopath who shot four people. I have no doubt that Lamb was a psychopath, but, excuse me, he was a beautiful psychopath. He was a perfect psychopath. Perhaps groomed from birth.

Like Peter Woodcock, Lamb knew how to read people. Many of the patients we oversaw were there for a thirty-day assessment. They had been sent by the courts, just like me. Most of these guys were trying a *One Flew Over the Cuckoo's Nest* routine, thinking it would be better for them to be in a nuthouse than a prison. Lamb saw through it right away. Fakery never fooled him.

Doug Billings was quiet and thoughtful. He was polite and never interrupted. When asked his opinion, he was empathetic and emotional. Doug was the opposite of a psychopath. He was an empath with bouts of psychosis.

I don't know why I was placed into that mix once again, but I adapted quickly and willingly, giving my opinion on each file.

On two occasions, I had to push the panic button, so to speak. Patients were set up to get violent so we could cuff them. I saw the drug squad inflict as much pain as possible from a hypodermic in the buttocks. I knew it already from experience. How could I just watch it happen to someone else?

There was a new variation of the choke with a rolled up towel around the neck. Maybe the old way was too dangerous? A wet towel over the face and twisted from behind worked as well.

Decades later, I heard about a torture technique called waterboarding. It reminded me of Oak Ridge. I wonder how many interrogation practices were tested on patients in Oak Ridge.

About two weeks into my thirty-day assessment, Barker walked into our ward meeting accompanied by Peter Woodcock. Peter was so happy to see me. He thought it was a good thing I was back in Oak Ridge, like I had returned to summer camp or something.

"You two have a lot to catch up on," Barker said. "You can stay here and chat."

He and the other three teachers left to go on his rounds.

As soon as they were gone, Peter moved his chair closer to me. "Karl was disappointed you didn't stay with them," he said. "What happened?"

"I got strung out on speed," I replied. "I didn't think they wanted me around anymore, so I split."

"Well, that's too bad," Peter said. "Karl had plans for you. But you know he was keeping an eye on you when you went home."

"How do you know that?" I asked.

Peter looked at me like he was surprised I didn't know. "I know everything that happened after you left us," he said. "The Brotherhood comes to visit more often now, sometimes twice a month. They're trying to get me transferred to another hospital. Karl has people all over the world, you know. Every time they visit, I ask about you, and they always know where you are."

"They're spying on me?"

"Of course they are. You know about them. Now they will always know where you are and what you're up to."

Peter smiled. "Escaping from jail and almost having a shootout with the police was so cool. You should have killed that old man, you know. You will have to kill at least one person to be truly accepted by the Brotherhood. Killing one person only makes up for you being in the world. Every one you kill after that makes you better."

"I don't want to kill anyone," I said.

"Oh yes you do," Peter replied. "Everybody wants to kill someone. They just don't admit it and are too afraid to do it. Some of us understand how worthless life is. It's better to die young, when you're innocent."

I didn't like hearing that, but I thought he might be right.

"How many did you kill?" I asked.

"I can't tell you," Peter replied. "The doctors know, but I can't talk about it or everything will change for me. I have an agreement."

"Okay," I said, trying not to sound interested. "Where did you meet Karl?"

"I didn't meet Karl. I have always known him."

His reply was strange, but I didn't push it.

"My real name isn't Peter Woodcock you know," he added. "They gave me that name. I know I'm German. I'm working on changing back to my real name. Doctor Barker said it's too risky, but I'll do it if I can talk to a lawyer. I hope they'll move me to the farm some day," Peter said wistfully. "I'm sure I'd like it there."

"What farm?" I asked.

"Oh, you know, the farm," Peter said. "You've been there. Doctor Barker showed me a picture of you riding a horse."

"Well, that was nice of him," I said. "Where did he get the picture?"

"It's his farm," Peter answered, surprised I didn't know. "He lives there with his wife and daughters. Sometimes he brings patients to stay there for a while. I'd like to go, but I don't think he trusts me around his kids."

Peter smiled that slow, evil "Brotherhood" smile I had seen before. I knew without a doubt that if he got the opportunity, he would murder again. I realized I should not turn my back on him. He could try to kill me just to get a little attention.

JUST THEN, BARKER CAME BACK into the nursing station with Lamb, Michael, and Doug in tow. He told Peter to go back to his ward.

As Peter walked out, he flashed me a peace sign. "See you later, man."

I did see him later, much later, twenty-five years later, when he was fat and nearly blind. And he had killed again.

Dr. Barker smiled at me. "We have decided to move you to 'F' ward. We think you should be an observer in the Compressed Encounter Therapy Unit."

I noted his use of the word "we," meaning Michael, Matt, and Doug, along with Barker, were making the decisions about treatment.

The Compressed Encounter, or "CAPSUL," evolved from the sun room program. It was the same misguided idea but more intense.

A room at the end of "F" ward had been transformed into a windowless plywood box about ten feet square. The walls and floor were padded and soundproofed. In one corner was an open toilet. Above this "capsule" was a room with a one-way mirror and video recording equipment. Decades later, a CBC reporter told me the camera was state of the art for the time. It was better than what CBC had. Four small, circular holes were in one wall. Straws could be inserted from the outside and liquid food sucked through.

Four or more patients were stripped naked and locked into that room, sometimes for several weeks. It was brightly lit twenty-four hours a day. It was impossible to tell if it was night or day. No distractions. Only various drugs. Lots of LSD and sometimes even more exotic drugs like mescaline. Occasionally, alcohol was added to the liquid food. Surely a recipe for trouble, but that's what Barker wanted.

He took me to the room above the capsule and showed me how to operate the video equipment. The room was comfortable. A big, soft chair overlooked the one-way mirror in the floor. The camera pointed down at the four naked patients. It was an ugly situation. Any normal person would have been disgusted by that view.

"All you have to do is watch them and turn on the camera if anything happens," Barker said.

"What do you mean 'if anything happens'?"

"Anything unusual like sexual activity or loud arguing. If a fight breaks out, just let it go unless it looks like someone might really get hurt. It doesn't happen often, but if it does, you'll have to use this."

He opened a small cabinet and took out a can of mace. "Just a small squirt through the feeding hole. You need to stay awake."

He pointed to a prescription bottle on the table. Benzedrine, speed, the drug that led to my crash and burn the last time I got out of that place. Bennies were like candy at Oak Ridge. I didn't want to go down that road again.

I was expected to stay awake all night and film possible deviant behaviour or decide if an outbreak of violence was serious enough to tear gas the patients. I wasn't nuts. This situation was nuts.

Let me quote an excerpt from a paper authored by Barker and Michael Mason. I think it's relevant to understand how far Barker was willing to go. It's called "Buber behind bars."

> But in situations where patients are quite properly being held against their will until they change, it seems humane and helpful to use force.
>
> At least to the point of increasing their range of choice, of increasing their awareness of themselves, and others, to the point where as far as can be determined, what they do, they self-consciously choose to do.
>
> The validity of force depends on this assumption. If the process were one of eradicating a set of disapproved ideas and washing in different social values, then we would be committing offences as grievous as those involved in setting up the Third Reich—Indeed, the more sinister, because of their subtlety.
>
> On the other hand, if our patients did not choose to deviate from society's norms, but rather were driven to such deviations by internal un-resolved conflicts, then we should help them resolve such conflicts by every means at our disposal, including force, humiliation and deprivation, if necessary.
>
> Physical force brought our patients to our hospital, physical force maintains him there, and this force will not be lifted until he changes his behaviour in a

recognisable way... as communication approaches a maximum, the permissible use of force also approaches a maximum.[2]

This paper, and a number of others published around the same time, provides a glimpse into the state of mind of Dr. Barker and his minions. When he speaks of maximum use of force, I tend to interpret it as murder.

"Don't fall asleep," Dr. Barker said on his way out of the observation room. He sounded cheerful, but I knew it was a threat. If I fell asleep, there would be consequences.

He locked the door behind him. I didn't expect to be locked in. What was I supposed do if these caged nut bars tried to kill each other? I didn't even want to look through the one-way mirror. It was perverse voyeurism.

A thick log book sat on the table, a pencil stub inside. Funny, they put the lives of these four Guinea pigs in my hands, but they didn't trust me with a full-length pencil.

I considered using the can of Mace to blast my way out of here. I knew I had no chance though, and they probably wanted me to try it.

I picked up the log book and started to read from the beginning. It was obvious several people had written parts over a period of time. Some of the notations were clear and well-written. Others were messy and illegible. Some was just the crazy, disconnected ramblings of a speed freak. Most of the entries were descriptions of homosexual encounters with the time and date of the video recorded. Some of what I read was clearly rape. There had to be hundreds of hours of tape. Who was this record for?

Under the chair was a small piece of carpet. I picked it up and put it over the one-way mirror. Now it was a no-way mirror. I was not doing this!

I picked up the log book and wrote "FUCK YOU" on the last page. Then I went to the far corner, lay down on the floor, and went to sleep.

Sleep didn't last. How could I sleep above that?

I sat up and wondered if I knew any of the guys below me.

I took the carpet off the spy hole and looked down, hoping I wouldn't see something disgusting. Below me were four drugged-up mental patients who could try to kill each other at any moment. If I don't watch over them, who would?

All of them were around my age. I recognized one of them, Victor Hoffman, from my previous encounter groups. I had talked to him for several hours during

---

[2] Barker, E.T., Mason, M. (1968). Buber behind bars. *Canadian Psychiatric Association Journal, 13,* 65.

my first eight-month stay at Oak Ridge. I had been placed in a "dyad" with him. He had talked about being spied on from above. I thought he was a paranoid psychotic nut back then. Now I was spying on him from above.

Hoffman really was nuts, but more than nuts, he was dangerous beyond your imagination. He had killed an entire family in Saskatchewan. Nine or ten, mostly shot in the head. Mother, father, children, babies. He murdered them all one after another in cold blood. He said the devil made him do it. He stuck to that story. I met him more than a year after his murder spree.

Prior to one of our marathon encounter therapy sessions—the one where I wound up in a dyad with Hoffman—one of the patient-teachers told me that, "Victor is delusional, and we should try to dissuade him of his delusions. Use logic. Try to trip him up."

Logic had nothing to do with Victor Hoffman. His delusions were organized so perfectly that it was impossible to dissuade him. He claimed to have personal contact with the devil and a host of demons who told him what he must do. His story was very convincing. He didn't sound like the usual psychotic raving about the devil. He was calm and well organized. I think he influenced many patients who came into contact with him.

Hoffman was as cold as a razor blade. Unlike Peter Woodcock, who was essentially a weak and simple person, Hoffman had empty eyes. Look into the eyes of a goat or a snake, and there is no connection to human empathy. The same was true of Hoffman.

Nothing I could say could convince him the evil he spoke of was only in his mind. If there are forces of good and evil in this world, Hoffman chose evil, or evil chose him. He claimed the choice was not his. A few hours of conversation with him convinced me he might be right. It was possible to be possessed by evil.

I have crossed paths with a few nasty characters in my life, but Hoffman was by far the most dangerous. Not only because he could kill you without a moment's hesitation but because he could convince weaker people it was the right thing to do. Why would they put him into this box with three other naked patients? I knew they could do nothing to help him. If this confrontation accomplished anything, it would be the conversion of three others to Hoffman's twisted beliefs.

As awful as the view from my perch was, I had to watch it unfold under my feet. I was sure Hoffman would kill the other patients if they angered him. I had to pay attention. It was up to me to be the lifeguard. How responsible would I be if I was sleeping when he killed one of them? I really wished they had hanged him.

The capsule was mostly soundproof. From my observation post, all I could hear was muffled voices coming through the one-way mirror. There were headphones on the video camera. I would have to record to hear anything, but I didn't want to hear what he was saying. I had heard Hoffman's story before, how he had communicated with devils and demons all his life. It was creepy, and I didn't need to hear it again. Just watching the encounter and his body language was enough.

Hoffman sat in front of the others with his legs crossed in a lotus position like some kind of guru. He made continuous, odd hand movements, like he was trying to teach the other three how to do it exactly right. Hoffman had the others in thrall. I knew there was no way they were giving him any kind of therapy. More than likely, he was teaching these young mental patients the Victor Hoffman technique.

I didn't know anything about the other three. They were young, maybe late teens. I think they were court assessment cases. I have no idea what crimes they were accused of, but I would really like to know what crimes they committed after being initiated by an evil son of a bitch like Hoffman.

This was so wrong.

I tried to stay awake all night without touching the bottle of Bennies. I knew if I start doing speed again, it would make me crazy. I was sure it was better to take my chances in Kingston Pen. I had learned how to survive prison culture at Burwash, so I thought I would be okay in the Big House. I suppose most prison inmates, even the killers, committed their crimes for profit or passion. The killers in Oak Ridge did it for pleasure. I never knew when someone like Hoffman or Woodcock might decide to kill me.

I did fall asleep a few times with my face against the one-way mirror. Each time, I awoke with a start. Below me, nothing had changed. They sat in the same position all night. I thought Hoffman was initiating his captive audience somehow.

Finally, Michael Mason opened the door, and daylight poured in, hurting my eyes. He told me I could go back to my room.

I had made it through another Initiation or test with nothing bad happening. I was relieved to be back in my own cell. I could safely get some sleep.

THE CELL DOORS OF PATIENT-TEACHERS were usually left open during the day, but when I woke up, I found I was locked in. Something was wrong. I had a bad feeling.

The ward was quiet. No one was in the hallway as far as I could see in either direction. I thought I had better stay calm and wait. It was the last week of my thirty-day assessment. I didn't want to do anything to draw attention.

At around five o'clock, the door slid open, and three attendants and a nurse came in. They didn't say a word. Two of them grabbed me by the arms and pulled my clothes off. The other one gathered up my personal things and put them in a plastic bag. Books, clothes, watch, everything. The room was stripped bare.

They put the crazy man gown on me and trussed me up in full restraints, wrists and ankles. The nurse injected me with a "Don't care 'bout nothin'" drug. Then they went out and slammed the door behind them.

Not a word.

I didn't find out what had happened until I got hold of my clinical records more than twenty-five years later. They claimed I wanted to stay in Oak Ridge and were afraid I would act out in some way to make that happen. I think there was more to it than that bullshit excuse. I will get into it later.

For the next few days, I was kept in a semi-conscious state. One morning when they opened the door, it wasn't for another injection. They took me to the shower room and then gave me my street clothes. Then they took me to the front gate and handed me over to the bailiffs. They took off the seatbelt restraints and put on normal handcuffs and leg irons. I was off Kingston Penitentiary.

23

KINGSTON PENITENTIARY (KP) WAS BUILT IN 1833 WHEN REHABILITATION WAS NOT ON ANYONE'S agenda. It was a place of punishment, an oppressive, medieval dungeon designed to make you repent of your criminal ways. In 1971, a riot that lasted for five days tore the place apart. Steel, stone, cement, and brick were broken and twisted with rage and bare hands. I was dragged into it not long after the place had been wrecked. This is what happened to me there.

THE FRONT GATE WAS HUGE, made of wood and steel. There should have been a drawbridge and a moat. There were crocodiles, but they wore uniforms. In those days, KP was known as a dumping ground for bad guards, guards who liked their job because they got to hurt people every day.

The gate closed behind me, and before my chains were taken off, something hit me in the back. A boot, a fist, I don't know. I went horizontal and crashed to the floor.

"Go boy, eh?" a voice behind me said. "You won't be escaping from here."

A boot stomped the back of my head and smashed my face into the stone floor.

My mother never taught me much, but one thing she insisted on was that I brush my teeth regularly. I always had a toothbrush, even when I was homeless. I felt my front teeth go through my bottom lip and smash to pieces.

Then blackness.

THEY CALL IT THIRTY DAYS in the hole. It was a hole, all right, but I think it was longer than thirty days. That's what you got for escaping. Prison guards took it as a personal insult.

The "hole" was a cement or stone box about ten feet square. I couldn't tell what it was made of. The floor felt greasy, polished by more than a hundred years of the oil on men's skin. A hole in the middle of the floor served as a toilet.

No water was visible, but it flushed automatically with a great gurgling sound every few minutes. A dim light bulb hung from the ceiling, too high to reach.

My bottom lip felt bloated and flopped around. All of my front teeth were gone. Just when I thought I had nothing left to lose, I lost my teeth. Once again, I went to that place in the corner of my mind. Un-focused eyes. This time I didn't feel like fishing.

By then, prisons had abandoned bread and water. It was considered cruel. What I got instead was a "restricted diet." I think it came twice a day, although I didn't know day from night. A tin tray was shoved through the slot in the door. One slice of bread and a chunk of something they called meatloaf. It looked like spam, but it smelled like dog food. I'm sure it was dog food. And a cup of weak tea with too much sugar.

I couldn't eat anything for a few days. Finally, I got hungry enough to figure out how to break up the dog food into little pieces and sort of shove it down with a finger.

It didn't take long to develop bed sores. There was no comfortable way to sit or lie on the hard floor.

Then one day when the slot opened to deliver food, I heard the guard whisper, "You can ask for a Bible." It was the only human voice I had heard for the entire time I was in the hole.

"I want a Bible," I croaked the next time the slot opened.

Thirty seconds later, a Bible was pushed through.

"All you had to do was ask," the guard said.

You bastards, I thought. *All you had to do was tell me!*

I think it was some UN human rights thing. All prisoners need to have access to a Bible. But how would I know that?

I've already said this, but to be clear, I am not a religious person. Sometimes I wish I had what it takes to be a believer, but I don't. Believing in God would be like believing my father would come to take me home. I knew it wouldn't happen.

Of all the books I read in Burwash, I never opened a Bible. Right then though, having a thick book with so many pages was as close to God as I would ever get. If I wasn't sleeping, I was reading, from Genesis to Revelation and then back again.

This is an odd thing: The book that defines Christian and Jewish beliefs was written not only as history but also as the road to salvation. In my case, it did save me. But still, I don't think God is watching over us. Honestly, I don't know. I'll have to wait a while longer to find out.

ALL THINGS PASS. GOOD TIMES turn bad, and sometimes bad times turn good. My thirty days in the hole came to an end, and I was alive.

They took me out and led me to the shower room. I saw my face in a mirror for the first time in I don't know how long. It was a shock. My first thought was that girls wouldn't like me anymore. I was ugly. But then, I wouldn't be seeing any girls for a long time.

I was issued prison clothes, always too big, and a newcomer's kit, all folded up military style, boots on top. Sheets, blanket, comb . . . toothbrush. Ha! Thanks a lot!

They took me to a cell block with two guards following. Other prisoners watched from their cells as I walked past. They could tell I had just gotten out of the hole. Maybe it was the way I walked or the pasty colour of my skin. They shouted words of encouragement.

Thirty days in the hole gave me instant status. The hole was a prison within a prison. It was so bad it made a normal cell look like luxury. The bed wasn't exactly a "Beauty Rest," but it was a big improvement over a stone floor.

I didn't plan on writing a prison book, but part of this account has to deal with my time behind bars. It amounts to five years out of sixty-five. It's not what defines me.

Believe it or not, prison is not all pain and suffering. There are good times as well. Sometimes you meet the best people in the strangest circumstances. Sometimes you laugh and sing with them, even get drunk on prison "red eye."

The single biggest fear that keeps many people out of prison is the threat of being ass-raped by a big, black drag queen. I can tell you, it is a myth. I never saw it, and I never heard of such a thing happening. Prison is a dangerous place. If that sort of thing was common, the murder rate would go through the roof.

True, some people in federal prison belong in Oak Ridge, but few in Oak Ridge belong anywhere but a secure mental health facility. Committing a crime does not mean you are crazy. The fact is, most prisoners get along quite well with each other. People form groups based on common interest. I met some memorable people in prison, people who were solid and trustworthy. I will tell you some prison stories focusing on the good people who contributed to my development as a human being.

Seeing as most of KP had been destroyed recently by a riot, what was left of it was used as an assessment center. Prisoners did not stay for long. They were sent to one of three other institutions, all in the Kingston area.

Millhaven was a new maximum security joint. It was bad, reserved for the most dangerous, hard-to-manage prisoners; Collins Bay was medium security, although it had a forty-foot wall around it with guard towers; Joyceville was also medium security. It was reserved mostly for older prisoners. It was contained by a fence and razor wire.

The classification officers interviewed me a few times. I fully expected to be sent to Millhaven. What I had done was considered a violent escape. I also looked bad with my smashed bottom lip and missing teeth. I was likely saved from Millhaven by my answer to one question: "Do you want to go to school?"

Collins Bay had a very progressive school program. The teachers came into the prison from regular teaching jobs. They were real teachers. The classrooms were the real thing, too.

Collins Bay it was.

24

MY FIRST JOB ASSIGNMENT AT COLLINS BAY WAS THE LAUNDRY, A STINKY, NO STATUS JOB. HOWEVER, working the laundry did allow me to find clothes that fit me. It didn't last all that long, maybe six months.

One day, I was told the warden wanted to talk to me. That was very unusual. The warden's office was in the administration building outside the main security perimeter.

It turns out someone reviewing my file read about my machine shop experience in Burwash and the gun I had made. Part of that course included drafting. I knew how to use a drafting machine and make blueprints to scale. The warden himself appointed me to the works department. It was office work in a real office. He also told me the gun I had made was in a forensic museum in Ottawa. He seemed a little proud of me.

"Can you promise me you won't try to escape again?"

Why on Earth would a warden of a federal prison ask a prisoner like me to promise anything, and why would he believe me? Who knows? Turns out he knew more about me than I realized.

MY MEETING WITH THE WARDEN took place seven months or more after I was in the hole. After that experience, I became fearless. I decided I would not cut my hair until I was released.

There were rules against long hair and beards, but I ignored them. I was hassled constantly by some guards, but I never complied. I developed an attitude about my hair. Like Samson, as long as I kept my hair un-cut, I believed my strength would grow with it.

The warden asked if I would cut my hair. I simply said, "No."

He nodded. "Okay."

And that was the end of it.

I was never hassled again.

I took up weightlifting and boxing. I had no front teeth, so it was impossible to hurt me with a punch in the face.

Some prisoners were almost pro boxers. One guy bragged about winning Golden Glove-sanctioned matches. He was a good teacher.

My new job at the works office was in the administration building. I was given a "blue pass." That is pure gold in a prison. A blue pass allowed me to go wherever I wanted inside the prison grounds. All I had to do was flash the blue paper, and the gate would open.

I worked that job for more than a year. Guards got used to me moving around the institution. Inmates also knew I could move easily from cell block to cell block. Often, I would carry notes from one inmate to another. They were called "kites."

Speaking of kites, I started a tradition in Collins Bay that may still go on today. Using pieces of straw from a broom, thread from the tailor shop, and a typewriter ribbon, I taught myself how to make a really cool paper kite.

Many inmates also learned how to make them. We flew our kites in the exercise yard. We fastened a razor blade to the tail and had kite fights by cutting the others' string. It was great fun. Sometimes twenty kites were in the air. It was harmless, and the guards never tried to stop it.

One day, I got a visit from two serious hard cases. These guys were both mafia, the real thing, hit men doing life for murder one.

"Dominic wants to talk to you," one of them said.

He didn't need to say "Dominic *Racco*." Everyone in Collins Bay knew who he was. Racco was a "made man" in the Toronto mafia. He got special treatment even in prison. Years later, he was shot dead along the railroad tracks. Dominic would have become the godfather otherwise.

They gave me his "address," his cell and block number. I didn't hesitate. I went right away.

His cell block was different than all the others in Collins Bay. They had solid wood doors, and the cells weren't open in the front with bars. I think the entire block was filled with lifers and important people, rich men who'd killed their wives or something. At any rate, it was a special place. These inmates did not mix with the others. I could go there though. All I had to do was carry a file folder, a tape measure, and a pencil, and I could go anywhere, except, unfortunately, out the front door.

My first attempt was bad timing and scary as hell. The shower room was at the front of the range. As I walked past, I heard a strange grunting sound. I looked to my left and saw a guy being murdered. He was on the floor with two or three guys standing over him, stabbing him over and over. He wasn't moving, but they kept stabbing.

I froze in mid-step and took two steps backward, hoping they hadn't seen me. They were busy with their task and did not look up. If they had, I'm sure I never would have met Dominic Racco.

I went back the next day and met with him. I already had a good idea why he wanted to talk to me. I had a blue pass. I could be useful.

I was really nervous, and he knew it. It turns out he was a friendly, casual guy. He didn't make any demands at all. He outlined what he wanted me to do, but he asked several times if it was okay with me.

Racco and his people ran the drug trade in Collins Bay. Oh yes, there is a drug trade in prison. Big time. He controlled all of it from his cell.

I had easy access to an area behind the visiting room. Inmates going to the visiting room had to pass that area after they were searched. It was easy to make a quick transfer from my pocket to theirs. It was money, lots of it. I think the drugs came in through the guards. But because there wasn't much to spend money on in prison, it had to get out somehow.

I never asked questions. I just moved the money wherever they told me. I know I was set up a few times to test my honesty. I always passed. Who the hell would try to rip off the mafia in prison?

Maybe the guy I saw in the shower getting his.

They offered me almost any sort of drug you can imagine: heroin, cocaine, speed, pot, all of it easier to find in prison than on the street. I didn't want to get tangled up in any of it except for pot. Smoking a little "boo" never seemed dangerous to me. Racco and his people trusted me partly because I declined the hard stuff.

Like Dave, they also sold single joints, but in prison you could make money selling singles.

I became the official joint roller. They had to be consistent in size and quality. I had to provide a certain number of rolled joints from a one-ounce bag. The rest was mine. It was a good deal. I always had pot, and other inmates never fucked with me. You can't ask for a better situation in prison. Mafia protection.

In time, I found out it wasn't just the blue pass that got me my lucky break. It was the Italian connection from my hometown. I don't know if it came from Joe or one of the others who owned the town and the hockey arena brothel, but someone put in a word for me.

The arrangement went on for more than two years

I MET SOME OTHER MEMORABLE characters during that time. I'll tell you about Jarvis—not his real name, of course, but that's what everyone called him. Jarvis was Black Muslim or Nation of Islam, as it is called today. He came to Canada a number of times to rob banks. He said banks were easier to rob in Canada. The money went back to the US to help fund Elijah Muhammad and the Black Muslim movement. People talk a lot of bullshit in prison, but he showed me a picture of him in a chauffeur uniform standing beside Elijah, who was very old at the time. I believe he was as connected as he claimed.

Jarvis was also the most racist and militant person I ever met. He hated white people, but we got along, because he thought I was black at heart. I never thought about it that way, but then again, Jarvis was the first black person I had ever met.

One of the good things in Collins Bay was band practice. It had a well-equipped music room—drum kit, PA system, amps, everything was there.

I had played guitar since I was a kid. I wasn't very good, but I liked music, and I wanted to practice. Four of us got together and practiced two hours a week. We wanted to be a blues band, but none of us could sing worth a damn.

That's how I met Jarvis. One day, I walked past him in the yard. He was sitting on the ground singing *a capella*, and man, he was good. I asked if he wanted to come to our practice. He gave me a doubtful look.

"What, a blue-eyed blues band?"

I shrugged. "Yeah, I guess so, but none of us have blue eyes."

He agreed to give it a try, and the next week, he showed up.

It was magic from the start. Jarvis didn't play any instruments, but he knew how to arrange music. We became at least as competent as your average bar band. We called ourselves "Not Often," because we played only once a week.

One of our gigs was the prison Christmas concert. It was the only day of the year that visitors were allowed into the auditorium to mix with the inmates. When it was our turn, we rocked the place. It was jailhouse rock, the real deal. They clapped and asked for more, and we kept giving it.

The next day, I saw Jarvis with a towel wrapped around his neck because his throat was blown out from singing.

I knew Jarvis was a Muslim, but I didn't have a clue what that meant. The only thing I ever heard about Muslims was from my father when I was about nine years old. He came home from work and told me there was a new guy at work who had some strange religion.

"Mooslim," he said. "They worship some little god named Allan."

That was all I knew.

I told you I read the Bible at least twice when there was not much else to do, so I checked the prison library and found a Qur'an.

I didn't object to anything I read in that little book. It was easier to read than the Bible, and if you could believe in God, the Qur'an made sense.

I showed it to Jarvis at the next band practice and told him I had some questions. He was pleased I was reading the Qur'an.

"You are a seeker of the truth," he said, "so you will find it."

The last time I saw Jarvis, he said, "You need a Muslim name. You will be Hakim, because you are wise. Don't forget it. One day, it will save your life."

I haven't eaten pork since that day forty-five years ago, out of respect for Jarvis.

We became friends over hours of religious discussion. He was waiting for the revolution he knew would come. It would be the end of the white man and his world domination.

My experience of "white man's justice" was about the same as most black people's. Black Irish. I understood what it was to suffer oppression not for what you did but for what you were.

After the Christmas concert, everyone knew us. Even the guards showed a little respect for "Not Often."

The music room had an old, upright piano, but we couldn't find anyone who played. I suggested we look for a piano player from outside the institution. Quite a few outside people were already coming in for various rehabilitation programs. I presented a good argument to my boss, and he agreed easily. We even discussed the possibility of doing outside concerts. It took a while and there was lots of red tape, but the idea was approved.

Enter Cynthia.

She came from St. Laurence College music department. She was nineteen years old, full of talent, and had an adventurous spirit. She played piano standing up. Cynthia took "Not Often" to a whole new level and gave all of us something to look forward to every week.

When Cynthia was in the music room the boys in the band outdid each other trying to be polite and civilized. No cursing, and we always said "please" and "thank you." We weren't pretending; we meant it. All of us loved her.

How I wish we had been able to record some of the music we made. I know we were good, because we were inspired.

Everything ends eventually. How this ended was a sad day all around.

Racism exists in prison, as it does anywhere. Blacks usually hung out with blacks and whites with whites. I had one black friend, but I hung out mostly with whites. In those days, there wasn't a big percentage of blacks in Canadian prisons, but in the years I was in Collins Bay, the ratio of black and white slowly increased. I'm sure this has been studied. The formula is predictable and certain. When you reach the dangerous ratio of black and white, you get trouble.

I got trouble, all right. A race riot in the dining room. I wound up on the black side of it.

Tension between blacks and whites had been building for a while. It blew up in the cafeteria. A fight broke out. A black guy got stabbed in the eye with a fork. The dining room erupted in seconds. Everyone was fighting, black on white.

Jarvis was at a table with three other brothers. They were attacked by a white mob. Jarvis was knocked backward to the floor. Two guys grabbed his arms and held him down while another picked up a chair to smash him.

I had no time to think. I jumped to my feet and drop-kicked the guy with the chair. The other two let go of Jarvis and came after me. Jarvis leaped to his feet and came to my defence.

Let me be clear, I don't like violence. This was the only real fight I have ever been in aside from boxing in a ring.

We stood back-to-back and fought them off. We took our lumps, but we prevailed.

Until the tear gas came.

I'll never know if anyone was seriously hurt. There was lots of blood on the floor.

The riot squad came and put an end to the battle. Everyone was separated and locked up—blacks in one cell block, whites in another.

I was in the white side, where I heard threats coming from up and down the range, all aimed at me. The black side didn't like me either.

A few days later, they started shipping people out to other institutions. I figured I would go to Millhaven, where, sooner or later, I would get shived.

When my turn came, I was alone on the transport bus. I didn't know where I was going until I got there.

Not Millhaven.

Joyceville.

25

JOYCEVILLE WAS ACTUALLY A BETTER PLACE THAN COLLINS BAY, BUT NOT FOR ME. I DIDN'T HAVE A BLUE pass or mafia connections or music or Cynthia to look forward to.

I started back in the laundry.

Build myself up, improve my surroundings, and then burn it to the ground. That's what I had been doing since I left home. After it went down the drain, I would go over and over what I had done to cause it.

I contemplated Dr. Barker's diagnosis. Could he be correct? If I was a psychopath, how could I prove it to myself one way or another? I didn't believe it was true. I was the only person who knew what I felt inside. I didn't want to take advantage of anyone; I wanted others to take advantage of me. I could do things, I could make things, I had talent, and I could learn. I received no enjoyment from the pain of others. I wanted people to like me. Those were not typical traits of a psychopath. On the other hand, wouldn't It be better if I was a psychopath? I was sure I would not suffer as much if I was as cold as a reptile.

Now that I think about it, in a way I have been studying the psychopath phenomenon for almost fifty years, long before it became a popular subject. I have no degrees or professional standing, but I have my own theory. Psychopaths are not mentally ill. They are an evolutionary adaptation. If you know how to spot them, they can be useful. I'm sure the ratio of psychopaths in the western world has been increasing over the years. Why? I will have more to say about that later.

I WENT BACK TO SCHOOL. The population in Joyceville was mostly older than me. The academic programs were different. I could choose whatever college-level courses I wanted to take. In my last year there, I took every course available, even economics, micro and macro. I learned how to make balance sheets the old-fashioned way. I also learned how central banking systems work, what money is, bookkeeping 101, and, of course, psychology.

The psych lab even had a white rat. We learned operant conditioning in a maze. The rat became my pet. Surprisingly, rats can be very affectionate.

I took a course in art history. From that, I discovered I had some drawing talent. What I lacked in technical skills I made up for in imagination. I entered one of my paintings in a prison art competition and won second or third prize. It went on tour across Canada. That was encouraging, but I never got the painting back.

I kept to myself in Joyceville. Despite all of the good people I had met at Collins Bay, it was safer not to make friends in prison.

Time passed, as it does. Looking forward, it was painfully slow. Looking back, it was the blink of an eye.

The medical experiments were something that stood out. There was an outbreak of hepatitis A. Prison is an ideal environment for hepatitis to spread. All inmates were told to monitor themselves for symptoms. The result being everyone thought they had it, including me.

I went to sick bay because I didn't feel so good. No symptoms, just vague unease. They took some blood, and the next day they told me I was being sent to the Kingston Armed Forces Hospital.

Prison inmates make good lab rats. Endless amounts of skin to play with. I had to leave my own lab rat in the care of another inmate while I spent the next six weeks in building B-62.

A simple blood test will reveal hepatitis. They would know right away. They never told me what was wrong with me. They just kept doing tests every day. Liver biopsy, spinal tap, bone marrow biopsy, lymph node biopsy. Stabbed, prodded, and poked with thick needles, cut and then stitched up. Every day brought some new level of pain I had never experienced. Some required full-on surgery. The most painful things you can imagine. Always a room full of interns watching the procedure.

The main doctor was a woman in uniform. Major or Colonel something. I don't recall her name, and it's just as well. She used inmates to teach interns the most painful medical procedures, things for which no one would volunteer. She called me "Sport," but not in the traditional definition. I think she used the word in the lesser known "genetic defect" definition.

I woke up one day to find two teachers from Joyceville standing beside my bed. I was thankful someone was actually concerned about me. An intern was pulling a long green drainage tube from my armpit. I puked all over the teachers.

The doctors always talked about what they thought it could be, diseases that could kill you, discussing it among themselves like I wasn't even in the room. I let them do whatever tests they wanted to do. They never came up with a diagnosis.

Eventually, I was sent back to Joyceville feeling worse than before I went into building B-62.

It was morphine withdrawal. For the past six weeks, they had given me morphine almost every day. No one bothered to tell me about the withdrawal.

Fortunately, there was no contraband morphine to be found in Joyceville. I got over it and continued doing time.

I APPLIED FOR DAY PAROLE so I could attend art school at St. Lawrence College. I showed my paintings to the teachers who volunteered their time in Joyceville. They backed me up, wrote letters to the parole board, and encouraged me.

But I was turned down. No reason, just rubber stamped. "DENIED."

Then one day, it happened. Out of the blue, I was called to the classification office and told I had been accepted at St. Lawrence College. I would be transferred to Portsmouth House, and I would attend art school. It was the best day of my life up to that point. It was like my birthday, Christmas, and winning a million dollars all at the same time. I wasn't just getting out of jail, I was getting into art school. I would be an artist!

That was the turning point. My suffering was almost over. Now I was on a quest; I had something to prove. Arrangements were made for my transfer to Portsmouth House. But for one last ordeal I had to endure, I had a release date.

For more than four years, I had no front teeth. I got used to it, but transitioning to the real world where people didn't have a big hole in the front of their face needed to be addressed.

What remained of my teeth were fine. I never had a toothache, and I could eat almost anything. They offered to fix them, but it was all or nothing. If I wanted front teeth, I had to let the rest of them go. Reluctantly, I agreed, but the scariest part was I had to go back to Kingston Pen to have it done. I had to be locked up in the same dungeon where they were smashed out years before.

Even though I was about to be set free, I was treated the same as any prisoner coming into Kingston. I arrived in handcuffs and marched past the same spot where it all began.

I looked at the floor, and a shiver went up my back. They would have one last chance to kill me. Maybe they would. Maybe I wouldn't get out at all.

I was locked in the same dismal cell and told I had to wait until the following day. No sink or toilet, only a narrow metal bunk. Nothing to do that day but think about how they would extract all of my teeth at the same time. I didn't eat or drink anything. Sleep was impossible.

Early the next morning, they came for me. I believe that is what it feels like to walk the last mile. I thought there was a good chance I wouldn't make it through the experience. In no hurry, I walked slowly toward the infirmary.

The place looked old and dirty. Too many coats of green paint. As usual, no one said a word to me. I was an object, and this was a routine surgery—or execution.

I was shaking from head to foot like I had been doused in ice water.

"Just relax," someone said.

The needle went in, and that long, black cloud came down.

But I didn't die. I heard a loud rushing in my ears and woke up. It felt like seconds later. I tasted blood running down the back of my throat. My mouth felt like a baseball was stuffed into it.

Someone standing beside the gurney was talking to me, but I couldn't understand what he was saying. The rushing in my ears was too loud.

I was taken back to Joyceville for my last six weeks in custody. I had a full set of dominos in my mouth, but it was several weeks before I could eat anything more than soup and wet bread.

They say when you get out of prison, don't look back or you will be back. Despite all the time I spent in Joyceville, I have no idea what the front of the place looks like. Like Lot fleeing Sodom, I didn't look back.

26

JOYCEVILLE PROVIDED ME WITH A NEW SUIT AND TIE. A PRISON SUIT. IF YOU SEE SOMEONE WEARING one, you can guess where he just came from.

A guard drove me to Portsmouth House. Called a "halfway house," it was actually a historic Kingston house made of stone and stained glass, a beautiful piece of architecture. It was a temporary home for about fifteen men on day parole.

Let me say right away, Portsmouth House was a life saver. More than any other single thing, that house and the people who ran it likely saved me. After my time there, I never again found myself on the wrong side of a locked door.

On my first day, I had a long meeting with the director. He told me the rules of the house, and then he said something that really stuck with me.

"I have read your file, and I think you have suffered a great injustice. No doubt you're angry at the world. There are two ways you can go, young man. You can look for revenge or you can do your best to prove them wrong. Direct your anger constructively, and you'll be okay. You're free to go."

Free to go? Yes, I was free to walk out the front door, go out to the street, and walk left or right. I could go wherever I wanted as long as I returned by ten at night.

I stood on the sidewalk looking back at the house and straight up at the sky. It looked large and unreal.

I wasn't angry about injustice that day. I was overwhelmed just to be free.

I looked down at my ill-fitting brown prison suit and felt embarrassed. I had saved about three hundred dollars from my five years of prison labour. Yes, they do pay you in prison, but not much.

Everything had changed in five years. Cars had changed. People dressed differently. I had to ask the bus driver how much the fare was. I was embarrassed to ask. I thought it would reveal me.

Oh, and I still had my Samson hair. I didn't see anyone with long hair like mine. For so many years, I had defied authority and refused to cut my hair. I suffered for it, but I kept it. Now it felt wrong. I went directly to a barbershop in downtown Kingston and had it all cut off. Afterwards, I felt lightheaded, like gravity had been reduced.

Next, I went to a clothing store and bought a three-piece denim suit. It was a cross between hippie and well-dressed. It felt right for me. I told the sales clerk he could throw the brown suit away.

As I walked up the main street, I kept looking at my reflection in store windows. It wasn't vanity; it was amazement. Was that really me walking free?

I spent my first day of freedom wandering around Kingston and looking in stores, just picking things up and handling them. So many things I hadn't seen or touched for so long.

THE RESIDENTS OF PORTSMOUTH HOUSE had to do their own cooking. I bought some simple things I thought I could deal with.

I had a few possessions from Joyceville, some paintings and a box of acrylic paint and brushes. I had a week to wait before enrollment in St. Lawrence College, so I asked the director if there was a room I could use to do my art.

"Yes," he said, "you can use the sun room."

I cringed at the term "sun room" but realized that one was different from the one at Oak Ridge. By the time I had it all set up, it became "my studio." I loved the idea of having a studio.

ENROLLMENT DAY CAME. I DON'T know how to describe what that day was like. I was older than the other students, but no one seemed to notice. This was a real school where people learned useful things, not like my high school in the Sault. This place didn't smell like stale bananas and gym socks. It wasn't an empty, make-do room in prison turned into a classroom.

All of the students were rushing around trying to find various classrooms, dropping their books and papers on the floor, all clumsy and new.

I loved it.

ST. LAWRENCE COLLEGE WAS A short bus ride from Portsmouth House. In the first week, one of the residents who was leaving gave me a bicycle. It was perfect transportation for me. I fell quickly into a routine of school, homework in my studio, and exploring the town.

Something was on my mind though: Cynthia, the piano player from Collins Bay. She lived in Kingston, and I knew her last name. I thought she would be easy to find, but I was reluctant to try. Would she remember me? Would she think I was stalking her?

There were only two numbers with that name in the phone book. One of them had to be hers. I took a deep breath and called the first number. A man answered, and I chickened out and hung up.

I didn't try the second one.

A week went by, and I kept thinking about her. I talked to a few girls at school, but I didn't want anyone to know I was in Portsmouth House. More than five years without much communication with girls had left me a bit insecure to say the least.

One evening, without thinking, I picked up the phone and dialled the first number again. A woman answered. I asked for Cynthia.

"One moment please."

And there she was. It was her all right. I knew her voice.

I didn't know what to say. She said "hello" twice before I blurted out, "Do you remember 'Not Often,' the band?"

"Of course I do," she said, "It was my band. Do you know anything about them? It ended more than a year ago. They told me I couldn't go anymore."

"I'm Steve," I said. "The bass player. Do you remember me?"

Of course she remembered me. I don't think it's an experience any young girl would forget.

I told her I was in Portsmouth House and attending St. Lawrence College. She wanted to meet up right away. She knew where the house was.

"I'll come and get you," she said. "I can be there in twenty minutes."

I had to tell her I had a ten o'clock curfew. "I can't go anywhere."

"Can I come into the house?" she asked. "I have so many questions, I can't wait."

We were allowed visitors in the house anytime, so I told her it was okay. "Come on over."

And she did, in twenty minutes, maybe less.

I knew there was a deep psychological thing going on. Some girls are attracted to bad boys. Anthropologists have an explanation, but I didn't care. I was just glad she wasn't afraid to see me.

Our first meeting was full of hugs and kisses. The last time anything like that had happened was with Debbie. That was a long time ago.

She was very sad when I told her what happened in Collins Bay. She had had no idea why the band practice had ended. No one had told her anything.

I didn't expect it to have happened like that, but Cynthia and I were together for the next two and a half years. Eventually, we moved to Toronto together.

Cynthia had a car. I didn't even have a driver's licence. She was happy to drive us all over the area. She was in her first year at Queens University, and I was at St Lawrence. It was perfect but for one thing.

I had no money.

My school expenses were paid by parole services. It was a good deal. I could buy all the paint, canvas, and art supplies I needed at taxpayers' expense. Residents of Portsmouth House also got twenty-five dollars a week in pocket money, but it wasn't enough to take a girl to a movie and dinner. Cynthia was nice about it, but I always felt bad when she had to pay.

Other than lack of cash, life in Portsmouth House was like being a millionaire. I was living in a mansion. Only one unfortunate incident happened during my stay.

Portsmouth had a beautiful, full-sized pool table, not the rinky-dink basement-sized table. This one was an antique, and we used it a lot.

One evening, several residents were playing along with Cynthia and me. One guy I didn't know so well kept slapping Cynthia on the ass when she bent over to make a shot. He thought it was funny, but it was pissing me off.

I turned to another resident with whom I was friendly. "If he does that again, I'm going to give him a smack."

My friend was tough, big, and full of tattooed muscle. He didn't hesitate. He went straight for the jerk and punched his lights out. One shot, and it was devastating. I'm sure a guy like him could have killed someone with a single punch. It was just luck he didn't, but he sure made a mess. He was charged with another offence and sent back to prison, likely Millhaven.

I thought it was my fault. I never should have said anything to him. I didn't care much about the jerk who got his nose broken, but if I had taken care of it myself, maybe the tattooed muscle would have had a second chance.

The thing is, Cynthia didn't freak out at all. Her reaction was surprise but not fear or revulsion. Did she like the idea of men fighting over her? It should have been a clue for me, but love is blind.

27

I FINISHED MY FIRST SEMESTER AT ST. LAWRENCE AT THE TOP OF MY CLASS. I HAD A DISCIPLINED EXIS-tence, lots of time to study. My only distraction was Cynthia, and I got distracted as often as I could.

Sometimes in an empty classroom at Queens.

I was twenty-six, and Cynthia was nineteen. I was an immature twenty-six though, because I had missed the past five years of normal development. Even so, I didn't like to sneak around like a teenager looking for a place to hide with my girlfriend.

By Christmas, I found myself losing interest in school and wanting to take care of myself. In the break between semesters, I went looking for a job. I found part-time work in a grocery store, stocking shelves and slinging sides of beef from a truck to a freezer. I was making a little money, and my expenses were low. I was able to save some and actually open a bank account. I was twenty-six, and it was the first savings account I ever had.

I felt like Stephan Leacock.

> *When I go into a bank I get rattled. The clerks rattle me;*
> *the wickets rattle me; the sight of the money rattles me;*
> *everything rattles me.*

I HAD READ THIS FUNNY story some years before I ever set foot in a bank. It was exactly how I felt. Banks still intimidate me. I'm sure they think I came to rob them. Anyway, I did go into the cathedral-like building and asked them to keep my humble cash where I wouldn't spend it.

I didn't go back to St. Lawrence. My job became full-time, and I got more satisfaction from saving money than I did going to school. The director of Portsmouth House had to fill out all sorts of forms and write letters of support, but he was on my side.

In a few months, I was able to rent an apartment in downtown Kingston. I think Portsmouth House was happy to see me go, not because I was bad but because I was doing exactly what the place was meant for.

Cynthia was living at home with her parents. They didn't like me at all. I had dinner at her house once, and I could tell they disapproved. Who could blame them?

On the day Cynthia moved in with me, I bought a big waterbed. The bed itself didn't cost much, but the frame was expensive. The box said, "We recommend using a frame."

"Recommend," so that meant I didn't really need one.

Wrong!

We filled it up and watched it pulse like a big amoeba. That night we gave the wave motion a good workout, but we woke up in the middle of the night drowning. The bottom seam had split wide open. A wave of water hit the wall and washed back over us. We literally woke up under water.

I leapt to my feet naked, grabbed the split seam with both hands, and lifted the bed as high as I could, trying to keep what water was left inside the bag. I managed to stop the flow, but both hands were full, and I couldn't let go.

It was heavy. I didn't know what to do.

"I'll call the fire department," Cynthia said, soaking wet.

It took a while for them to get there. All the while, I was struggling to hold up the bed. Wrapped in a sheet, Cynthia let them in. Just imagine how this looked to the firemen.

Never mind.

They had a good laugh and syphoned the rest of the water out the window with a fire hose. All the water that washed over us had disappeared through the floor to the building owner's office below. I was sure we would be kicked out.

The next morning, I crept past his door. He came out and asked if I had spilled some water.

Oh-oh!

"Yeah," I said, "we had a little accident last night."

"No big deal," he replied. "I found a little water on my desk. No harm done."

Oh man! All that water must have gone through the walls and straight into the basement. What a relief.

CYNTHIA HAD TO BUY A bicycle. It turns out her car actually belonged to her mother. When she moved in with me, she had to give it back. Bikes were okay until the weather got cold. Then we had to get around by bus.

We were satisfied getting by on my grocery store wages. I knew Cynthia had some money stashed away, because she paid her own way at Queens. We never talked about money.

The winter of 1976 passed without event. Christmas was fun but sad. Cynthia had to choose between holidays at home with her family or staying with me. She stayed with me. It was the first time in her life she wasn't home for Christmas and the first Christmas I had in my own home.

We set up a tree and decorated it with things we could find or make without spending money. Cynthia gave me a guitar, and I gave her an Underwood typewriter. Cynthia was a writer. She was always writing in her journal. She recorded everything, and she had a way with words. I wasn't much of a guitar player, even though I had played since I was around fourteen. We worked out this funny routine. I would play some chords, and she would play her typewriter like a musical instrument. Sometimes she would type lyrics in rhythm, using typewriter keys as a form of percussion. It was a neat sound.

When spring came, Cynthia told me she was leaving Queens and enrolling at Ryerson. That meant she would be moving to Toronto. Secretly, I was tired of Kingston anyway. I had a job, and I was saving money, but Kingston was boring.

I still had to report to my parole officer every two weeks. I wasn't sure if they would let me go. Technically, I wasn't allowed to go outside a twenty-five-mile radius of Kingston without permission, but they let me go. I just had to report to a parole office in Toronto as soon as I was settled.

Cynthia's mother relented on the car and let us borrow it. We drove to Toronto for a weekend and looked for an apartment. I also used her car to get a driver's licence. That rite of passage came a little late for me, but the feeling was the same.

We had accumulated more furniture and junk than we could carry in a car. I rented a U-Haul, and off we went. I didn't look back at the town of Kingston when we passed the city limits.

28

I WAS TIRED OF SLINGING SIDES OF BEEF AROUND. THE DAMNED THINGS WEIGHED MORE THAN I DID. I found a job in a picture-framing store. I thought about calling the guy I worked for when I got out of Oak Ridge, but I didn't want to take a chance on drifting back into speed and cocaine. Besides, I never liked the guy anyway.

We had an apartment in an old house on Bernard Street. It was close to Yorkville Village, but by then the Village scene was gone. It had been gentrified to the max.

I met my neighbours in the house and others on Bernard Street. I joined the "Bernard Street Gang." At its height, we had about twenty-five members. We even had jackets made with embroidered colours on the back. The graphic was my creation—a spooky demon head with sharp teeth.

I didn't live for work in those years. I lived for weekends. We gathered every weekend at a club called "Why Not" on the corner of Bernard and Avenue Road. Don Franks, also known as "Iron Buffalo," owned the place. His band played every night. We locked the doors after hours, and sometimes we partied 'til dawn. I'm sure we bent the rules, and we may have broken some hearts, but we didn't break the law. We didn't rob banks or deal drugs.

The Bernard Street Gang had some interesting members. One of them was John, Canada's only schizophrenic, bar-certified lawyer. He was fine for the most part, but if he didn't take his medication, he would do strange things, like stand at the bus stop on his way to court with his briefcase in hand but no pants. Our group also included Hans Zander, artist, author and serial seducer of everyone; and Dennis, a high school teacher whose wife left him because he lost his licence for drunk driving. He never drove again in his life. Then there was Robin Harp, the best harmonica player ever. His girlfriend stole the only picture I had of "Not Often." I wish I still had it. A certain environmental scientist named David was also part of our crew. He's pretty famous now. Richard, a rich guy who owned a drapery factory on Davenport Road joined us as well. He bought a lot of rounds. Finally, Coco and Angel, two irresistible black girls who lived in the house with Cynthia and me. Yes, irresistible they were! Then there was me, ex-mental patient and freshly-released ex-con still on parole. I thought it better not to talk about that.

Sometimes the Bernard Street Gang would go on road trips or camping expeditions. We also got into model rocket building and launching. It almost got us into trouble, but the cop let it slide. Just a broken window. It was a summer like no other. Up to that point, it was the best of times. In the fall, Cynthia went to the Ryerson School of Journalism.

One day, we heard on CHUM radio that the Rolling Stones were coming to Toronto for a recording session. The radio station had a contest where we could write and tell them why we should be picked to go to a private recording party with the Stones. Like I said, Cynthia had a way with words. She wrote the letter, and we forgot about it.

We were getting dressed to go out one night when the phone rang. It was CHUM-FM. We had won the contest.

"Come to the radio station on Young street by eight," the caller said. "Don't bring cameras or recording equipment."

Oh man, what a score!

We were loaded on a bus with about twenty other people. The windows were covered with paper. We had no idea where we were going. The bus pulled into a narrow alley, and we were ushered up the fire escape. It was the El Mocambo. I knew the place well, but I had never gone in through the fire escape.

The place was packed. We got a table close to the stage, close enough to get splashed by a glass of water thrown by Mick Jagger.

They started off stage with the thumping first chords of "Honkytonk Woman." They played for three hours straight. That was my day in rock 'n' roll heaven. Later, I heard that Margret Trudeau was at the table next to us. I didn't notice her, but I can tell you that two of the voices cheering and clapping in the background of "Love You Live" are Cynthia and me.

I missed Woodstock, but the gods of music did compensate. I still have the vinyl.

29

ONE DAY, WE WERE TALKING ABOUT MY HOMETOWN WHEN CYNTHIA CONVINCED ME TO CALL MY MOTHER. I knew her phone number, always did. My mother was a simple woman, not a lot of words. Her life had changed. This is what she told me.

Bill had left her after another big argument. He went straight to the tail race and jumped in. I told you, that water. I guess he didn't last long. Of course, Bill's last act was to lay the blame for his miserable life on my mother.

Anyway, Bill was dead, and my mother was fine. She bought a small house and had savings and a pension. She sounded a bit drunk, but she was happy. I gave her my number and address. She acted like I had been away at college for summer. Didn't ask anything about the past five years.

A few weeks later, my long-lost brother Garry called me. I was stunned. I didn't believe it was him. I had long since resigned myself to the fact he was dead and gone. I made him answer a bunch of questions that only Garry would know. He said he was living in Vancouver, and he had just called our mother. She had given him my phone number. Garry told me he was coming to Toronto to do a show.

"A show?" I asked. "What show? What are you doing?"

He wouldn't tell me. "You'll find out when we get there."

"We?" I asked. "Who's we?"

"You'll see."

Two weeks later, they came to our door—Garry and his partner Billy. They had driven across Canada in a silver Lincoln Continental rag top. Gas was cheap then.

I'm sure if I had passed Garry on the street I would not have recognized him. He was skinny like me, and he had the Smith nose, but I would have had to look closely. By 1977, gays were no longer hiding. They were out front and flaunting their gayness. The word "gay" no longer meant happy and carefree. Garry and Billy were "flaming fags," at least that's how they described themselves. It didn't bother me at all. I knew Garry had been gay since I was a kid.

He looked rich. His clothes, his watch, his diamond pinky ring with one absurdly long fingernail. (It took a while for me to find out what that was used for.) But most of all, the Lincoln, an impressive land yacht.

Billy, as boys go, was drop-dead handsome. I call him "boy," but he was close to thirty. Looking back on the short time I knew him, I can say he was one of the most talented people I have ever met. Writer, singer, artist, entertainer, athlete. Everything he did, he did with style.

I had a lot of catching up to do with Garry. First thing, how could he afford a Rolex watch and a Lincoln Continental? This is what he told me.

When he left Sault Ste. Marie, it was Joe and the Brotherhood who guided him. He said Bill had threatened to kill him because he was queer. Joe helped him with money and a plane ticket to San Francisco.

When Garry arrived, he was picked up at the airport by Ira Magee, who was a stage hypnotist. Much older than Garry, Magee was a "chicken hawk," an old man who liked young boys. He was connected with Hollywood elite, the dark side of it. His hypnosis shows were popular at the mansions of the Laurel Canyon weirdoes.

Soon, Garry became "the talk of the town," like the Lou Reed song, "Take a Walk on the Wild Side." He was a small town boy. Easy to corrupt.

It was said that Ira Magee could turn a straight boy gay in five minutes with a few "hypno-tricks."

That's a scary thought.

Ira took Garry under his wing and made him his assistant. He also taught him his trade and gave him a stage name: Steve Hyslop. I never could figure out why he stole my first name. It caused confusion for years to come.

Garry met Billy at one of those Laurel Canyon parties. He told me details I didn't really want to know. He also dropped some names of people who may still be alive. Sons and grandsons of Hollywood actors going back to the silent era.

Billy was a whipping boy, literally. He enjoyed pain. Well, not really, but he enjoyed others who enjoyed watching his pain. He was covered with scars in places that didn't show.

I asked Garry to tell me more about the Brotherhood. "Maybe I worked for them in the Sault and in Toronto."

"I don't think anyone knows who they are," he said, "but I know they're everywhere. Almost like a guardian angel for me."

I told him about Oak Ridge and Peter Woodcock and Toronto. I also told him what happened in the Sault with Dave and Debbie and Joe, the Memorial Gardens, hockey players, the "employment agency," all of it.

"Do you think the Brotherhood is bad?" he asked. "They weren't bad for me."

It took twenty years for me to understand that Garry was already committed to the dark side when I met him that day.

Garry had no way to prove he was Canadian. He didn't have a birth certificate or a social insurance number. Everything he had was American. He didn't care. He came back to Canada in 1974 and had been using what Ira Magee taught him. He was preforming in gay bars, getting paid in cash and making a fortune, spending it as fast as he made it.

He also told me he had been in jail for a while, too. He was in New Brunswick doing a show and had gotten involved with a kid who was underage. He got busted right in his dressing room. He bailed himself out, but he had to pay everything he made from the gig.

"I think the club owner set me up," he said.

He left New Brunswick, never to return. There was still a warrant out for his arrest, but the warrant was in the name of an American who didn't exist. Garry Smith had no history.

THE NEXT EVENING, WE WENT to his performance. It was at a sleazy bar on King Street. It wasn't a gay bar, but the clientele was weird.

When Garry was on stage, he was totally transformed. His costume was all flashy silver, and he had a black cape. He did a few magic tricks to get the audience pumped up. He had two antique magic props made of spring steel, a disappearing walking stick and an appearing walking stick. If you didn't know how they worked, it looked magic. His voice was completely different, too, a deep baritone with a commanding ring. When he barked an order, people followed.

He started by asking for volunteers. More than twenty-five people rushed to the stage. Out of these, he picked about a dozen. He whispered something in the ear of the rest and then sent them back to their tables.

He sat the volunteers on folding chairs facing the audience. First, he did some simple tests on all of them at the same time. He knew what he was looking for. He asked them to clasp their hands in front with fingers locked. Then he told them to squeeze tighter and tighter as he counted from one to ten. As he counted backward from ten to one, he told them to try to loosen their hands.

"But you can't," he said. "The harder you try, the more stuck they become."

It was amazing to watch all of them struggle to get their hands apart. A few separated their hands right away. He sent them back to their table. A good number of volunteers remained.

Then Garry, or Steve Hyslop, asked the room for complete silence. It was a difficult thing to accomplish in a nightclub like that, but he got what he demanded.

Not a sound.

With his back to the room, he started the hypnotic induction. Everyone on stage fell into a trance. I was amazed by that, and at that moment, I was proud to be his brother.

Once everyone on stage had their chin in their chest, Garry turned to the audience. "Now, what should we do with these poor, helpless people?"

"Take their clothes off! Take their clothes off!" the crowd yelled.

Of course.

Garry smiled and nodded with an exaggerated theatrical wink. He knew exactly what he could get away with. He turned to the volunteers. "When I tell you to wake up, you will wake and do exactly what I tell you to do. When I tell you to sleep," he made a loud *pop* with his tongue, "you will sleep." It wasn't a request; it was a command.

He worked one person at a time while the rest remained in a trance. To some, he said, "You are the best stripper in the world. Everyone wants to see you perform."

And they did, both men and women. He never let the women go too far, just enough to prove they would do it. At the crucial moment, he would command, "Sleep," and make that loud pop. The woman would freeze like a puppet just before taking off her shirt or pants. He would allow the men to get right down to their underwear. The audience screamed and cheered. Garry knew the fine line he was treading. Entertaining but legal.

By the end of the show, everyone on stage was doing something foolish. Men were giving birth while women helped. Some bounced around the stage clucking like chickens.

In the end, he told them when they woke they would not remember any of it. With each group, he gave one subject a post-hypnotic command, something he or she would do after returning to his or her table, such as take a beer from someone's table and drink it or light up an invisible cigarette. It always worked, and he always got a standing ovation. The volunteers didn't remember anything, so they were not embarrassed about acting like fools.

Cynthia and I were blown away. I had never seen anything like it. I always thought my brother was sort of weak. He was older than me, but I had always been the stronger one. When I saw him in total command on stage, I knew he had developed some serious and powerful character.

GARRY AND BILLY WERE STAYING in the Four Seasons Sheraton, the most expensive hotel in Toronto. As I learned more about my brother, I realized he always had to have the most expensive of everything—not because quality mattered but because he needed to impress everyone around him.

The day after the performance, I went with them to a recording studio. Garry had booked the studio for two hours at great expense. He recorded an LP in one take. No dubbing and no corrections. He even brought cover graphics he had designed himself. My brother had to do everything himself. He didn't know how to delegate.

He had five hundred copies pressed, waited a few days to pick them up, and then headed back to Vancouver.

"Come with us," he said before they left. "You'll like Vancouver more than Toronto."

"I can't leave Toronto," I said, "I'm still on parole for at least another three years."

I was tempted to just up and leave, but I stayed.

It was good to know I still had a brother, but something about Garry made me uneasy. It wasn't that he was gay. Something below the surface didn't feel right. He had something missing. It also bugged me when people called him "Steve." It felt like he was jealous of me or trying to take over my identity. But he had turned into a very interesting guy.

UP TO THEN, I HAD been fine getting around Toronto by public transportation, but after driving around in Garry's Lincoln, I wanted a car of my own.

Sibling rivalry, I guess.

I had saved enough to buy a used Chevy Nova. It was no Lincoln land yacht, and it was a bit rusty, but it could go like hell. Once in a while, late at night, the Bernard Street Gang would go racing down the street in it. If I had that car today, it would be a classic muscle car.

Meanwhile, I was thinking about Vancouver. I had tried to get there ten years earlier but had wound up in Oak Ridge. Getting to the coast was unfinished business. I had an image of the west coast, like a magnet drawing me.

I recalled Hugh Morrison telling me something about Vancouver. I think he said he had lived there in the past. I wanted to look him up, but I thought I had been a disappointment to him and his wife.

Then there was the Brotherhood. Garry had been influenced by them as well. Was it the same group to whom Peter Woodcock had introduced me? Was it something from which I should stay away?

I knew I should talk to Hugh, but I kept putting it off. For some reason, the more I thought about calling people from the past, the less likely I was to do it.

Back then it was easy to find a phone number. Just call information and give the operator a name. One day, on impulse, I did it. I got his number and dialled it right away.

Hugh answered on the first ring. He must have been sitting right beside the phone. I had no idea what to say. I told him who I was and asked if he remembered me.

"Oh yes, I remember you," he said. "Where are you?"

I told him I was in Toronto. He asked a bunch of questions. I thought he was trying to determine if I was going to be a nuisance. I didn't mention having been in prison.

"Yes, I have a job," I said, "and I'm living with my girlfriend."

His demeanor changed when I told him about Garry and hypnosis.

"My brother wants me to move to Vancouver."

"We should go for lunch," Hugh said. "Shall I pick you up?"

We met at an outdoor restaurant in Hazelton Lanes. It was the summer of 1978, a beautiful, hot, sunny day.

From our table, I could see the back window of the apartment in which I had lived almost a decade before, the apartment for which Karl had paid. Hugh knew this apartment. I wondered if he had chosen that restaurant because of the view.

It was within walking distance of our Bernard Street apartment. Hazelton and Yorkville had changed. We seldom went there. It had lost its character.

Hugh was already seated at a table when we arrived. He got up, shook hands with me, and bowed to Cynthia.

"Charmed," he said and motioned for us to sit. "What would you like to drink?" he asked, as though he was the waiter. "Do you still not drink alcohol, Steven?"

I looked at Cynthia. She smiled.

"A glass of wine would be fine," she said.

I nodded. "I'll have the same."

Hugh ordered for us. I was reminded of our last meeting. Hugh was better at ordering food and dealing with arrogant waiters. Like bank tellers, waiters intimidated me. I was happy to let him take care of it.

"So, what have you been up to since we last met?" he asked.

I didn't know what he knew about my recent past, and I didn't want to tell him.

"Getting an education one way or another."

He nodded as though he knew my education had come from the "Crowbar College." He didn't push it though, maybe because he didn't know how much Cynthia knew about me.

He was very curious about Garry. He asked a lot of questions about Laurel Canyon and where Garry had lived in Hollywood. I told him some of what Garry told me about his adventures after leaving the Sault. I didn't tell him Garry had mentioned the Brotherhood.

Hugh told me he knew Ira Magee and had seen his stage act. He commented on what a small world it was. "Your brother was Magee's apprentice!"

I realized all of this fit together somehow. What was I missing?

He asked what part of Vancouver Garry lived in.

"The West End," I said. "Do you know what it's like there?"

Hugh nodded. "Yes, the West End. Gay people tend to live in the West End."

I hadn't told him Garry was gay. How did he know? Or did he know?

THE PSYCHOPATH MACHINE

He practically ignored Cynthia. He asked her a few things, like what she was studying, but he didn't seem interested in her.

Conversation came around to what I planned to do in the future.

"I'd like to travel," I said. "I've never been outside Canada except a few miles across the US border."

"It would be good for you to do that," Hugh said. "You should go to Central America. Learn Spanish."

He said a few sentences in Spanish. I didn't understand a word.

"I can help you with that," he said. He picked up a briefcase from beside his chair and wrote down a name and address in Guatemala. "This is a friend of mine. Go look him up. It's a guaranteed adventure."

He put the note into a small, white book and handed it to me. "I wrote this book" he said. "You don't have to read it, but I want to give it to you."

Lunch came to an end.

Hugh looked at his watch. "I better get going."

He shook hands with me and wished me luck. Then he kissed Cynthia's hand and said, "Goodbye."

It didn't look silly. He was like that.

I never saw Hugh Morrison again.

30

WE HAD FUN IN THE SUMMER OF '78.

The Bernard Street Gang drank and partied too much, but we were young. I could stay up all night and still be at work in the morning.

My job was uninspiring. The framing store was inside a mall, so I didn't see the sunlight most days. I was turning into a night crawler. Cynthia continued at Ryerson.

The "Why Not" club closed, and Don Franks moved his band to George's Spaghetti House on Dundas Street. It was a great place but not within easy walking distance of our apartment. A few times we left the club well after hours. It was impossible to find a taxi, so we had to walk.

One night, a group of people came into the club and sat at a table close to us. One of them, a woman, was particularly striking. She wore a full-length, black velvet cape with a hood that left her face in shadow but for her bright red lips.

One of the men went to the stage and talked to Don. Then she went on stage without introduction and said a few words to the band members. She pushed the hood of her cape back and sang the most beautiful rendition of "Bridge over Troubled Waters."

It was Roberta Flack.

All my hair stood on end!

TWO YEARS HAD PASSED SINCE I got out of Joyceville. I was living a stable life, but I was still reporting to a parole officer once a month.

This parole officer was nothing like the Portsmouth House guy. He wasn't much older than me. He was full of his own importance and always seemed to be looking for a reason to throw me back into prison. I didn't like him, but I had to put up with his attitude for five minutes a month.

Winter came. It was February of 1979. Cynthia had gone to New York City for a school field trip. I was on my own for a week. It was bitterly cold, and I just stayed home or went to work.

One of Cynthia's journals was in a magazine rack beside the couch. The book was narrow and tall with a picture of a giraffe on the cover. I picked it up and flipped through it. What I read changed everything.

I should have just left it alone, but something caught my attention: a graphic description of the day my parole officer paid a visit to my apartment when I was at work. Cynthia was in bed with that bastard within minutes. She wrote about it in detail, like a dime store romance novel.

Everything came crashing down around me. It wasn't the act itself; it was the betrayal. We weren't married, and I had no contract with her, but getting it on with my parole officer? That was a thoughtless and dangerous thing to do.

I understood that some girls were attracted to bad boys. It occurred to me Cynthia might not see me as a bad boy anymore. Was she trying to make me do something bad, or was she just trying to make me go away because I wasn't bad enough? Why had I tried so hard those past two years, only to be betrayed?

In a daze, I collected my clothes and left the apartment. I left behind everything, even the guitar Cynthia had given me.

I found a room in a skid row hotel on Queen Street. The Rex. No TV, no phone, no mini bar, no view, just cockroaches. It should have been called "the Wrecks." I sat there for three days. I didn't go to work, and I didn't eat except for a bag of potato chips from a vending machine. What was I going to do?

I thought seriously about going after the parole officer. I was ready to go back to jail. Nothing and no one outside could be trusted. Then I thought about what the parole officer had said to me in Portsmouth House.

"You can look for revenge, or you can prove them wrong."

They were wrong. They had always misjudged me. I was not going to let them be right.

I had to get my car out of the hotel parking lot or pay. I didn't even want the car anymore.

On the fourth day, I closed my bank account and took the car back to Bernard Street. I parked carelessly in front of the house and left the keys in the ignition.

The lights were on in our apartment, but I just walked away.

I had about fifteen hundred dollars in my pocket. It was a lot of money back then, to me anyway. It made me feel like I had some options at least. What if I hadn't saved that money? I would have been doomed for sure.

It's so strange how some things just happen if you let them. As I was walking back to the Rex, I realized I hadn't eaten much in the last few days. I didn't want to pass out on the street, so I walked into a Christian drop-in center to eat something.

It wasn't a normal café with tables and chairs. There were couches and coffee tables. I ordered something, and when the waitress brought it to me, she asked, "Do you know the Lord Jesus?"

Oh boy. Well, I had gone in there. I should have expected to be Bible thumped.

"Yes, I've heard of him," I replied with a smile. Smiling hurt my face, but I was trying to be nice.

She was a blond, blue-eyed girl with that shiny Christian face. You should know by now that I have a soft spot for waitresses.

I talked to her for more than an hour. Then, just for fun, I said, "I'm going to Vancouver tomorrow. Do you want to come with me?"

She looked totally surprised. "Yes I do," she said. "Tomorrow? But I don't have money."

"I have money," I said. "We can fly tomorrow if you're serious. I'll get you a ticket."

I told her to meet me at ten the next morning in front of the Rex. She said she would be there, but I didn't believe her.

The next morning, I checked out and started walking toward the York hotel to catch a bus to the airport. Then I stopped, thinking I'd wait a few minutes just in case. And there she was, backpack and all.

"I'm ready," she said. "Can I really go with you?"

"Let's go," I said.

Suddenly, I didn't want to take a bus. I flagged a taxi.

In the 1970s, you could still go to the airport and buy a ticket with cash. That's what we did. We didn't have to wait long for the next flight.

When we were settled in our seat, she turned to me. "I've never been on an airplane."

"Neither have I," I admitted.

My life up to that point had taken some strange turns, and now it had just taken another one.

My new friend's name was Debbie.

31

THE FLIGHT FROM TORONTO TO VANCOUVER WAS AROUND FOUR HOURS. WE TALKED NONSTOP THE ENTIRE way. I didn't know anything about Debbie except that she was cute and blonde and up for adventure. At least I wasn't alone and thinking about Cynthia. With Debbie sitting beside me, I was heading toward something instead of running from something.

I called Garry from the terminal when we landed. I didn't tell him I was in Vancouver. I teased him a bit with questions about Vancouver, and then I said, "Okay, sounds nice. Can you pick me up at the airport?"

"Of course," he said. "When are you going to come?"

"I left Toronto around five hours ago. I'm in the Vancouver airport right now."

I thought I heard him bounce off the roof.

"Billy! Billy! Get the car. My brother's here!"

That was around the end of February. Toronto was bitterly cold. Every day was minus something. When Debbie and I stepped out of the airport, I was amazed at how warm it was. The sun was shining, and it felt like spring. Even the sky was different. Bigger and bluer. I could smell the ocean, too. I had never seen the ocean, but I knew the smell.

Garry and Billy arrived in less than half an hour. They were surprised to see us standing outside. They thought it was cold.

We had no luggage, only Debbie's backpack and a bag of clothes I had taken with me when I left my apartment. I realized I had nothing, but I did have money in my pocket.

Garry drove the scenic route from the airport to the West End. The view from upper Granville Street was spectacular. Snow-capped mountains behind the city skyline. Even the grass was green on the front lawns of the houses we passed.

It had been a decade since I had set out on the road to Vancouver. Now there I was, ten years older, less carefree and a lot more cautious, determined to get revenge on everyone who misjudged and abused me. I would find revenge by proving them wrong. Here was a new beginning.

Debbie hardly said a word all the way into town. She was just smiling in wide-eyed wonder.

"Where did you two meet?" Billy asked.

"We don't really know each other," I said. "We only met yesterday. We thought it would be a good idea to travel together."

I didn't say I paid her way.

I found out two things on the flight from Toronto: 1) Debbie didn't really believe in "The Lord Jesus Christ," and 2) she had no money. Not a dime. She was either a very brave and adventurous girl or she was crazy. Turns out she was crazy, but I'll get to that.

Garry stopped at English Bay before driving home. I wanted to dip my foot in the ocean. By then it was getting dark. Only a few people were on the beach. I thought this was strange. By Toronto standards, it was a warm, beautiful evening—not sunbathing warm, but it made Toronto look like Siberia. The beach should have been full of people. I cupped my hands and drank some cold Pacific Ocean water, quickly realizing that it's true, you can't drink sea water!

Garry's place was close enough to walk to English Bay. Nelson Street close to Denman. It was a spectacular place. There were three houses side by side. Each house had three apartments. They were all designer cedar, vaulted ceiling, spiral staircase to a loft with a great view of the mountains. Altogether, there were four bedrooms and two lofts.

He showed us to a small bedroom in the back. "Is this okay?"

I hesitated.

"It's perfect," Debbie said. "So beautiful."

"It's great," I said, smiling like a Cheshire cat. I couldn't wait for bedtime.

The first thing Garry did was break out the BC bud. Billy liked to roll specialty treats. Two or three papers joined together to make a foot-long joint.

I had heard about the legendary BC bud in Toronto but had never actually tried it. I wasn't smoking much pot in Toronto, mostly because I didn't have a connection with a dealer. Other than the odd joint I mooched from a Bernard Street Gang member, I did without.

Pot smoking, like drinking alcohol, is an acquired taste. If you don't do it regularly, you can wind up face-down on the carpet. There is a three-hour time difference between Toronto and Vancouver. Debbie and I were jet-lagged as it was. After a few tokes, we were zonked! We were asleep before we got to the back bedroom. Two days, and I still didn't know this girl at all.

We were awake before six in the morning, still on Toronto time. Then I did get to know Debbie. She was... enthusiastic. I was afraid she would wake up the entire house. I didn't know how soundproof our room was. I said Debbie never talked about "the Lord Jesus" again, but she did that morning. Sort of. There was no "Lord," but she did call out his name quite a few times. The thought occurred to me that this girl was a little strange. I had no idea how strange until later.

Eventually we had to get up. Four or five people were scattered around the apartment sleeping on the floor. It reminded me of my place on Hazelton. A crash pad for hippies. Not hippies this time though. Stepping over the half-naked bodies of gay boys was a little unsettling. A few of them looked like they should have a chalk outline around them, but they were breathing.

Garry's place was always busy with people coming and going. I didn't find out until later that Billy was the local dealer. Every night was party time for Garry and friends. Mostly gay boys. Night crawlers of all kinds. Strippers, hookers, drag queens. A Moulin Rouge of weirdness.

I managed to find a coffee machine and got it going. Meanwhile, Debbie was sneaking around lifting blankets and having a look at what was under them, a big grin on her face. This girl was kinky. That was all right though. Cynthia had been sort of conservative.

By nine o'clock, everyone was still sleeping. We got tired of tiptoeing around and decided to take a walk.

Finding our way around Vancouver was more difficult than Toronto. Bridges and water to cross everywhere. It wasn't a simple north/south set-up, and there was no subway. We didn't go far for fear of getting lost.

Our first week in Vancouver was nonstop partying. Garry introduced me to his friends as his brother Steve. It always caused confusion, because they were used to calling him Steve. It annoyed me, but I was having so much fun I let it slide. I considered changing my name but decided not to let Garry steal it.

Garry had developed a huge ego. He had to be the center of attention, the star. Everyone around him knew he was the guy with the drugs, the money, and the nice apartment. I realized in a short time that Garry bought his friends. They were all sycophants.

Billy was different. He knew Garry's other side—the frightened, insecure, abused boy. Billy was deep. Garry was shallow but popular.

In the first week, a lot of gay boys hit on me in various ways. I'm not homophobic, but I know I'm not gay. I didn't have to punch anyone's lights out to let them know. Most gay men simply have better manners than straight men. All I needed to do was tell them once.

"You can drool over me all you like, but don't touch."

The first time I was in a gay nightclub was an interesting experience. The place was actually a lesbian bar, but men were there, too. It was called "BJ's," an odd name for a lesbian bar. Later on, I worked there as a doorman and bouncer. It was some education! Bouncing an angry dyke isn't something you want to try.

BJ's was a small basement bar, famous for its drag shows. I didn't know what to expect. I had never seen a drag show.

We had a table up close to the stage, but Billy wasn't with us. Just Garry, Debbie, and me. The star of the show was "Diana Ross." It took a while for me to get it. This Diana Ross was Billy! It was truly amazing. He looked and moved exactly like the real thing. Of course, he was miming the lyrics, but if the real Diana Ross had seen him, she would think she was looking in a mirror.

A few minutes after his show, he came to our table and sat down, still in drag. Minus the Afro wig and high heels, he was a gender contradiction. Billy was a blond, blue-eyed Aryan boy, but that night he was a brown-skinned woman. Hollywood makeup artist was another one of his talents.

32

THE FIRST THREE WEEKS LIVING WITH GARRY AND HIS ENTOURAGE WAS A REAL EYE OPENER. IT WAS THE wild West End all right. Davie Street was lined with hookers, some almost naked. Pretty much everything they had for sale was on display. This nightly circus started just around the corner from Garry's place. Most of the girls on the corner got used to me or Debbie passing by and didn't solicit us.

One evening as we passed a group of drag queens on the corner, one of them made some wisecrack.

"Be nice or get out of my neighbourhood," I said.

He/she puffed him/herself up. "I don't mind fucking your girlfriend."

Now, this freak really pissed me off. I wasn't a conservative, gay-bashing redneck, as I'm sure you can see, but something about this challenge really got to me. They may not look like it, but drag queens can be vicious and dangerous. There were too many of them for me to handle on my own.

"Stay here," I said. "I'll be right back."

I went to the back of the house and picked up a broken axe handle.

As I rounded the corner, they saw me coming. I walked quickly toward them, looking serious and determined. They did exactly as I hoped they would do. They ran like hell in all directions. Hiking up their mini-skirts, one of them jumped right out of his high-heeled shoes. I stood there laughing but trying to look fierce.

The gay boys in my brother's house learned not to mess with me, and now I had established myself in the neighbourhood.

Billy didn't act gay around me. It was as though he could turn it off and on at will. He was a dual personality. I thought it was possible he didn't know he had at least two distinct personalities. Sometimes I could see he didn't remember things that had happened when he was in drag.

Garry paid for everything. He didn't ask me to contribute rent or food money. The money I had was spent mostly on buying clothes and essentials for Debbie. It ran out in the first two months.

Debbie's behaviour was becoming increasingly erratic. It's difficult to explain why, but I knew something wasn't right with her. For one thing, she was a nymphomaniac.

Even though the boys who hung around the house were all gay, they liked to flirt with Debbie. They were always fussing over her makeup and hair, talking like a bunch of girls. Debbie liked the attention and started treating them like servants.

Garry also had female friends, but they were all lesbians or strippers. I didn't know anything about lesbians. I found out there are dykes and fems. I discovered the fems were temporary or part-time lesbians. It was a lifestyle experiment for them. They usually grew up, got married, and had kids. Dykes, I suppose, are born that way. They try too hard to act like men, or at least how they think a man acts. They don't usually get along with real men. That's understandable, because for the most part, men hate them.

The dykes hit on Debbie constantly. I didn't like it, but Debbie didn't mind. I tried to make sure none of them was alone with her.

I had to find a job. It had been more than two months since I had an income. Because Garry paid for everything, I felt like I was losing my independence.

I applied at three picture-framing shops and got the position at all three. I had to choose. One was within walking distance of Garry's place. The owner offered a deal I didn't really understand at first.

"I'll pay one dollar a corner in cash," he said.

A picture frame has four corners. If it has a matte, that's eight corners. A framed poster with a double matte would make sixteen dollars for me. It sounded good, but I wasn't sure.

Clem, the owner, came to regret making that deal, but he lived up to it. Before long, I was pumping out more than fifty prints a day. I was so good at mass-producing framed posters that I changed the nature of Clem's business. He rented a warehouse, and it became my domain. It wasn't within walking distance, but I was making so much cash I could take a taxi to work every day.

I knew living with Garry and his sycophants wasn't good for Debbie, but she liked the wild side. She was becoming like them, and I was thinking it would be better if she went back to Toronto.

It became obvious to everyone that something was wrong when she got caught in the sauna with two neighbourhood kids—a girl around ten years old and a boy around eight. I'll never know exactly what happened.

Their parents called the police. After some tense discussion, they didn't charge her with anything, but they suggested she get professional counselling. Debbie didn't understand why everyone was so upset. She said they were only having fun.

By that time, I knew Debbie was nuts. I didn't know if it was something new or if she was nuts before I met her. Even her face was changing.

It took a lot of convincing, but I talked her into going to Saint Paul's Hospital. She was interviewed for maybe five minutes, and I guess she passed the test.

A few days later, I came home to find an astonishing sight. Debbie was sitting alone in the center of the living room. Around her she had taken all the soil from the house plants and dumped it on the carpet. She had formed the dirt into concentric rings and symbols. It was a huge mess.

But the worst thing was the ladder. Somehow she had taken a big aluminum ladder from the backyard, maneuvered it up the stairs, and placed it in the living room—one end in the corner of the high ceiling, the other end on the floor, corner to corner.

Cleaning up the mess took hours. Garry had to hire a carpet cleaner. We couldn't figure out how to get the ladder back outside. It was too long. We had to get a carpenter to take out the window and frame to move the damn thing. It remains a mystery how she ever got it in there in the first place.

We could not find any help for this girl. We tried every agency we could think of. All she had to do was act normal during a short interview, and they thought she was okay. Ten minutes later, she would be babbling craziness. It wasn't safe to leave her alone.

I had to go to work, but I didn't trust Garry's flaky friends to watch over her.

Debbie refused to give me any information about her family. I knew her last name, but it was a common name. I had to trick it out of her. I told her I wanted to play a little game at the public library. I got a Toronto phone book and started going through names randomly and asking if she knew anyone by that name. When I got to the pages with her last name, she pointed out the number. It worked; I had her parents' phone number.

Then I had to scare her into wanting to go back to Toronto. I didn't know what else to do. I told her the police were going to arrest her for molesting children. She was already paranoid, in the clinical sense, and she was almost in a panic when I took her to the airport. I'm not sure if she had much of a grip on reality at all. I don't know if Debbie even realized she was leaving Vancouver.

As soon as the plane got off the ground, I called her parents and told them to meet Debbie at the airport. "She's sick," I said. "You need to help her."

I never found out what happened to her. I called the same number about a week later, and it was out of service.

Afterwards, I thought about how easy it had been a decade earlier for me to get locked up in a nuthouse. Now it was impossible to get any help for Debbie at all. I also felt a heavy weight of guilt. Had I caused her transformation? Was I responsible for putting her in an environment that made her go crazy?

I'll never know.

I do know that I was told several times over the years by a number of people that I don't know a good woman from a loser because of my mother. I don't know if that's true or not. People come and go in and out of our lives all the time. I think it's all about finding the right combination.

Debbie would be over sixty years old now. She may have had a happy life and be a grandmother several times over.

I hope so.

I STAYED ON AT GARRY'S place for a few more months. It wasn't the same with Debbie gone, and it wasn't a good environment for a straight guy.

At first, it was amusing to watch the nightly circus, but it was getting uncomfortable. Billy was the only one who knew I was never going to give in to the gay boys. He would put them in their place a little more forcefully than I did.

"Hey, do you want to be black for a day?" he asked one day.

"What do you mean?" I replied, "like in drag or something?"

He laughed. "No, no, not drag. I can show you what it's like to be a black man. White people don't understand, but when you're black everything is different."

As I said, Billy was a makeup artist. He had everything in his kit to turn me into a black man. I had grown some hair and had got it permed recently into a big Afro (I know, I know, but it was the end of the 1970s. It was a common thing then.) So Billy went to work with his makeup, and in less than an hour, he told me to go look in a mirror.

What a shock. I didn't recognize myself. It wasn't like the black face I got during my escape from Burwash. I didn't look like Al Jolson. Face, arms, and shoulders, all chocolate brown. Even the palms of my hands were just the right shade.

It took some cajoling, but Billy talked me into going outside for a walk down Davie Street.

I thought everyone would stare at me like some kind of freak. But no. What I found out that day gave me some insight into being black in a white man's world. I know this may anger some people, but I learned something I never forgot.

In 1979, there were very few black people in Vancouver. As I strolled down Davie Street, lots of people on the sidewalk, I noticed a few things right away. The main thing was that people don't look you in the eye when you're black. There's none of that quick flash of eye contact that happens all the time. When you walk a busy sidewalk with people coming toward you, there is silent communication that keeps people from bumping into each other, always an unspoken challenge of who will yield right of way.

Not when you're black. The oncoming traffic will part before you like the Red Sea. It didn't take long to understand. White people are afraid of black men. Since then, I have tried my best to be colour blind.

IN LATE SUMMER OF 1979, I woke up to a big fight going on in the living room. Billy had got into it with one of the flakier boys. He threw him out and all his clothes behind him.

A few days later, an Immigration Canada officer and two cops showed up to deport Billy. Fortunately, he wasn't home. Billy was American, and he had no legal status in Canada. Everyone knew the punk he threw out had ratted on him.

Billy decided to go back to the US on his own to avoid being deported. I heard him typing all night. Before he left the next morning, he gave me a folder with all of his music lyrics. I still have it. So much talent just collecting dust these past thirty-five years.

Soon, it became clear that Billy was the one who had kept Garry from falling into chaos. Garry acted like he ran the show, but the only show he was capable of running was on stage. It didn't take long for BC bud to turn into a hardcore cocaine addiction.

I started looking for an apartment.

33

I WAS MAKING GOOD MONEY, AND I LIKED MY JOB. I MOVED OUT OF GARRY'S PLACE ON THE FIRST OF September. I was twenty-nine years old, and it was the first time I had lived in my own apartment by myself. The apartment was in a nice, old building next to Hy's Restaurant on lower Davie Street close to Denman, a two-minute walk from work. I furnished it in modern Salvation Army with bricks and board shelves. I could have bought nice furniture, but I was becoming a cheapskate. The more cash I put in my pocket, the less I was willing to spend.

I enjoyed living by myself. I was a rare commodity in the West End—single male, not gay, and employed. I met a few girls during that time but I didn't want anything serious. As soon as I told them they couldn't move in with me, they were gone.

Two weeks after I signed the lease and moved in, I got a letter from the parole board. I was still on parole, and I had left Toronto six months earlier without permission. I was in breach of parole conditions. I could be sent back to prison without even going to court. The letter ordered me to report to the Vancouver parole center. In the back of my mind, I always knew they would catch up with me.

I went the next day not knowing if I would walk out of the building or not. The interview was brief. The parole officer asked why I had left Toronto. I told him about Cynthia and the parole officer. He didn't comment. He asked if I had a job. I thought he already knew. Then he told me I was free to go, and I didn't have to report any longer. That was it. I was no longer on parole. The day ended far better than I thought it would.

I went directly to the post office and picked up a passport application form. I didn't know if I was eligible or not, but I thought I would give it a try.

THE SHOP I WORKED IN also sold art supplies. I got a good deal on tubes of paint and canvas. Over the next few months, I painted a lot, at least one canvas every few days. I had a vague idea of putting together a show.

I thought about buying a car, but there wasn't much reason. I hardly ever left the West End. A bicycle was more practical.

There was a place in the basement where I stored my bike. One day, I was snooping around in the boiler room and found a crawlspace in one corner. It was too interesting to ignore.

I climbed in. Lighting my way with a Bic lighter, I worked my way hunched over to the end of the building. I found a similar opening, but I also found a half-sized door. I tugged it open and, to my amazement, found I was looking into the pantry of Hy's Restaurant. It was full of industrial-sized cans of food.

For a second, I thought, *I'll never have to buy food again!*

But no! What the hell was I thinking?

I closed the door and forgot about it.

At the time, Hy's restaurant was the most expensive in Vancouver. I couldn't afford to eat there, and even though it was right next door, I had never seen the inside.

The building was a beautiful, old stone mansion. Built around 1900 for the Rogers sugar magnate, it was a historic site. I never did find out why it was connected to my apartment building by a secret tunnel.

THE WEST END WAS A great place to live. Everything was close by, and entertainment was everywhere.

I stopped going to Garry's place. He was on tour a lot, and his apartment was getting trashed when he was out of town. When he was in town, he spent most of his time hanging out in gay bathhouses, even though people knew of the AIDS epidemic by then. Billy was what had kept Garry from self-destructing, and he was not coming back. I just kept my nose to the grindstone and saved money.

The guy I worked for was cool. He was ten years older than me and had traveled the world. He had lots of tales to tell. He was also a cokehead. What was it with picture-framing stores and cocaine?

I knew the danger, but every once in a while, I indulged. My rule was, "I will never buy coke. Put a little under my nose and I'll join you, because I'm no prude. But I won't go looking for it, and I won't pay for it."

I worked Christmas Eve. Well, not exactly worked, but I was at work. Clem was making bags of money, and he liked to share the good news.

He was an interesting contradiction. He was a capitalist through and through, a self-made businessman. He liked to make money, and he knew how to do it. The guy was also amazingly generous. The entire day before Christmas, he put on an open-house party in the store, complete with a catered buffet and free booze, including some good single malt scotch. Anyone walking down Denman Street was welcome.

Who does that?

New Year's was different. Just one big downtown party. Club to club, music and drinking. Like half the population of Vancouver, I woke up on New Year's Day with a hangover. I lounged around doing nothing most of the day.

One feature I really liked about my apartment was the bathroom with the high ceiling and the white tiles. If I turned on the hot water in the shower, the room could be made into a sauna, which was a good cure for a hangover.

At around five in the evening, I had just started to heat up some leftover spaghetti when the doorbell rang. I heard a muffled female voice through the intercom. The damned thing never worked very well, but I heard the name "Garry." I pressed the button to let whoever it was in.

My apartment was on the ground floor just around the corner from the front entrance. It would take no more than ten seconds to get to my door. I waited at the door for several minutes. No one showed up. I went into the hallway, but I didn't see anyone. Then the door to the garbage room opened, and she came out. The door was like an internal fire escape. It went to the top floor with a landing and utility room on the second floor. Why on Earth would anyone go up those stairs? It was obvious my apartment was on the first floor.

She came in, said, "Happy New Year," chatted about nothing for a few minutes, and then left.

I was puzzled. I didn't know her other than from seeing her at Garry's parties a few times. She was older than me, and, frankly, I wasn't interested in bedding her. I thought she was sort of creepy.

Maybe twenty minutes later, the fire alarm went off. It was an old building, and the fire alarm went off a lot. I didn't pay any attention for a while, thinking it was another false alarm. Then I opened the door and smelled smoke. I also saw smoke pouring out from around the garbage room door. The hallway was full of smoke.

All I had time to do was grab my wallet and a few things I could carry. I stood on the sidewalk in front of the building along with half the population of Davie Street and watched the building burn to the ground. Davie Street was full of fire trucks, hoses, and flashing lights. People running everywhere.

I tried to get back inside to rescue my paintings, but the firemen blocked the door. I ran to the back lane where I could see my apartment window. I tried to get in that way, but I would have had to break the window. I didn't want to do it.

Just behind the apartment they were building a new condo. It was partly finished and mostly open framing. I jumped the construction fence and climbed to the top. I was above my building and could see the rooftop. By that time, the fire was blazing. Sparks and then flames broke through the roof.

From my vantage point, I could see the ladder hose pouring water on Hy's restaurant next door. They were soaking down the roof of that building but doing nothing where the fire was coming through on my building. From the street in front, I'm sure it looked like they were trying to put the fire out. I saw the Vancouver fire department allow my building burn to the ground while they protected the building next door.

I went back to Davie Street and joined the crowd. I told a few people what I had seen from the back. All of the apartment residents were milling around, not knowing what to do. Then, standing beside me, I saw the woman who had come to my door that evening.

"I guess you need a place to stay?" she asked.

I thought she was hitting on me. It didn't occur to me that she had started the fire. It took a while for me to get around to that.

"It's okay," I said, "I can stay in a hotel."

Then she handed me a key. "There's a house just around the corner. They're going to demolish it, and there's no one in it now. You can stay there for a while; no one will mind."

I put the key in my pocket, thanked her, and walked away.

The first night I did stay in a hotel. I had money, but I didn't want to spend it on hotels, so I checked out the house. On the way there, I walked past what was left of my apartment. There was no point even trying to recover anything. It was all gone.

I called Garry. There was no answer, so I decided to stay in the abandoned house until I could figure out what to do.

34

THE HOUSE WAS A TYPICAL, THREE-STOREY, WOOD FRAME VANCOUVER HOUSE. THE HOUSES ON BOTH sides were also empty. It looked like they planned to demolish all three and build a condo.

I tried the key, and it worked.

Inside, it smelled like an abandoned house—wet, rotten wood and stale air. The house had been divided into apartments: two on the first floor, two on the second, and one on the top. I flicked the switch inside the door, and the lights came on. That was good. If it had electricity, it would be liveable for a few days even though it was cold and damp.

I tried the apartment doors on the first and second floor. They were all locked. I thought about kicking one open, but I wasn't sure if I would be breaking and entering.

The third floor was open. It was a small apartment with a sloped ceiling and dormer windows. It was carpeted, so I thought it would do.

I went back to work the same day. Of course, Clem had heard about the fire. Everyone in the West End had. He told me to take as much time off as I needed. I think he was happy to not have to pay me for a while. I was doing piece work, and he was already stuffed full with inventory.

I went downtown and bought a sleeping bag and a few things I needed. I just wandered around for a while thinking about what to do. I was homeless again, and it felt just the same as it always did, sort of empty. But this time was different. I had a lot of money in my pocket.

The house had electricity, but there was no heat. The first night, I slept on the floor with my head buried in the sleeping bag.

Sometime in the middle of the night, I woke up to a strange sound: a low murmuring of female voices coming from the second floor right below me. It sounded like three or four people chanting. There was also an occasional thump like something falling on the floor. I put my ear to the floor and tried to make out who or what it was. I had locked the downstairs front door with a bolt on the inside. Even if someone had a key, they couldn't get in.

I was scared shitless. I wasn't thinking about haunted houses or ghosts. I was thinking I could be in trouble if anyone found me there. I stayed quiet, pulled the sleeping bag over my head, not even tempting to go downstairs and investigate.

I woke up to a bright, sunny January day. I crept down the stairs, stopping to listen at each door. Not a sound. The house was definitely empty. The bolt on the front door was still locked.

I smelled the remains of the Angus apartment as soon as I stepped out the door. It was less than three blocks away. I went to take a better look at the remains.

They had put up a metal fence around the rubble. The brick walls had not collapsed completely, but the roof had caved in.

I went to the back where my apartment used to be and climbed up on the fence. Through the blackened and broken windows, I saw the devastation inside. It would have been better if I had not seen all of my paintings still leaning against the walls, totally destroyed.

I was very sad, but I didn't want comfort or help from anyone. I just wanted to go back to Toronto. Or something.

Hy's restaurant was untouched. Of course! I knew they had protected it and let my place burn. I understood, we renters didn't matter. They didn't even know if my bones were mixed with my paintings. No one ever asked if the guy who lived in room 106 got out okay.

I thought about my bicycle buried under all of that rubble. Funny, the bicycle never mattered much; it was just transportation. But thinking about it made me cry for the next few hours. I walked the back streets for most of the day so no one would see.

Just before dark, I bought a flashlight and went back to the house. I didn't want to turn on any lights in case someone noticed.

It was colder the second night. When I looked out the third-floor window to the street below, I realized it had started to snow, just a light dusting on the street and sidewalk. It looked pretty under the streetlight. It reminded me of Toronto.

I read a book by flashlight, bundled up inside my sleeping bag. Eventually, I fell asleep.

I was startled awake by a loud pounding on the front door, like a fist hammering five or six times. Then the old-fashioned doorbell rang. It was the sort of doorbell where you had to turn a little, key-shaped brass knob on the outside to make a mechanical bell ring.

More pounding. I thought it was the police.

I peeked out the window to the street below. I couldn't see the front door directly because of the porch roof, but what I could see creeped me out!

The street and sidewalk were covered in fresh snow, but no footprints led to the front door. It wasn't possible to get to the door without leaving footprints.

More pounding. Too many times for it to be someone just knocking on a door. It sounded angry.

I leaned against the wall inside my sleeping bag and stared at my feet. I was thinking about ghosts.

The pounding stopped. I waited a while and then looked out the window again. No footprints.

I don't think I slept until daybreak.

The next day, I started looking for an apartment. There were a lot to choose from. I picked one that was no different from all the others, a typical one-bedroom in a boring, three-story building. I laid down a hundred bucks for a deposit. The manager told me it would take a few days to clean up the apartment, and then I could move in.

In the light of day, the empty house didn't seem so creepy. I thought I would just deal with it for two more nights.

I went shopping for essential household things I would need to replace. I bought a futon and arranged to have it delivered.

That evening, I returned to the house before dark. The place seemed to smell worse than before, like something was rotting between the walls. The third floor wasn't as bad. I decided to take a chance. I turned on all the lights and heated the apartment using the electric stove in the kitchen.

All of the kitchen stuff was left behind. The drawers were full of knives and forks. The cabinets had dishes. Most of it was good, so I thought I would keep it for my new place. I recall the silverware was real silver. That was before the price of silver went through the roof.

After heating a can of soup, the place felt better. Two more nights, no problem. I decided the noise and the pounding on the door was just kids fooling around.

I went to sleep early, because I had nothing to do but wait. I wasn't as wound up and stressed out as I was the first few days after the fire. I knew how to start over. I had enough experience at new beginnings. Everything would be fine. I slept soundly—for a while.

I woke up in near total darkness standing beside the furnace in the basement. I didn't know where I was. I was freezing cold, standing there in a T-shirt and underwear. For ten seconds, I stood there confused and shivering. Then I realized I had a fucking crowbar clutched in my hand. It fell to the floor with a clang. I have no idea where it came from or how I had got into the basement. I had never sleep-walked in my life, and I haven't since.

A bit of light was coming through a small, dirty window high on the wall, just enough for me to see the old furnace and ducts all around me. Everything was covered in spider webs.

I looked around frantically for a way out. I found the stairs and climbed, my knees turning to water. The door at the top was locked. I slammed my shoulder into it with my heart pounding so hard I thought it would stop. The door flew open, and I crashed to the floor on the other side.

I was under the staircase that went to the second floor. I took the stairs three at a time, catching my big toe on something and almost ripping my toenail off.

No time for pain.

I got to the third floor, got dressed as fast as I could, grabbed my few possessions, and ran out the front door.

When I hit the sidewalk, both feet went out from under me. I crashed my head hard on the ground, almost knocking myself out. I had no idea what time it was. There was no light on the horizon yet.

I made my way up Davie Street to an all-night restaurant. A few people were sitting at booths. No one noticed another night crawler with disheveled hair and a pounding heart. I sat there drinking coffee until dawn wondering what I was going to do. My big toe was throbbing, and I felt blood in my boot. I didn't want to look at it.

I have no explanation for that event. I have no idea what happened. Was it stress from the fire? Possibly, but that wasn't the first time I had experienced extreme stress. It's just how it happened and what caused me to get out of Vancouver.

I forgot about the apartment, the futon, and all the other stuff. I went to the airport to catch the next flight to Toronto.

But I didn't go to Toronto.

35

AT THE AIRPORT, I LOOKED UP AT THE DEPARTURE BOARD FOR THE NEXT FLIGHT OUT. I HAD NEVER BEEN outside Canada. Why not try Mexico? It had always been a good place to run.

Flying was so different then. Not even a metal detector. All you needed to do was go to the airport, buy a ticket, walk up the stairs, and go. Family could even come into the cabin to see people off and then leave just before takeoff. Canadians going to Mexico didn't even need a passport. A birth certificate would do.

But I did have a passport. I had applied, and to my surprise, I got it. I didn't think I was eligible with my past and all. No one even asked to see it.

After getting settled in my seat, I noticed all the other passengers were wearing light clothes, summer clothes. It was January, and I was wearing winter clothes.

I sat in a window seat. The airplane was nowhere near full, but a couple in their forties sat next to me.

"Have you been to Mexico?" the woman asked.

"Um, no, I've never been anywhere," I said. "This is the second time I've been on an airplane. I've never been outside Canada."

She got really excited, like she wanted to tell me all about Mexico. She said they were going to Mexico City for a "cultural holiday." They usually went to resort towns. I wanted to know anything I could find out about Mexico. All I knew was what I had read in books or seen in movies.

"What's a cultural holiday?" I asked.

"Well, it's nice to sit on the beach and enjoy the ocean," she said, "but there's more to Mexico than that. Mexico City is full of art galleries and museums. You can spend an entire week looking at beautiful art and architecture."

I didn't know that. I expected cowboys and dust and cactus. I got enough of that later, but Mexico City was a surprise.

"Why did you choose Mexico City for your first visit?" she asked.

"It was cheap," I said. I didn't mention it was the next flight out of Vancouver. I felt like I was running away from something, I didn't know what. I can't identify a single cause, but a series of things were just bad karma. At any rate, I was about to land in Mexico City, the best culture shock adventure you could imagine.

As soon as I walked off the airplane, I knew I wasn't dressed appropriately. It was hotter than anywhere I'd ever been. I was wearing a winter leather coat, blue jeans, and cowboy boots. I had nothing to carry other than a school bag with what I had rescued before the fire. At least I could take the coat off and carry it. There was also an unfamiliar smell in the air. Not a bad smell, a plant smell, and food. Heat waves rose up from the black tarmac, creating mirages. I got cooked walking from the plane to the terminal.

Everyone in front of me moved quickly through customs. When I got there, I stopped and presented my passport with both hands, like it was a bank book or some other precious thing. This was an important moment for me. It was the first time I would get a stamp in my passport, a rite of passage even though I was thirty. The uniformed guy just looked annoyed, stamped my passport, and threw it back in my direction—not hard enough to be aggressive, just Mexico.

Outside the terminal was a lineup of taxies and buses belching diesel smoke. Taxi drivers came at me from all directions.

"Hotel? Hotel? El Centro?"

The couple who sat beside me on the plane had told me where to find a cheap hotel, but I had no idea how much a taxi would cost, so I just jumped into one and told the driver where I wanted to go. Like an idiot, I didn't ask how much. My first Mexican lesson: always ask first. I wound up paying a hundred dollars for a ten-dollar ride.

He delivered me to an area in the city full of cheap pensions, rat's nest hotels, and ex-pat hippies. Everything was unfamiliar. I couldn't read the signs, so I just had to guess.

The first hotel I went into, I had no problem with English. I didn't feel like exploring, I just wanted a place to think about what I was doing. I took the room. I recall it was around six dollars. It had a good shower with lots of pressure. I found out just in time that in Mexico, "C" stands for *Caliente*—hot, not cold.

I was learning Spanish already.

My boots didn't come off easily. My right foot was in bad shape. I had mostly pulled the nail off my big toe. I had to take a shower with my foot outside, careful not to get it wet. I knew I had to find medical attention for it. It wasn't going to get better on its own.

Unable to put my boot back on, I went down to the lobby and asked where I could find a drugstore. I showed my toe to the guy behind the desk. He freaked out a bit, said something in Spanish, and then told me to sit down and wait.

He returned a few minutes later with his wife. She had a first aid kit. She was so sympathetic and careful. She poured something on my toe. It burned like hell, of course, but I knew it would do some good. She wrapped it up nicely, and it felt much better, but there was no way I would be able to put my boots on for at least a few days. I wanted to get out and explore Mexico City, but I had to sit around doing nothing.

Most of the hotel guests were young people, travelers and adventurers. I spent my first four days in Mexico talking to them and getting ideas of where to go. One of them gave me a pair of cheap sandals made from a car tire. At least I had something on my feet.

My toe healed quickly, and soon I was able to check out some of the tourist sights. The national art gallery was spectacular. It was easy to see that Mexicans loved art, music, and culture. Language wasn't a problem. I always found some English and made do with sign language when I had to. I already liked Mexico. This would be good!

A week in Mexico City was long enough though. There were plenty of things to do, but I wanted to explore the countryside, the "real" Mexico with cowboys and tumbleweeds. One of the young Americans told me I had to see the Teotihuacan Mayan ruins. I could have taken a tourist bus, but I got directions and took a regular city bus. It was stuffed with people, chickens, ducks, and blaring mariachi music. People smiled and nodded at me. Mexico felt friendly.

"Hey gringo!" someone called out.

From the movies, I thought "gringo" was a bad word, but I learned that if it came with a smile, it was friendly.

Years before, I had read a book called *Chariots of the Gods*. It was about Mayan civilization. It suggested that these monumental ruins were built with the help of aliens visiting Earth. After exploring Teotihuacan for a day, I thought that could well be true. How could this be built by people who didn't even have steel? It got me hooked on Mayan exploration.

While in Mexico, I had time enough to think about what had happened back in Vancouver. It seemed so far away. I was sure of one thing: the woman who had visited me was the cause of the fire. What happened in the abandoned house afterward, I'll never figure out. I had had some crazy things forced on me over the years, but waking up in the basement with a crowbar in my hand was the craziest thing I had ever done. I don't think I'll ever be able to explain it.

I went over all of my worldly possessions. There wasn't much in the schoolbag: some drawing pens, a sketchbook, and a few other books I was glad I hadn't lost. It was all I had apart from the clothes I was wearing. The only really useful thing was the name and address Hugh Morrison had given me before I left Toronto. The person was in Guatemala. I didn't know exactly where Guatemala was, only that it was south of Mexico. At least it was some sort of destination. I decided that's where I would go.

I showed the address to the hotel owner and asked if he could read it for me. It was in Spanish. He told me it was a formal introduction, something about honour. He also advised me not to go to Guatemala. He said it was very dangerous.

I thought "dangerous" was a relative term. Danger always seemed to be close behind me. I wasn't going to let undefined fear prevent me from traveling freely.

THE PSYCHOPATH MACHINE

I liked hitchhiking, and I was going to do it. I went shopping for travel gear: a backpack, a good belt knife, a travel book (by Lonely Planet, it came in very handy), and a cowboy hat.

I could get to Guatemala one of two ways. I could go directly south or I could go east to Yucatan and then through Belize. I decided to go to Yucatan, because that's where the best Mayan ruins were. It was impossible to hitchhike out of that mega-city, so I got a bus ticket to a small town just far enough to get me to a highway.

36

IT WAS SEVERAL HOURS TO THE COUNTRYSIDE. I PASSED MILES AND MILES OF SMOKING HEAPS OF garbage. As far as the eye could see, people were picking through the piles. Children dressed in rags hunched over, pushing trash around with a stick, looking for something to sell or perhaps for something to eat. They seemed to move in slow motion, like a vision of hell. That was my first experience of extreme poverty. Sadly, eventually, my world travels hardened my heart enough to make it bearable.

The bus stopped at a roadside cantina for a bathroom break. Apparently, the small town to which I had bought a ticket was some distance ahead, so I decided to start hitchhiking right there. I walked out to the highway, stuck out my thumb, and caught a ride before the bus left the parking lot.

All in all, hitchhiking in Mexico was easy and safe. Everyone I met was curious about this gringo. Often, they would treat me to a meal and a beer or two. I suppose danger was lurking in dark places, but I didn't think about it. I didn't think of myself as a tourist. I wanted to fit in with the Mexicans and not be noticed.

I stopped at a lot of places along the way. It took more than a week to reach the east coast. By then I had a suntan and didn't look so much like a new gringo.

Veracruz is an industrial port city. Tourists didn't go there, so there was no English at all. I had learned a few Spanish words, just enough to ask for a room and "How much?" Or "Where's the bathroom?"

I made my way down the Yucatan coast, stopping when I found an interesting place to explore. I visited every Mayan ruin I could locate. A few places had not been discovered or explored by anyone except locals. Often, I would be the only person climbing over huge pyramids covered in jungle.

A Mayan Indian truck driver with whom I was riding pointed to a field full of mounds covered in jungle, stretching as far as the eye could see. "Out there is a city."

Twice before reaching the Belize border, I was delayed by a pretty señorita. Sometimes it was hard to keep moving.

Chetumal is another industrial city, close to the Belize border. Not much in town was worth hanging around for, but it was my last day in Mexico.

From my hotel window, I saw a big, Spanish-style church in the distance. With nothing else to do, I decided to find my way to it by bus.

The church had nice architecture and stained glass windows, but after seeing so many Mayan structures, it seemed primitive by comparison. It was on a fairly high spot, and I could see where my hotel was and most of the city below. I decided to walk.

This gringo was walking through a sketchy neighbourhood. Run-down houses, men hanging out on street corners. Back then, I was fearless or just plain dumb.

I passed by three tough-looking hombres sitting on the curbside. I nodded in their direction.

"Hey, Ranchero!" one of them called out. He held up a bottle of rum and offered me a drink.

I didn't really want to drink rum from the bottle, but I thought I better be polite. I took a swig and passed it back with a smile. The other three took a swig, and then it came back to me. All the while they spoke Spanish as though I understood what they were saying. I remained standing, but they stayed on the curb.

People started gathering around, curious. Most were smiling at this unusual gringo in their hood. Before long, it was a crowd.

Then an older guy with a machete in his hand came forward. "English no good. English no good."

Things got ugly when he started slapping me on the chest with the flat side of the machete. Not hard but threatening.

The three guys got to their feet and came between us, all the while saying the same word over and over. They were telling me it was dangerous there, but I didn't know enough Spanish then to realize it.

A bus came down the hill. The hombre who had offered the rum grabbed my arm, put some coins in my hand, and pushed me onto the bus.

As it pulled away, I saw my drinking buddies arguing with the machete man. *Holy shit!* I thought. *I almost got killed!*

There was a lesson in that, and I learned it fast and never forgot it, but I didn't let that experience turn me against Mexico. It was the only dangerous situation I encountered.

The next day, I took a taxi to the Belize border. It was a short ride but the only way to get there.

Crossing was quick and easy. No questions. A six-month stamp in my passport, and I was back on the highway.

37

THERE WAS NOTHING ON THE BELIZE SIDE OF THE BORDER. NO TOWN, NO CANTINA, *NADA*. ONLY A FEW beat-up taxies offering overpriced transportation to Corozal Town. As always, I preferred hitchhiking. I got a ride from the first truck that passed by.

Belize was totally different from Mexico. Most of the population was black, and everyone spoke English, "Caribbean English," that is, which could be as difficult to understand as Spanish.

I must have arrived in Corozal during siesta time. I was hungry, but nothing was open. I searched a long time to find something to eat. The rice and beans I finally found came from the garbage can out back. They didn't look right.

A little girl stood beside the table and watched me eat. She had a sly look on her face. I think she was amused by the gringo eating garbage. Oh well, it was a poor country. Why waste food? It didn't poison me.

It took one day to explore Corozal. There wasn't much there, but everything was painted bright colours. The buildings looked British with a dramatic paint job.

The next morning, I was back on the highway heading south. It was hot, and there was no traffic. I walked a long way out of town.

I saw two guys coming in my direction—big, bad-looking Rasta men with dreadlocks. I hoped I wasn't going to have another brush with death.

"Hey mon, got any bullets?" one of them said when they were right in front of me.

"Bullets?" I asked. "No, man, I don't even have a gun. Do I need one?"

They both burst out laughing. Then one stepped forward and dropped something into my palm: two short, fat joints.

"Bullets," he said, still laughing. "Enjoy, mon."

They walked off.

Well, that was nice, I thought.

I continued on my way, lit up a "bullet," and enjoyed.

Still no traffic. I walked for more than an hour.

I heard live reggae music coming from a shack by the side of the road. A few Rasta men were standing out front.

I walked up to them. "Can we share a bullet, mon?"

I hung around for most of the day. Great live music and very friendly conversation. No threat there, just good people and good music.

Late in the afternoon, an American guy showed up. He was around my age. Everyone knew him. He was returning from the hospital in town, where he had been treated for an infection on his leg. He told me he had some land a little farther down the road. I could stay for the night if I wanted.

We walked through the jungle, followed one trail that led to another until I was pretty much lost. We passed by several grass-thatched primitive houses before arriving at this dude's homestead. All he had was a few hundred square feet of cleared jungle and a pup tent. I had expected more.

Just before dark, a guy came riding through my American friend's "homestead" on a big white horse. They knew each other.

The American dude wanted to ride the horse. He jumped on board, but the horse didn't like it. It took off, dumping Mr. American on the jungle floor, hard.

This crazy American had been clearing land with a machete. Lots of chopped-off bamboo spikes were sticking out of the ground like sharp knives, poking up a foot into the air. When he hit the ground, one of those spikes went between his armpit and his chest. It missed impaling him by inches.

He jumped to his feet laughing. I don't think he realized he had come an inch from a miserable end. I was sure he didn't have the sense to be homesteading in the jungle. I wondered what he was running from in the USA.

After dark, there was nothing to do. Mosquitos started coming, so I set up my hammock and mosquito net and tried to sleep. It was tropical warm, so sleeping outside wasn't a problem. Being surrounded by coconut trees in the dark was a problem. The sound of big, green coconuts hitting the ground kept me awake. Those things weighed maybe forty pounds. If one hit me on the head, I'd be done for. Here's a basic rule of jungle survival: Don't sleep under a coconut tree!

That wasn't the worst of it. It was the mosquitos that finally drove me out. My mosquito netting was useless. They got in from the ground. There was nothing I could do. Sleep was impossible.

It was still dark when I packed up my stuff and tried to find my way back to the highway. I came to one of the houses I had passed on the way in. An old guy was sitting out front, drunk as a skunk. I convinced him to show me the way. but I had to give him my flashlight so he could find his way back.

The mosquitos didn't bother him, but they were on me like a banquet. He kept offering me a drink from whatever was in his bottle. I kept telling him, "No thanks." It wasn't even daybreak yet.

"If you drink, the mosquitos won't bite you," the old guy said.

I thought it might be true. Mosquitos would likely get drunk or fly off and explode if they drank that guy's blood.

He got me to the highway. By then, a few streaks of daylight were on the horizon.

"There will be a truck carrying workers," he said. "Just wave your hand, and it will stop for you."

The truck came, and I flagged it down. People were stuffed in like sardines, poor workers who had to travel that way every day. By the time we reached San Ignacio, the sun was up.

I kept moving through Belize. So many Mayan sites to explore. I got to as many as I could without joining an organized tour group.

Less than two weeks later, I crossed into Guatemala. Everything changed again. No one spoke English, and the grinding poverty in the countryside was much more desperate than Mexico or Belize.

I made my way up to Tikal, back down to Lake Petén, and then to a place called Flores, a small island in the middle of the lake covered in classical Spanish architecture.

By the time I got settled into a hotel, I wasn't feeling so good. I thought it was the heat or something I had eaten. I didn't feel like exploring, so I went to bed.

A few hours later, I woke up sweating, puking, shivering, and sick as a dog. My head was splitting with the worst headache I have ever had. I couldn't get out of bed, not even to get to the bathroom.

For more than twenty-four hours, I was in and out of consciousness. I think what finally brought someone to my door was the smell. The smell of me dying!

38

I DON'T KNOW WHO TOOK ME TO A HOSPITAL, BUT I DO REMEMBER BEING HELD UP BY BOTH ARMS AND walked or carried through the streets. The sun was so bright it split my head if I opened my eyes.

It wasn't much of a hospital, a small, rundown clinic. Too many people and not enough beds. They placed me on a cot beside a big splash of blood on the green wall. I heard people crying and screaming in pain and desperation. I opened one eye and saw a man next to me with both hands cut off just below the elbow. How could that happen? I knew I was going to die, but I was calm, unafraid. I just didn't want to die in such a horrible place.

Then I heard an American voice right beside my ear. "You have malaria," he said. "Don't worry; you'll be fine."

I owe my life to that young doctor. He was a volunteer medical worker risking his own life to help the suffering Mayan natives.

Untreated malaria can kill quickly, but the treatment is simple and almost always effective. In two days, I felt fine. I was a little weak, and I had lost a lot of weight, but I was okay.

I stayed one more day with an IV bag in my arm. I was able to get out of bed and walk around the clinic. I don't know how that doctor and a few nurses managed to deal with so much chaos.

The doctor gave me a plastic bag full of quinine tablets.

"Eat these like candy," he said. "Don't forget."

I had a few short conversations with him when he was between emergencies. I wondered how it felt to know he was literally saving people's lives every day. I wonder how many lives that doctor saved, including my own. If he is still alive today, you would be lucky to have him as your doctor.

He told me a little about the situation in Guatemala. I didn't have a clue about political stuff. I didn't pay attention back then. I came to understand I was lucky to have made it that far hitchhiking through a very ugly civil war.

He also told me something about the nurses in his clinic. There was only one real nurse. The rest of the women in nurses' uniforms weren't nurses at all. They were sales reps for Borden.

"It's really bad what they're doing, but I can't do anything or the clinic will get closed. They give away a supply of infant formula to new mothers. The mothers' breast milk dries up, and they have to buy the formula. The real problem is these women can't afford to buy it. They have to water it down, and their babies get sick from bad water. I can't stop it; I can only treat the consequences."

What a horrible thing to do to those simple people. I had already met a few Mayans. I knew they were different, maybe different from any other people on earth. I had no idea how bad it was, but soon I discovered the depth of that genocide.

I recovered and continued on my way. I wasn't so keen on hitchhiking anymore. I had two choices to get to Guatemala City: a twelve-hour bus ride through rough jungle roads or a short flight on a tiny airplane. It was contrary to my cheap travel plan, but I took the flight.

GUATEMALA CITY WAS STILL RECOVERING from a big earthquake four years earlier. Many buildings were still just heaps of rubble. Typical of third world disasters, millions of dollars in aid that had poured into the country disappeared into the black hole of corruption. Even though I could see poverty, destruction, and desperation all around me, I still didn't understand how bad it was.

It only took a day to get tired of exploring destroyed churches and monuments. I had a name and an address. I had no idea who or what I would find, but it was a destination. It was a friend of Hugh Morrison's, so I thought I would go there and say hello. It would be good to find a friend in such a strange land.

Finding the depot and the bus to Antigua was easy. Unlike buses in Mexico, that bus trip was quiet and subdued. I felt tension and fear in the air. No blaring mariachi music. The people, mostly Mayan, were quiet or spoke only in whispers. The chickens in crates were the only sound. The buses were called "chicken buses" for a reason.

Half an hour out of the city, the bus was stopped at a military roadblock. Two soldiers came inside while at least ten surrounded the bus with machine guns pointed at the windows.

One pointed directly at me. I took off my hat and smiled at him. He smiled back, recognizing I was a foreigner. He lowered his rifle just enough so it wasn't pointed at my face.

One soldier stood beside the driver while the other came down the aisle looking at each passenger's papers. I showed him my passport. He looked at it carefully as though he was reading it. It was doubtful he could read at all, never mind English. He looked carefully at my face and then back at the passport. Then he handed it back with a smile, like I was on his side or something.

I'm not on your side, you bastard, I thought, but I smiled back at him and took my passport without a word.

A few seats behind me, he shouted something, drew his sidearm, and ordered two men to stand up. He pushed them toward the soldier at the front, who pointed his machine gun at them and ordered them off the bus. Then they let the bus go.

As we were pulling away, I heard two short bursts of gunfire. I didn't turn around, but I knew they had just killed those two men.

That was Guatemala in 1980. A corpse in every cave.

ANTIGUA WAS A BEAUTIFUL CITY. The streets were clean and well cared for. All colonial Spanish architecture. Central Square with a beautiful fountain. Most streets were paved with cobblestones. On the surface, it was calm and peaceful. It didn't look like a genocide was happening, but it was right there in front of me, as I was about to find out.

I decided not to look for a hotel and to go directly to the address Hugh had given me. I had no idea where it was, so I took a taxi from the bus depot. I showed the address to the driver. He hesitated for a minute and then drove off.

When we got there, I realized he had gone in a circle around several blocks and then ended up only a block or two from where we started. I could have walked. I really needed to smarten up about money. I didn't have an endless supply.

The address was just a number on a cement wall stretching almost the entire block. The wall was dirty with many layers of peeling paint. It didn't look like a house. No windows, only a huge wooden gate with a smaller door in the middle. There was a chain with a brass handle. It looked like the doorbell, so I gave it a pull.

I heard what sounded like a church bell through the thick wooden gate. A small window opened, and a woman's face appeared. She said something in Spanish. A question. She sounded annoyed or suspicious.

I passed the bit of paper through the window.

"*Momento,*" she snapped, and then slammed the window.

I waited on the sidewalk. In a few minutes, I heard metal bolts slide across the gate. It swung inward, and a middle-aged couple stepped forward, smiling and welcoming me inside.

The man was very excited. He kept repeating, "Seignior Morrison!" He shook my hand several times and patted me on the back, saying, "*Mi casa es tu casa.*"

I understood what he was saying: "My house is your house." It was nice to have a friend in Guatemala.

THE CEMENT WALL AROUND THE house gave no indication of what was on the inside. It was typical Spanish style. Better to conceal your wealth than to display it like western houses.

The man calmed down a bit and stopped speaking Spanish. He actually spoke English quite well. He introduced himself as Pedro and his wife as Guilda. Guilda didn't speak English at all, but Pedro said she could understand it if I spoke slowly.

The house was huge. Pedro showed me around room after room filled with heavy, antique Spanish furniture, all dark, carved wood.

"You are welcome in my house," he said. "You can stay as long as you like. A friend of Seignior Morrison is a friend of mine."

Pedro told me his daughter was a language teacher. She worked at the school downtown. "She is happy to teach Spanish for you."

I thought that would be great. I had already picked up some Spanish words, but I really needed some serious lessons.

The house was built around a central open area with rooms all around. Pedro showed me to one of those rooms.

"You must be tired," he said. "Rest for a while, and then Guilda will make a feast in your honour."

I sat down on the bed. What a day. Only a few hours earlier I had seen two men get murdered. Now someone was making a dinner in my honour. Things could change so fast in that part of the world.

39

I DIDN'T WANT TO SLEEP, BUT I THOUGHT I SHOULD STAY IN MY ROOM UNTIL SOMEONE CAME FOR ME. I didn't want to risk doing anything rude.

I took out my travel book and read the entire chapter on Guatemala. I learned there was a big volcano nearby, "Agua." I decided I wanted to climb it. The book said the view was worth the effort.

That evening, Guilda put on a feast. Only four people were at the table, including me, but there was enough food to feed ten.

I met Pedro and Guilda's daughter. She was in her late teens or early twenties, but I was disappointed. I always had my eye out for a pretty señorita, but she was not. She did speak passable English though.

Pedro asked many questions about Hugh. I didn't want to tell him about the way I met Hugh, so I was vague about mutual friends. I also told him about the fire in Vancouver. He was sympathetic, but something seemed a little fake about him. I can't put my finger on it, but he made me feel defensive. Pedro was warm on the outside, but there was a coldness in his eyes.

I asked what he did for a living. He paused a little too long before replying.

"I'm a truck driver," he said and smiled.

His smile didn't feel right. I knew truck drivers didn't have houses like his. But I was in strange land. I didn't understand half of what was going on around me.

Later that evening, after everyone had retired to their room, I heard a truck start up in the courtyard outside my room. I opened the curtain and peeked out.

Pedro and another man were standing beside a flatbed truck. The big gate was open, and I saw a few other men on the street out front. Pedro climbed into the cab and drove the truck out of the courtyard. The other man closed the gate from inside, but I saw four or five men jump onto the flatbed.

What were they up to? It was a strange time to be going to work. It looked like they were going to rob a bank or something.

Sometime in the middle of the night, I woke up to the gate opening. I peeked out the window and saw the truck come back inside. Pedro was alone when he stepped out of the cab. The other man who had stayed behind closed the gate. They talked for a minute, and then Pedro pulled a garden hose from the wall and turned it on the bed of the truck. They both spent some time cleaning it with water and brooms, and then Pedro drove it into a garage on the other side of the courtyard. When he came out, he walked right past my window. I clearly saw a pistol in a holster on his hip. I didn't think he was a truck driver. This was getting really ominous.

The next morning, I sat at the kitchen table with the family. Everyone smiled and talked in a mixture of English and Spanish. Just a normal Guatemalan family having breakfast.

I didn't think Pedro's daughter was very bright. She was a teacher, but I wondered how qualified she was. I needed to learn some grammar, not just words. I decided I would take some Spanish lessons from her anyway. I offered to pay, but they refused to take money from me. It was just as well, because I didn't learn anything from her efforts.

The second night was a repeat of the first. After midnight, Pedro and a few other men took out the truck and returned a few hours later. It could have been just a normal routine for a truck driver working the night shift, but I didn't think so.

I spent my days wandering around Antigua. Soon, I discovered it wasn't good to go to the central square early in the morning. Dead bodies were lined up in rows on the street. People passed by holding a cloth over their nose, but they didn't look. I had seen dead people before but never anything like that. It was a new butchery every night, put on display in the morning as an act of terror for the people to see.

There was a big fountain in the square. I was carrying a sketchbook. I had been making pen and ink drawings of the Mayan ruins I had visited. I was sitting on a bench trying to capture the fountain when I heard an American voice behind me.

"Nice drawing, man. Can I have a look?"

The guy was around my age, but right away I saw that he wasn't the same as the usual gringo traveler. He was clean-cut and athletic. My first thought was that he was a cop. Then I thought military, most likely.

"Sure," I said, handing him my sketchbook.

He took time to look at every page before handing it back. "Nice work," he said. He asked what I was doing in Guatemala and if I wanted a job.

"I'm not looking for a job right now, but what did you have in mind?"

"If you have some time, come with me, and I'll introduce you to some people."

I had nothing but time.

"Okay, let's go," I said.

I followed him to a cantina just off the town square. From outside, it was not a building you would notice. No neon signs or flashing lights, but inside it was a typical North American disco. It even had a big mirror ball and a dance floor.

The place was nearly empty. It was early afternoon, but it looked like it got busy after dark.

A few people were sitting at the bar. They looked the same as my new friend: short hair, military types. Two of them were older, middle-aged, a man and a woman. She was the only woman in the place.

My friend introduced me to the older couple. He didn't use my name. He never asked me, and he never told me his name either. He just called me an artist. They were archeologists from an American university working at a newly discovered Mayan site. Professor something and his wife. I spent some time at that disco over the next few weeks, but oddly, I never learned anyone's name. People addressed each other directly.

The archeologists asked if I would like to work with them at their dig. They needed someone with drawing talent to record the position of every object they uncovered. It was a tempting offer, and I almost took it. But I wasn't in need of money, and I wanted to keep traveling. There was so much more to Latin America. I think if I had taken the job, it would have changed my future. I probably would have become an archeologist. Anyway, I declined.

The disco bar was a good place to gather information on what was happening in Guatemala and south of the border. It didn't take long to discover most of the patrons were US military on leave, just relaxing in a nice, warm country surrounded by revolution and genocide.

Later, I asked Pedro about the bar. He looked surprised.

"A den of spies," he said.

TWO ENORMOUS VOLCANIC CONES TOWERED over Antigua: Fuego and Agua. Fire and water. Several people told me I should climb Agua. It was a good hike. Fuego was active. It wasn't possible to climb without risking being cooked. I met a young American couple who wanted to do it, so we set off together before dawn. A local bus took us to the trailhead.

The first few hours were easy, but it got quite steep farther up. These two were vegetarians—militant vegetarians, the sort who think meat eaters are killers. They didn't make it halfway up before they both turned green and gave up.

It was a grueling climb, and I almost quit, too, but I wanted to see the view from the top. I kept going alone.

It took around four hours to reach the crater. The view was worth the effort. It was the highest mountain I had ever climbed. Grouse Mountain in Vancouver did not compare.

The air was thin, and I felt lightheaded and shaky. I thought I had accomplished a significant climb. Then I saw a disappointing thing: a soccer field in the middle of the crater. Athletes actually climbed up there to play soccer because of the thin air. It made them stronger. And I had barely made it to the top.

Going down was easier but more dangerous. Gravity was on my side, but it was easy to get moving too fast. The trail, what was left of it, was loose sand without much grip. It was hard to put on the brakes. It also switched back at forty-five-degree angles.

Around half way down, two guys coming up tried to rob me at knifepoint. They smiled and waved in a friendly way until they were right in front of me. Then one pulled out a big knife and demanded my money.

I always carried my stash of American dollars in various hidden places, a money belt and a secret place in the lining of my boots. If I got robbed, it would be over. I would have to end my trip. I decided I wasn't getting robbed.

Without thinking, I jumped sideways off the trail into a steep, sandy stream bed. I landed on my ass and flew down like a waterslide without the water. I picked up speed fast. I'm sure the robbers thought I had committed suicide so as not to be robbed.

I dug my boot heels into the sand just in time. I slowed myself enough to regain control. It was a bumpy ride, but it was actually fun.

I reached the next level of the switchback in a few seconds. There was a sizeable drop from my waterless slide. I landed on my feet and looked up to where I had come from. I saw the two thugs way above me. I waved at them, gave them the finger, and continued down.

The survival skills I had learned in prison proved useful while traveling in Central America. Murder and violence were always lurking just around the corner. Human life didn't have much importance. I always had to assess every new situation and be aware, but I never let fear stop me.

I didn't know anything about the politics. Sometimes the bad people were on my side and helping me on my way. Often, the police or military was what you had to avoid.

The people were defensive and afraid, but they usually wanted to explain their situation to me, a gringo. They knew who the bad guys were and wanted me to understand and be on their side.

Pedro was a bad guy, a very bad guy, and I was about to witness it firsthand.

40

I WATCHED PEDRO'S ROUTINE FOR AROUND TEN DAYS. ALWAYS THE SAME NIGHTLY EXCURSIONS WITH THE truck washing when he returned.

One evening we were sitting in the courtyard drinking beer.

"What's happening in Guatemala?" I asked.

"These assholes are destroying Guatemala," he told me.

His explanation of the "Indian problem" wasn't the same as the things I was hearing from other people. Some Indians were organizing the peasant workers and causing problems for landowners.

I didn't want to go up against Pedro. He was my host, and I knew he was dangerous. I acted as though I understood and agreed with him. I told him Canada had had the same problem a hundred years ago. We solved it by killing most of them and putting the rest on reservations. Pedro didn't understand my meaning.

"No reservations," he said. "Guatemala is a small country."

I suppose he meant they intended to kill them all.

Pedro reminded me of people I had encountered in the past. He had an air about him, a look in his eye that difficult to describe. Like Peter Woodcock, Victor Hoffman, Matt Lamb. All psychopaths. Heartless killers.

It was late. We had drunk a lot of beer.

"Do you want to see how we deal with this problem?" Pedro asked.

I thought I knew how they dealt with it, but I didn't want to say no to anything Pedro asked.

"Sure," I said. "It's your country."

I spent most of the next day trying to learn a little Spanish from Pedro's lazy daughter, all the while worried about what would happen that night.

Here is what happened every night in those days in Guatemala. Simple, swift, and brutal.

I SAT IN THE CAB with Pedro driving and another guy on my right, sandwiched between them tight enough that Pedro's gun rubbed against my left thigh.

Three others rode on the flatbed, all armed with antique pistols that looked like they had seen years of mayhem. None of the other guys said a word to me.

We drove to a small village not far from Antigua. Pedro had an address or directions. He drove without lights and stopped in front of a mud and thatch house.

Three men in the back of the truck jumped off and ran into the house. One of them carried a steel pipe about four feet long.

I heard a brief scream cut off with a heavy thud. Then the sound of children screaming. They were silenced quickly as well.

The three men crashed out of the hut pushing a small, half-naked man in front of them. One of them dragged two girls by the wrist. I couldn't tell how old they were. Mayan people are very small.

They threw the man to the ground, and the guy with the steel pipe smashed his head with one blow. I think it killed him instantly, but he kept hitting him.

The two small girls didn't make a sound. The men tied the girls' hands behind them with bailing wire and threw them onto the flatbed. Then they picked up the man's limp body and threw him on top of the girls.

All the while, Pedro sat beside me watching my reaction.

I almost puked. I almost screamed. I almost attacked Pedro with my bare hands. I thought about trying to get his gun, but I didn't do anything. I just sat there and wished I was anywhere else.

I think Pedro had more work to do that night, but he saw I wasn't into it. He drove back to Antigua, making a stop at a house where the two girls were taken off the truck. Then he drove to the central square, where one of the men kicked the body off the truck, and then we drove away.

I guess someone else put the bodies in neat, grisly rows.

We returned to Pedro's' house. The same guy was there to close the gate and help clean the blood off the truck.

I didn't want to talk to Pedro at all, but I had to ask, "What happens to the two girls?"

"We export them," he said. "Just like bananas."

I went to my room and stared at the ceiling all night.

"Guilda monster" was always first to wake up and start working. As soon as I heard her rattling around in the kitchen, I got up, grabbed my backpack, and slipped out the front gate. I thought about going to the police, but I knew that if I did, Pedro and his men would likely kill me, too.

I found a cheap hotel on the other side of town. I was afraid to walk around during the day. Now I knew the people with whom I had lived for two weeks were psycho killers. I waited until after dark and then carefully made my way to the gringo bar.

The guy I had met in front of the town fountain was there. I didn't tell him what I had seen the night before. I just asked him about El Salvador.

THE PSYCHOPATH MACHINE

"Is it safe to travel there?"

"Of course not," he said. "It's not safe to travel anywhere in Central America. It's all a shithole. But you should go anyway. I'll give you a ride to the border if you do me a favour."

If he had been anything other than a clean-cut American, I wouldn't have done him any favours.

He told me he was US military working on border security between Guatemala and El Salvador.

"Yeah, it kind of shows," I said. "I knew you were Army right away."

"Not Army," he said, "but something like that. We're not official, but what we're doing is important. Do you want to help out?"

"Okay," I said. "But I want to get out of here tomorrow."

41

EARLY THE NEXT MORNING, I WAS SITTING BESIDE MY AMERICAN FRIEND IN A JEEP HEADING FOR THE border. It was about a three-hour trip.

Along the way, he handed me a fishing spear. I think it was called a Hawaiian sling, the kind with a thick rubber band and a pistol grip. He told me to put it in my backpack and just walk across the border. He said it was a test of how easy it was to get weapons across the border. Someone would take it from me on the other side and tell me what to do next.

I thought it was strange, but he seemed to know exactly what he was doing. Besides, it was only a spearfishing gun. It wasn't illegal, so I did it.

I received my stamp on the way out of Guatemala, walked some distance crossed a bridge, and then walked to the El Salvador border office.

I put my backpack on the table. The border guard opened it and saw the handle of the spearfishing gun. It looked like a pistol. He didn't take it out. He just called someone else over.

The other guy looked into my backpack, but he didn't touch it either.

"Harpoon?" he asked.

"Si, Seignior"

He said something in Spanish to the other guy and then stamped my passport and waved me on.

I walked a few hundred feet into El Salvador, and then another American walked up to me.

"Do you have something?" he asked.

I took the harpoon out and handed it to him.

"Good," he said. "Now, take this back to your friend."

He handed me something wrapped in a towel. It was heavy. I opened the towel and saw a gun—a real gun, not a "harpoon." It was an unusual gun, too. It looked like a cowboy six-shooter, but the barrel was at least sixteen inches long. It wasn't a sawed-off rifle; it was a pistol, about the same length as the spearfishing gun.

I was nervous about it, but it all looked well-practiced and professional. I walked across the border back into Guatemala.

The same guard waved me past. He didn't even stop me.

I gave the gun to the American and that was that. I got my free ride to the border and I could just walk back and forth with no problem.

That was April 1, 1980. One week earlier, Bishop Oscar Romero had been murdered in San Salvador. I think that long-barreled gun was the murder weapon.

THE BORDER CROSSING WAS MILITARIZED. It looked like Guatemala and El Salvador were about to go to war. It wasn't my fight, and I doubted the army would rob me, so I tried hitchhiking.

Cars and trucks rumbled past, but no one stopped.

A truck full of soldiers armed to the teeth slowed down to have a look at me. One of them waved a finger at me as though to say, "Don't hitchhike here, gringo."

I flagged down a chicken bus. I no longer had a destination. I was traveling south. I thought I'd just keep going until the money ran out.

I had to take three different buses to get to San Salvador. I didn't want to travel at night, so I stopped over in a small town. I couldn't find any hotels, so I just set up my hammock outdoors. It was okay, although I was worried about mosquitos.

I reached San Salvador the following afternoon. The city was in complete lockdown. Military police were at every street corner, and roadblocks were everywhere. I had my passport checked at gunpoint, and then a block away, the same thing happened again.

San Salvador was on edge. Everyone looked afraid of something. I didn't know about Romero. I didn't know that a week before the army had opened fire on civilians at his funeral. At night, there was machine gunfire in the streets and the occasional large explosion.

I didn't like San Salvador. I decided I would boot it south as fast as I could. Costa Rica sounded good.

I didn't want to pass through Honduras. I had heard Honduras was as dangerous as it got in Central America. I didn't want to let fear stop me, but it was just common sense.

I heard about a boat that crossed Golfo Fonseca from Playas Negras that would get me to Nicaragua, bypassing Honduras. I decided to take that route. Playas Negras is on a peninsula on the southern tip of Salvador. It was a long, hard, bumpy ride getting there, but it would save a lot of time if I went by boat. I thought it would be safer as well.

I waited at the dock for several hours. A small, open wooden boat arrived, and people piled in. The boat held about fifteen people. When it was fully loaded, the waterline was almost to the gunnels. I thought the boat would ferry the passengers out to a bigger boat that would make the two-hour crossing.

"Where's the ferry?" I asked the captain as I was climbing aboard.

He didn't understand what I was asking. *"Este es el Barco!"* he said ("This is the boat!")

This little, beat-up wooden boat with too many people on board was going to make a two-hour open ocean crossing.

Fine, I thought, *but not with me.*

They might do it all the time, but I couldn't swim. It wouldn't have done any good if I could. I would have just drowned slower. Reckless, lunatic bus drivers I was willing to trust, but not this.

Back I went, the long way to Honduras.

42

I DIDN'T THINK I WAS LETTING FEAR STOP ME. I WAS ACTUALLY WORRIED ABOUT HONDURAS. I TRIED TO get to Nicaragua by avoiding Honduras. It turns out Honduras was one of the friendliest countries I could have imagined.

Honduran people were always happy to give directions, feed me, or just drink beer, hang out, and make music. I spent a few days in Honduras but never had to pay for accommodation. I had to insist on paying something when I was taken home and fed. Guatemala was a poor country. Honduras was a desperately poor country. It became clear to me that poor people are often more generous than the rich. Honesty and morality are not connected to wealth.

Then again, maybe it's an inverse connection. I also understand Honduras is the murder capital of the world. I don't know if it was that way in 1980. My experience was different.

The border crossing to Nicaragua was confusing. Officials didn't know how to do things. They were mostly kids. Their guns were bigger than they were. They were Sandinistas, a happy, proud bunch of rebels, and with good reason. They had fought a revolution and won against all odds. They had tossed out the American-backed dictator Somoza. The brutal Somoza dynasty had ruled Nicaragua for more than forty years. He was lucky to have escaped the country before being "Mussolinied."

In my travels, I had never experienced the national joy those people showed me. You know how it is when a small country wins an international soccer match? All of Nicaragua was like that. Times a hundred.

A few hundred feet into Nicaragua, I saw a bunch of young revolutionaries standing by the side of the road. They were armed to the teeth, bandoliers of ammunition crossing their chests. It was a postcard of revolution.

"Hola," I said as I walked up.

"Che, Che Guevara," one of them said and pointed at me with a big smile on his face.

It wasn't the first time someone thought I looked like Che. I didn't mind. In fact, I cultivated the look. I even picked up a black beret along the way. I offered them a Marlboro, and then I gave the package to the oldest one. Marlboros were a good trade item all over Latin America.

I pointed at their rifles. "Nice."

They stood up straight at attention and presented their arms. It was so cool. One of them held out his AK-47, offering it to me. He pointed out to the field and made shooting sounds. He wanted me to try it. And I really, really wanted to.

The gun was set on full automatic. I almost lost control. The recoil wasn't so bad, but on automatic it threw me back a bit. He reached out and flipped the lever to single shot.

For the next hour, we shot at Coke bottles. It became competition with the Gringo Che. They were teenagers, but I was sure they had seen combat.

When it was time for me to hit the road, I demonstrated my plan by sticking my thumb out in a hitchhiking motion. No need to hitchhike. One of my Sandinista friends held up his hand and stopped the first truck that passed. He said something to the driver and then motioned me to get in. It was amazing and touching when he offered me money from his own pocket. I reached into my pocket and handed him ten dollars instead.

"For ammunition," I said.

I kept waving until they disappeared behind me in the dust.

In 1980, I was a leftist revolutionary. I have grown up since then, but I do hope those kids survived the coming trouble in Nicaragua.

I HEADED FOR MANAGUA, THE capital. I expected a city. What I found was a pile of rubble. The city had been destroyed by a major earthquake in 1972. Eight years later, it still had not been restored. Aid poured in from around the world, but it had gone into the pockets of the Somoza government.

On the highway to Managua, I saw evidence of that corruption firsthand. Mile after mile of banana plantations with primitive huts built over open ditches full of mosquitos. People living in poverty you could not imagine. But the highway! The highway was paved with interlocking bricks. Mile after mile of expensive patio stones. The Somoza government called it "urban renewal." Of course, the Somoza family owned the business that made those bricks. No doubt it is the nicest stretch of the Pan-American Highway. American aid built it while the people who lived on either side of it died of malaria and brutality. The bananas were more important. The earthquake and the exposed corruption led eventually to the revolution.

When I arrived, Nicaragua was a happy place. It was hard to understand how people living in those conditions could be so full of joy and optimism.

On the outskirts of town, I noticed some factories and buildings had been blown to pieces while others remained untouched. I asked the driver what was up with that. He told me only the businesses owned by the Somoza regime were destroyed. It was a selective and justified revenge. They had won their revolution, but they had no idea what misery was in store for them for a decade to come.

I learned not to take sides on political matters. People wanted to explain their politics to me. As a foreigner, my opinion mattered to both sides. When I saw that corruption and desperation, it was hard not to take sides.

There wasn't much to do in Nicaragua. It wasn't even a functioning civilization. All I could do was marvel at the destruction. Everywhere was the smell of gunpowder and cordite.

I kept moving south.

MORE THAN THIRTY YEARS LATER, I obtained a Canadian government document that seems to show someone was tracking me during that period. The document was addressed to the director of Oak Ridge, inquiring if he knew my whereabouts. Below the signature on that document are the words "Special Project." If I told you the government was tracking me, you would probably think I'm paranoid. But I have this document and others that prove they were.

43

I STAYED A FEW DAYS AT THE SOUTHERN TIP OF LAKE NICARAGUA AND THEN HEADED FOR COSTA RICA.

At the border post, I was told to sit in a chair. An official asked a few questions while a nurse snuck up on me and poked a needle in my arm. The uniform behind the counter gave me a handful of white pills and told me to take them right there in front of him. This was Costa Rica's anti-malaria program.

A few hours later, I got as sick as a dog. I had to get off the bus in a small village and find someplace to rest. Backpackers had to put up with it or not go to Costa Rica.

The contrast between Nicaragua and Costa Rica was amazing. The grinding poverty of Nicaragua ended at the border. Costa Rica was wealthy and organized. I liked Costa Rica, but I also saw the inverse connection between wealth and humanity.

Tikkas saw themselves as superior to the rest of Central America. For good reason, I suppose. I had made friends with people in desperate circumstance, but Tikkas didn't welcome travelers like me.

There was no visible military presence on the streets. No roadblocks or tension in the air. No death squads. The police didn't even carry guns.

Oddly, I could buy a pistol in almost any corner store. No licence, and no questions. Just buy it and stick it in my pocket. Costa Rica was the only place I ever encountered such leniency, but it was also the only Central American country where I didn't need a gun. There was little or no crime. The only reason I didn't drop a hundred bucks on a Saturday night special was I couldn't take it with me into Panama.

It was nice not having a destination. I just followed whatever road looked worth following. I hitchhiked my way through northern Panama without any problems. I caught a ride on the back of a big rig flatbed. It was a little dicey. I'm sure the driver tried to shake me off, but I held on.

He dropped me at a crossroad in the desert. There was nothing there but a gas station and a cantina. Only truckers stopped there, but I had fun drinking beer with them. I spent the night outdoors on my hammock.

From Panama City, I had to decide if I would fly to South America or go back home. I didn't really have a home. The last place I had called home had burned to the ground. I wondered if someone was stalking me, if it was safe to go back to Vancouver. Nothing was drawing me back to Canada. My only problem was money. I had no return ticket. I would find myself in a real pickle if I couldn't get home.

There was that word again, "home." It had been five months. For the moment, "home" was my hammock. I decided to keep going until the wheels fell off.

I had to fly from Panama City to Bogota, Columbia. No choice. The Darian Gap is a hundred miles of jungle separating Central and South America. It was an economic barrier as well as a physical barrier.

Bogota was dangerous, really dangerous, but it was also cheap. I could get a decent hotel for a few dollars and a good meal for one dollar.

I found a restaurant not far from the hotel. The entire place was "cocaine décor" with tinfoil and mirrors everywhere. Everything sparkled like crystal. Only men were in the booths. They were all packing guns, and they all wanted to buy me a drink.

I found myself jammed into a booth surrounded by drug dealers. They were a friendly bunch of bad guys. Every one of them had a few gold teeth and a pirate smile.

One of them spoke a little English. He asked me strange questions like, "Do you know karate? Do you have a knife?" The sort of things you'd want to know if you were planning to mug someone.

"I need to take a leak," I said, and then I worked my way past them out of the booth.

As I passed the owner at the front counter, I asked him to get a taxi and let me know when it was out front. The owner knew what was happening and, lucky for me, he helped me out.

I returned to the booth and acted normal. I just stayed cool and kept smiling. A few minutes passed, and then the owner signalled from the front door. I got up like I was going to the bathroom again with at least six pairs of eyes on me.

When I got close to the door, I made a dash for it. The taxi was parked right in front, two wheels on the sidewalk with the door open. I dove in head-first.

"Vamoose! Go, go, go!"

The taxi took off just as six bad guys ran out the front door. They chased the taxi, waving fists in the air. I left them in the dust. They looked plenty pissed off.

My hotel was only a few blocks away. I thought it would be better to find another place on the other side of town. I was glad I hadn't left anything behind and that the room was cheap. Not a big loss.

There was nothing in Bogota except cocaine and pot. I was out of there the next morning.

I had mostly hitchhiked my way from Mexico City. I had passed unscathed through a close call with a machete, a genocide, and a revolution. I wasn't a seasoned traveler when I started out from Vancouver. I'm sure I did some really dumb things, but I made it through.

South America was another story.

44

HITCHHIKING WAS TOO RISKY. I DECIDED BUSES WERE THE WAY TO GO FROM THERE ON. WOULDN'T YOU know it? That "safe" transportation almost got me killed.

I found the bus depot and headed south on a beat-up local bus. The seats were hard, and the road was rough. I climbed up onto a shelf just below the rear windows. It was long enough to stretch out and relax. It was a bumpy ride, but I started to feel sleepy. I rested my head on my backpack and was out in a few minutes.

The next thing I knew, I was being dragged by both arms down the aisle of the bus. My head was pounding, and I couldn't hear from the loud rushing sound in my ears. I was half-carried off the bus and lowered to the ground by the side of the road.

Someone slapped my face on both sides. I gasped and puked a few times. I came to my senses and realized I had almost killed myself with carbon monoxide fumes. If someone had not noticed, I think I would have been done for in just a few more minutes.

Was I just lucky? I don't believe in luck. We create our own fortune, good or bad. I don't know how I survived so much bad judgment. Possibly my experience in Oak Ridge and prison. Who knows how many close calls I had and didn't even realize?

I kept moving through Columbia. Every town had an air of danger.

Ecuador was a treat. Quito, the capital sits at an elevation of close to ten thousand feet. I was right on the equator. I expected a steaming, hot Amazon jungle. Instead, I froze my ass off. I had no warm clothes. Apparently, Quito is always cold.

By then I was getting tired of being a stranger in a strange land. I wasn't homesick. I couldn't be; I didn't have a home. I was also running out of money, and I had to make a decision. Head to Peru or go back to Canada.

Before I left Vancouver, Clem told me that if I ever needed help, just ask. I didn't think much of it at the time. I was flush with cash. Things had changed. I found a Western Union and sent a telegram. "Need a thousand dollars. Will repay with interest."

Two days later, Clem wired three thousand and a phone number in Lima. The telegram said, "Call. He will explain."

My problem was solved. I was going to Lima! Not only that, I was flying.

The beat-up airplane reminded me of the ferry I didn't take in Nicaragua. I was sure I could see daylight around the rusty bolts holding the seats in place. I decided to put my faith in the pilot's desire to get home to his wife and children.

The in-flight lunch was a bologna sandwich and a paper cup of Coke. After a short flight, I was in Lima, but not for long.

Before leaving the airport, I had purchased a ticket to Vancouver. I thought it was better to be sure I had my way home arranged.

I decided to treat myself to a twelve-dollar-a-night luxury hotel. The room even had a telephone, something I hadn't seen or used in half a year. I called the number Clem had given me. It turns out a lot was going on behind the scenes that I didn't know anything about.

Clem was in some business deal with these people, the cocaine business. They sent a car to pick me up, and then they robbed me at gunpoint. They got everything except two hundred dollars I had stashed in my boot. Then they dropped me off in the middle of nowhere.

Several hours later, I found my way back to the hotel. The clerk behind the desk said my friend had left something for me. He handed over a stuffed llama about ten inches tall, a typical tourist souvenir made of real llama hide.

I went to my room and tried to call Clem, but it was impossible to make an international phone call. I looked closely at the llama and noticed one of the seams wasn't right. I split it open and found a small bag of white powder inside. That was it. I was out of there! I dumped the cocaine down the toilet and threw the llama out the window.

They took me apart at the airport, complete with rubber glove treatment. They knew I was coming. I had been set up. But I had nothing. I had a direct Air Canada flight from Lima to Vancouver. Some people called it the "midnight express." They had to let me go.

The plane was mostly empty, plenty of seats to stretch out on. Half an hour into the flight, a guy came and sat in an empty seat beside me. I had seen the guy at the Air Canada desk when I arrived in Lima. He wasn't an airline employee. I think he was DEA or RCMP. Anyway, he checked me out carefully. Whatever training this guy had, I'm sure he could spot a nervous drug smuggler. I wasn't smuggling drugs, but I was nervous. I didn't know what awaited me in Vancouver. I felt like I had been chased out of town six months earlier, and now I had just lost three thousand dollars of drug money.

45

I ARRIVED IN VANCOUVER EARLY IN THE MORNING. EVERYTHING LOOKED SO CLEAN. I REALIZED HOW different Canada was compared to third world countries. I had to leave it for a while to understand.

When I passed through customs, I expected another shakedown, but they just waved me through. They didn't even look in my backpack. I could have kept that bag of cocaine, and I wouldn't have been so broke. But I was glad I had dumped it down the toilet.

I waited at the airport for a few hours. Nothing was open yet, and I didn't want to spend what little money I had on a hotel room.

I went directly to the picture-framing store. A shit storm met me at the door.

One of the employees saw me come in. He rushed up, grabbed my arm, and pulled me outside. In a panic he told me Clem had been busted the day before. They got him on his boat with a suitcase full of money, several kilos of coke, and two South American drug dealers. The employee assumed I was involved somehow. He told me the police were watching the store and that I had better get the hell out of there.

So I did.

I thought the police were after me, too, but I hadn't done anything. I wasn't a drug smuggler. I had no idea what was going on, but I was smack in the middle of it.

I didn't know where to go, and I didn't have enough money to do anything, so I went to my brother's place.

I had to drag him out of bed; he wasn't an early riser. Garry didn't even know I had gone to South America. I tried to explain the situation, but he seemed dazed from his never-ending party. I convinced him to hand over whatever cash he had in the house. I told him I needed to disappear again. I didn't say where or why. He was happy to just give me a wad of cash and go back to sleep.

I spent most of it on a plane ticket to Toronto. I didn't know any other place where I could hide. I didn't even know what I was hiding from. I only been in Vancouver for a few hours and already I was back on a flight to Toronto. I didn't want to live in Toronto.

I didn't realize what six months on the road had done to me. I had a bad case of scabies and probably lice as well. For the past month, I had been scratching my legs raw. I didn't understand why I couldn't find a job. If I had taken a critical look in the mirror, perhaps I would have understood.

I had no money to rent an apartment, so I stayed at the Salvation Army, likely spreading my South American bugs to everyone. That went on for more than a month. When you're down and out in Toronto, you stay that way.

Then, for the first and only time in my life I went to a welfare office. All I wanted was a ticket back to Vancouver. I knew what it was to be treated like a nutcase. I knew how it was to be a petty criminal. I understood rejection and isolation. None of that compared to the dehumanizing treatment I received at the welfare office. I will starve to death in the freezing rain before I subject myself to that again. Eventually, they relented and got me on a flight back to Vancouver.

When I returned, I discovered the police weren't looking for me. Everything was back to normal. Clem wasn't in jail, and I got my job back.

I don't know how he did it, but all charges were dropped against him. They caught him red-handed, but he somehow got away with it. He was a respected businessman with five pounds of cocaine. I was a dirt-bag who went to prison for stealing cigarettes. I'm not complaining about the way of the world, but it was certainly a learning experience. If I didn't want to be treated like a dirt-bag, I shouldn't be one. The past year had changed me forever. I decided I would become a respected businessman.

I went back to work at the warehouse. Same conditions, one dollar a corner.

Clem told me I owed him a thousand bucks, not the three thousand I had lost. He gave a vague explanation of what happened in Lima. It came down to this: The phone number he gave me was a business contact in Lima. He wanted cash, and it was convenient that I happened to ask Clem to wire money to me. Whoever picked up the phone when I called wasn't the right person. They saw it as an opportunity to rip me off. It wasn't my mistake at all, and I didn't have to pay for it.

I lived in the warehouse for the next few weeks. When I made enough money to get an apartment, I started to get my life back on track. I went to the bank, got a brand new one-thousand-dollar bill, folded it up, and handed it to Clem. He stuck it in his pocket without even looking at it.

"I like that colour," was all he said.

Clem always respected me after this screw-up. I also learned something about the virtues of capitalism. Clem was ten years older than me. He showed me his old passport from when he was my age. He had traveled through southeast Asia on his own—India, Thailand, Nepal—a yearlong adventure. And look at him now. He had a big boat, a business, and several condos in the West End. He was rich! I could do that, too, I thought.

I went to work and saved my money like Scrooge. A year and a half later, I landed in Bangkok on another adventure.

I would like to tell you about all the wonders and horrors I saw in Thailand, Burma, India, Nepal, and Sri Lanka, lessons on humanity and inhumanity, success and excess, personal growth and enlightenment. I smoked in an opium den in Rangoon. I climbed the highest mountain pass in the world, Thorung La. I sat under the Bodhi Tree where Buddha, himself, found enlightenment. I played my harmonica in the Taj Mahal. All that and more. But I'm writing for another reason. I don't intend this to be a travelogue. Now that you know my past, I want to tell you how I arrived where I am today and why I had to write this book.

46

THE YEAR WAS 1983. I WAS WORKING AT THE PICTURE-FRAMING FACTORY, SAVING MONEY AND PLANNING my next adventure. By that time, I knew the best thing I could do for myself was travel the world. I learned so much that I thought I would never tire of it.

One evening out of the blue, my phone rang. It was a voice from the past. Her name was Irene, and she had been my girlfriend in 1968. Before Oak Ridge. The story she told me changed my world again. You see, Irene was pregnant when I hit the road and wound up in Oak Ridge. I had no idea.

My daughter was born in 1969 as I was being brainwashed and tortured by Doctor Barker. They didn't tell me anything. Someone from the Salvation Army told Irene I had killed myself and that she should forget about me. A few years later, Irene found out it wasn't true, but it was too late. She had married someone else. All I had was her name tattooed on my right shoulder.

Irene found me through my mother. She could have done that at any time in the past sixteen years, but she was afraid to tell my daughter her father was not who she thought he was. Irene had separated from her husband. Soon, my daughter would turn sixteen. Irene wanted to tell her the truth, but she was afraid. Irene asked if I would come to Toronto to help her explain.

I was on my way the next morning.

I met Suzan for the first time sitting at the kitchen table. My heart almost stopped. I thought I was looking into some kind of mystical mirror that had turned me into a sixteen-year-old girl. I knew she was my daughter beyond any doubt. I know about that "nature" versus "nurture" argument. For me at that moment, nature won hands down.

Suzan had no idea who I was, but she knew something important was happening. Irene was dying to tell her, but she was afraid. Suzan and I just kept looking at each other. She was trying to figure out who this stranger was. I wanted to blurt it out, but it was up to Irene. I took her aside a few times and insisted she just do it. I told her if she didn't, I would go back to Vancouver, and that would be the end of it. Irene knew she had to tell her; she just needed encouragement.

Finally, she looked Suzan in the eye. "Wolf is not your father. Steve is your father. I hope you don't hate me."

Suzan didn't show any shock or surprise. She was silent for a moment, and then she stood up and walked around the table.

"I knew it," she said. "I've been waiting for this all my life." She hugged me. "I love you, Dad."

I don't think anyone can imagine how I felt. A spot that had been empty for sixteen years was filled, something I didn't know was lost until I found it. And she was stunningly beautiful—except the poor girl had my nose.

We went for a walk together, holding hands. Now she knew I wasn't some creepy guy staring at her across the kitchen table. She had these mannerisms, like walking backward in front of me while talking. I'm the only other person I ever saw do that.

We went shopping downtown. She looked at a Michael Jackson red and black leather jacket. I told her to try it on.

"It's way too expensive, Dad."

"It doesn't matter," I said. "It looks too cool on you. You need to have it."

I was so glad I had learned to save money. I wanted to buy her everything she wanted. I also wanted to know everything about her. Suddenly, I was the father of a beautiful, sixteen-year-old girl. How did that happen?

I thought about Doctor Barker. Did he know about Suzan? Had he concealed this life-changing information? What sort of man would do that? I realized I had to do something. I couldn't continue to hide my past. I decided to move back to Toronto.

I returned to Vancouver and gave away my furniture and anything else I couldn't carry on an airplane. I was back in Toronto in less than a week. All the while, Suzan's face was on my mind.

Irene thought we could get together again, but it didn't seem right. We had nothing in common except Suzan. We became friends, and we still are today. She phones me every year to remind me of Suzan's birthday.

I didn't need to find a job right away. I was glad I had saved some money; my travel plans could wait.

I found an apartment, actually a coach house behind a big mansion. The place was a mess when I moved in, but I put a lot of effort into fixing it up.

During that time, I was reading a Toronto newspaper, looking for furniture when I saw a small notice asking people who had had a bad experience with Canadian psychiatric hospitals to attend a seminar at the University of Toronto. I thought it would be an opportunity to find out something about Oak Ridge.

It was held in a lecture hall with a large audience. They had an open microphone, and anyone with something to contribute was given time. I didn't have any notes, and I really had no idea what I would say, but I went to the microphone and started talking about what had happened to me in Oak Ridge. I'm not good at public speaking. I was nervous, but I just let it pour out. I talked for ten or fifteen minutes. I guess I didn't realize how passionate I was. When I walked away from the microphone, the audience stood up and clapped. Everyone in the room was anti-psychiatry.

When it was over, I realized others understood something very bad had happened to me. I thought I needed to look into my past and stop trying to forget about it.

As the room was clearing out, a guy walked up and handed me a video cassette.

"I'm a camera man," he said. "I work at CTV. This video is important. It's embargoed by the network. As far as they're concerned, it doesn't exist, and I didn't give it to you."

With that, he walked away. I looked at the cassette. All it said was "F Ward."

On my way out, I picked up a brochure labeled "Citizens' Commission on Human Rights (CCHR)." They sounded important. I had no idea it was a Scientology organization. I didn't know anything about Scientology other than the creepy personality tests they promoted on Yonge Street. I knew I had been tortured, but I had no idea what I could do about it. At least I got an opportunity to talk to someone who was on my side.

I bought a car, an old beater, but it worked. Suzan and I drove to Sault Ste. Marie, where I introduced her to my mother and my father. Yes, by then, my father was also living in the Sault. He had long since recovered from life with my mother. He did more than recover; he had prospered. He re-married and had three daughters. Our reunion was something to remember.

I came to understand how wrong I was about him, and he realized the same about me. I was the wayward child, and he was the best man I had ever met in my life. It was my mother who almost did him in. I know my ability to overcome adversity came from him, proving to me it's nature, not nurture. He was totally blown away by Suzan. She was his first grandchild, and he couldn't stop smiling. He acted like a kid.

My mother was okay, but she was already an alcoholic working her way toward the end. Bill was gone, she had bought a small, one-bedroom house where she lived alone with her dog. Her only friend was a drunken Indian named Ralph who stole what savings she had bit by bit. All she did was sit at the kitchen table and drink vodka from morning to night.

Suzan was overwhelmed to discover she had a much bigger family than she realized. I also discovered things I never imagined. Going to a PTA meeting at Suzan's school, for example.

Some of the Bernard Street Gang were still around. John the lawyer was less crazy than he used to be. Better medication, I suppose. Now Dennis the high school teacher was the crazy one. He had become a recluse who didn't want to leave his apartment. Hans the artist was still seducing anyone in a skirt. Jeff Healey was a new member. Some say he was the best guitar player in the world in 1984.

Our new hangout was a club on Queen Street called Chicago's. Good times and good music. The bar closed at two in the morning. No one was ever ready for last call.

Generally, we would head for a "booze can," an after-hours club. Like an old-fashioned speakeasy, they were illegal, but they were everywhere.

My coach house evolved into a booze can on weekends. I built a bar and sold beer, but I didn't feel like a gangster. We kept it low key and didn't attract attention.

I stayed in Toronto until 1986. Suzan changed so much in that time. I didn't get to see her grow up, but I did see her change from a child to a woman. She found a boyfriend, and, of course, I didn't like him. Then she stopped coming around. I'm sure this happens to every father eventually, those teenage years of rebellion. For Suzan and me, it was condensed into three short years.

When she moved in with her boyfriend, I decided it was time for me to head back to the west coast.

47

I KEPT IN TOUCH WITH IRENE, AND ONCE IN A WHILE, SUZAN WOULD CALL. IT WASN'T LONG BEFORE I found out I was a grandfather. I wasn't even close to forty yet.

My job at the picture-framing warehouse was waiting for me when I got back to Vancouver. Clem was always happy to have me as a one-man production line. I worked alone in the warehouse.

One afternoon, two men in suits came in and asked if I was Steve Smith. They knew who I was, and I knew they were cops. They didn't need to identify themselves, cops give off a certain aura.

They said they were with Ontario Provincial Police (OPP) from Toronto. They asked if I was a member of the Church of Scientology. Then they asked about an Oak Ridge patient named Bob Dean.

This is creepy, I thought. I knew who Bob Dean was. I had seen the guards in Oak Ridge murder him. I had talked about that when I went to the Scientology seminar at U of T. I told the police the same thing I had said then.

I saw two guards drag Bob Dean, unconscious, down the hall with a towel twisted around his neck. They threw him into a cell right across from mine and slammed the door.

The next morning, they dragged him out and put him on a stretcher. I was sure he was dead. His skin was a horrible grey colour.

They thanked me for my assistance and left.

I was stunned. Where did they get the idea I knew something about that murder? That was more than fifteen years earlier. And how had they known where to find me? More and more, I was seeing indications that someone was keeping track of me.

I was frightened at first, but when I realized I had done nothing wrong, it turned to anger. I decided I would get to the bottom of it no matter what it took.

The first step turned out to be easy. The cops had asked me about Scientology. The only connection I had with them was the seminar in Toronto. I discovered that the police had raided the Scientology headquarters shortly after I attended that seminar. Many files were taken, and I was certain one of them contained my name.

I found a newspaper article about the police raid in the public library. I had never researched anything in a library, but soon I discovered how helpful a librarian could be. They loved to find a curious mind they could help out. I had a name, "Elliott T. Barker." What could they help me find out about him?

I learned about professional publications. Doctors like Barker always publish their research. After several hours of digging through abstracts of the *Canadian Psychological Association Journal*, I came up with one of Barker's papers. Once I had one, I was able to follow the citations, and others were easy to find. I wrote the volume numbers on a piece of paper, and the librarian would go to the stacks and bring the bound books to me.

Every time I found something authored or co-authored by Barker, I could not believe what I was reading. It read like a confession of abuse and torture.

One of the publications, "Buber Behind Bars," was co-authored by M. H. Mason. Wait a second, I thought. Mason wasn't a psychiatrist or a doctor. He was a patient at Oak Ridge, the same as me, except I don't think he had just stolen a car. He had done something much worse. As bizarre as that was, the content of the paper was even more disturbing.

Since my time in Oak Ridge, I read a lot of books, some written by raving madmen like Adolf Hitler. "Buber Behind Bars" reminded me of such writings. It was a manifesto written by someone who hated society and wanted to transform it into his image. I could understand a certified madman like Michael Mason writing it, but Barker?

I buried myself in volumes of professional journals. Every time I found something new, I realized more and more what a sick, twisted man he was. Titles like, "The Hundred Day Hate-in," "Defence Disrupting Therapy," "LSD in a Coercive Milieu Therapy Program," and more. I read and photocopied all of it. I understood beyond any doubt that what had happened to me should never have happened in a civilized country, and I was going to do something about it.

48

MY BACKGROUND DIDN'T GIVE ME A LOT OF CREDIBILITY. I WAS, AFTER ALL, JUST AN EX-CON WITH A history of mental problems. What could I do? If I brought up the subject, I could see people dismissing me and anything I had to say. I had embarrassed myself more than once already. I needed more than Barker's published papers. I needed clinical records. I had to find solid proof that I had been tortured with drugs. Ideas of truth, justice, and accountability were meaningless without credibility. I had to become a believable person despite my past.

That understanding was a revelation. It changed the course of my life. I knew I needed to become successful and independent or no one would believe me. I never wanted to define myself as a victim. I didn't expect compensation. I just wanted to clear my name and hold those people accountable.

I had heard of something called freedom of information (FOI) requests, but I had no idea how to go about it. I didn't have a typewriter, and even if I did, I had no typing skills. My handwriting was slow and painful, but I began writing everything I could recall in a grey notebook. That was almost thirty years ago. Today as I write this, I'm still doing the same thing, although the world has changed in so many ways.

I knew Scientology was a cult I should stay away from, but there was no other organization that hated and criticised psychiatry. I went to their office on Hastings Street with copies of Barker's publications and my handwritten story.

It was difficult to get past the front desk. I waited more than an hour while someone upstairs read what I had given them. Eventually, a girl led me to the CCHR office. She reminded me of the Beatles song, "Girl with Kaleidoscope Eyes."

I'm sure I didn't seem believable in that first meeting. I was nervous and inarticulate. But the CCHR believed my story. They were on my side from the start, because they knew much more about psychiatry than I did.

They had office equipment: a typewriter, a fax machine, and a photocopier. For the first time in my life, I was in a professional-looking situation, and they believed my story.

They told me about Linda Macdonald and nine other Canadians who had sued the CIA successfully. They were victims of CIA-funded brainwashing experiments conducted at McGill University in Montreal. CCHR thought the experiments conducted at Oak Ridge were very similar to that case. They told me anyone using LSD for research in those days was reporting results back to CIA or other intelligence agencies. I didn't know about any of that, but it sounded possible to me.

CCHR helped write letters and do a proper FOI request. I wanted all of my clinical records from Oak Ridge, and, by golly, I got them. Everything. Even more than I expected. I think someone in Oak Ridge's archives was on my side. Someone wanted to reveal what had happened there. Finally, I had proof, not just the ravings of an ex-lunatic.

Amazingly, other patients were named in those records—Peter Woodcock and others. Giving me those records without blocking out their names was a breach of patient confidentiality. I was happy to get those records, but at the same time, it demonstrated how Oak Ridge operated outside any laws or regulation. The records were extensive. Just a casual reading proved numerous breaches of standards of treatment and most likely outright criminal assault.

What was I to do with all it? A lawsuit? I was in Vancouver, on the other side of the country. How could I find a lawyer? Besides, I didn't have money to pay a lawyer.

I thought back to the visit I had received from the OPP. They had found my name in the Scientology files taken in the Toronto police raid. I didn't want the Scientology people to get copies of my records. I was thankful for the help they had given me, but I had to get those files from them.

I went to their office and told them someone had stolen my copies. Fortunately, only one guy was in the office. He took the file out and told me he would make another copy. I took the folders out of his hand and walked out. They chased me, but they didn't dare lay a hand on me. My heart was pounding when I blended into the crowd on Hastings Street. Now I was on the list of people unfriendly to Scientology. That was fine with me. They had their own agenda.

I recall reading science fiction by L. Ron Hubbard. That was during the period in prison when I would read anything I could get my hands on. "Pulp fiction," it was called. It's a good thing my first encounter with Hubbard was mediocre fiction. I don't like organizations that keep files on people.

    Now I had Barker's published papers and my clinical records. I still didn't have to be a lawyer to help determine if a lot of unethical, if not criminal, things happened at Oak Ridge. I thought my best option was publicity. I needed to tell everyone what happened. Tell these things to the world, and justice and accountability would surely follow.

49

I DIDN'T SPEND EVERY WAKING MOMENT OBSESSED WITH IT. I GOT ON WITH MY LIFE. BIT BY BIT, I established a foundation of small successes. But I kept nudging my "case" forward, too.

The Vancouver Sun published a two-page center spread with my name and face displayed prominently. I thought there would be a huge reaction. I thought people would recognize my face in public. I even worried about losing my job. Nothing happened good or bad. No one even noticed.

Sometime later, I managed to get on a radio talk show with Jack Webster, a gruff, harsh Scotsman. He read the consent form Barker had forced me to sign and then gave me a look.

"You would have to be crazy to sign this."

I thought he was confusing the cause and the effect. I didn't know what to say. Live on air, I said CCHR helped me get those records. Webster hit the roof.

"What are you doing proselytizing Scientology on my program? Get him out of here!"

They practically frog-marched me out the door. I found myself standing outside the studio with my briefcase full of documents, humiliated.

Lesson learned. I never mentioned Scientology again.

I don't know how many letters I wrote by hand trying to find a lawyer who could understand the case I was sure I had. Nothing but rejection. I understood clearly. With my history of mental illness, nothing I said would be believed. It was such a diabolical situation. If only I could get someone to read all I had gathered in my briefcase.

There was an entry in my clinical record. I don't know who wrote it. No signature. "Smith has grown his hair long and has taken to wearing high-heeled boots. He is suffering from the hippie syndrome."

That's right, *hippie syndrome.*

Are you kidding? Who in the world thought being a hippie was a "syndrome."

Was I a psychopath hippie? No matter how ridiculous the statement, it was a clinical record, and it damned me to dismissal. I was lucky to have those records at all. Oak Ridge was not inclined to hand them out.

I didn't surrender. I brought the subject up from time to time. I continued on a normal path in life. I just got a late start, that's all.

I found a new occupation. Picture framing wasn't a career; it was just something I was good at doing. Fortunately, Clem paid me well.

One day, I saw an advertisement in the paper for a "plastic fabricator." I had no idea what that was, but I thought I would apply anyway.

Sitting across the desk at a job interview, the shop owner asked what experience I had. As I was about to say, "None," he accidentally knocked a plastic brochure holder off his desk. I have very fast reflexes, perhaps learned in prison. I caught the thing before it hit the floor.

I looked up at him and smiled. "I'm good with my hands, but I don't know what a plastic fabricator is."

"You're hired," he said. "Can you start tomorrow?"

The falling brochure stand was another one of those "sparks" in the path of life. It changed everything and led to my independence.

Plastic fabricating is similar to fine woodworking. Most of the tools are the same. All of the skills I had learned, from working in the machine shop to picture framing, came together in my new job. I learned quickly.

The factory produced a lot of scrap plastic off cuts, a dumpster full of useful pieces each day. I took bits and pieces home to practice welding and design. I lived in an apartment, so I couldn't use machine tools. I needed my own workspace.

I took a chance and rented a six-bedroom house with a detached garage. I rented out five of the bedrooms, and the place paid for itself. I bought a table saw and a router from a second-hand store, built a few homemade workbenches, and the garage became Plasticsmith Inc. It wasn't long before I was making more money working at home than I did at the factory. I quit my job in 1989 and never worked for a paycheck again.

Keeping a six-bedroom house full of diverse people wasn't easy. Sometimes I would interview people, and everything seemed okay, but they would turn out to be hookers or drug dealers. It was hard to get rid of them.

Quite by accident I discovered Japanese working holiday students. They always paid the rent and kept the place clean. One of my Japanese tenants wrote a newspaper advertisement in Japanese for me. When I needed a new student, I put it in the local Japanese language paper. Only Japanese could read it, so I had no more problems with bad tenants.

One morning something extraordinary happened. I had just picked up a copy of the Japanese newspaper. Of course, I can't read Japanese so I couldn't tell if my advertisement was there. I was passing through the food fair at the shopping mall and saw this drop-dead beautiful Japanese girl sitting alone. I wasn't shy. Why not ask her to read it for me? The newspaper in my hand was a good excuse to talk to her.

We were married nearly a decade before I asked her why she talked to me that day and why she left the mall with me.

"Because you didn't look dangerous," she said.

She was fifteen years younger than me. The age difference didn't matter at all. That was twenty-five years ago. We have come a long way together since then.

We didn't get married right away. She was in Canada on a visa. Neither of us had much money, only boundless optimism. I had my little garage workshop. My rent and expenses were pretty much taken care of. We decided to go on a road trip.

50

WE DROVE MY OLD CAR FROM VANCOUVER TO MONTREAL, STOPPING AT SOME INTERESTING PLACES along the way.

One of those places was Oak Ridge.

I had told her about my past, but I think it lost something in translation. Or maybe I just didn't fit the profile of an ex-con mental patient.

We drove right up to the front door. Not much had changed. It still looked like a medieval prison, not a hospital. Oddly, the place didn't intimidate me at all.

I walked up to the steel door and knocked, hard. It opened right away. I'm sure we were being watched on camera before we got anywhere near the place.

The same sort of guard I remembered—big body, small head, and pants held up by suspenders—was standing behind the barred gate. He didn't say a word, just looked at me like I was not where I should be.

I said I wanted to visit Peter Woodcock.

He looked surprised, hesitated a moment, then said, "There's no such person."

He gave me such a fierce look I didn't challenge him. I just pursed my lips, looked doubtful, and walked away.

I didn't know Peter had changed his name to George Kruger. There really was no such person as Peter Woodcock, child killer. I'm still curious. How did someone like Woodcock legally change his name? I didn't think a prisoner could do that.

Oak Ridge was only one building in a large complex of hospital facilities. The hospital itself covered many acres. Some of the outbuildings were more than a hundred years old.

We drove away from the Oak Ridge building, found a place to park, and walked around.

I had heard rumors over the years of a hidden graveyard on the property. It sounded a little over the top to me. There's always a secret graveyard in these stories.

Well, we found it. In a large grove of trees, maybe three or four acres, right in the middle, overgrown by tall grass. We moved the grass aside and counted the grave markers. No names, only numbers, lots of them. The place was desolate and creepy. Who wanted to end up in a numbered grave hidden in the forest? Who were these people and how did they get there? Who had the record of a person who was now in a numbered grave? As far as I know, that has never been addressed.

We continued our road trip, making a stop in Toronto, where we met up with some old friends. Bernard Street Gang guys.

We visited Niagara Falls and stayed in a honeymoon suite. We weren't married yet, but I knew we would be.

When we returned to Vancouver, we decided to take a day trip to the US. I had already traveled the world. I had visited more than fifteen countries, from active war zones to peaceful, tropical paradises, from communist dictatorships to mountaintops where I could see the entire world below. I found out the hard way I was not welcome in America.

They locked us behind a steel door in a small room. Questioned me about my past, put me against the wall, took my picture, and then told me to get out and never come back. Worse, my future wife and life partner was ordered out of Canada. She had twenty-four hours.

I went to the airport with her. She was escorted to the departure gate by Canada Customs agents. With tears in her eyes, a last kiss, and she was gone.

I knew what they were thinking. They thought I was a bad guy, and this young Japanese girl was in peril. They needed to intervene for her own good.

The burning tire necklace was still hanging around my neck. Everything I had done to redeem myself had come to nothing.

But we didn't give up.

She went back to Japan. In three months, she got a new passport and came back. She became Mrs. Smith right away.

We went to Mexico for our honeymoon. We landed in Cancun and hitch-hiked down the Yucatan to Belize. We weren't poor hippies. I just wanted to show her the way I had done it a decade earlier.

Then we got behind the mule and continued to plow. I gave up the house, and we found an apartment and rented a small warehouse space. We hung up our sign and created Plasticsmith Inc. Each month, we barely made the rent, but we were satisfied to be poor and working together.

One day, we were driving down Hastings Street when I saw a huge pot leaf sign on a small storefront. That was an unusual thing. I wasn't sure if it was even legal. I stopped and went in to check it out. It was the beginning of Mark Emory, so called "Prince of Pot." They were selling pipes and bongs and a whole new marijuana philosophy. I had the equipment and the workshop to make acrylic bongs, so I started making them.

They sold like hotcakes. Suddenly, we were making more than the rent. We could even afford to eat out once in a while.

Our little business grew. We had no business experience, so we learned hard lessons along the way. The most important lesson was that if you appear to be desperate, people will take advantage of you. Confidence is more important than experience. You cannot gain experience if you don't have the confidence to step out and do it without experience. We had plenty of blind confidence, simply because we didn't know what else to do.

We were lucky to be there at the beginning of the emerging medical marijuana movement. I played around with creative pot-smoking devices. I knew marijuana had chemicals with medical properties, but I didn't think smoking anything was such a good idea. I had an idea to heat the herb gently without burning it. Just enough heat to vaporize the active crystals but not enough to create combustion.

I used a thirty-watt pencil-type soldering iron and replaced the tip with a brass bowl. I mounted it on a block of wood and enclosed the entire thing inside an airtight glass jar. It was a simple concept: heat with no air meant no combustion. I called it a "vaporizer." It was my first invention, and it took off like a rocket. We moved to a bigger warehouse and started hiring help.

51

I DIDN'T FORGET ABOUT OAK RIDGE. I HAD A BRIEFCASE FULL OF CLINICAL RECORDS AND BARKER'S PUB-lished papers. I still saw those publications as a confession of torture.

Once again, a small newspaper article opened up a new avenue of confirmation. A lot of Central American refugees were coming to Canada with horrible stories of torture and abuse. Amnesty International had set up a counselling program to help them. The advertisement advised people who had been tortured to contact a phone number.

I recalled my experience with Scientology. I didn't want to get involved in anything like that again. I knew I had been tortured in Oak Ridge. "Hydro therapy" was waterboarding no matter what clinical term they used. Interrogating people with mind-altering drugs was an international crime. Nowhere in the Geneva Convention did it say it was okay to do those things to mental patients.

I contacted Amnesty International and told my story. They agreed I was a victim of torture and accepted me into a counselling program. I was the only Canadian ever to be admitted into a torture recovery program. That was where I met Jeff Lyon, surely the most compassionate man I have had the pleasure to know.

By that time, everything was moving in a positive direction. My wife and I were establishing a successful small business. Everything was looking up, but I still had a black hole in my soul. Hours of deep conversation with Jeff clarified what I needed to do. It wasn't revenge. It wasn't compensation. What I needed to do was hold these people accountable for what they had done.

I was more than accountable for every mistake I made in my youth, but I would never be content knowing Oak Ridge and Barker could hide behind clinical "standards of treatment." Their reputation was still intact. I had to pick myself up by the bootstraps and prove my reputation. I had to go after their reputation.

I THINK I STARTED IN the right place. I wrote a letter to the Ontario College of Physicians and Surgeons. Handwritten and full of spelling mistakes. I didn't send copies of any documents, only my recollection of Oak Ridge and questions about whether or not the "treatment" I had received was acceptable.

I waited six months or more for a response. When I finally heard from them, it was a brief, half-page letter informing me that none of what I claimed ever happened. No action would be taken.

I was stunned. How could they dismiss me so easily? I had the documents. It was right there in the records, signed by Dr. Barker and all. I was angry! They couldn't ignore reality to protect one of their members.

I appealed to the Health Professions Board (HPB), a governing body that oversees the governing body. This time I sent copies of my clinical records. With the help of Amnesty International, it was typed up properly with no spelling mistakes.

Months later, I heard back from them. HPB was careful in how they worded their response, but they had to send it back to the College of Physicians and Surgeons along with a number of recommendations. I thought I was dealing with two mutual admiration societies. I didn't like the sound of it, but what could I do?

It went on way too long trying to find a resolution with those governing bodies. Was it hopeless? It looked more and more like they were hiding something bigger than my case.

It was 1996. That year, something extraordinary came into the world: the Internet. I suppose it was around long before I heard of it, but that was the year I bought my first computer. A dial-up connection, some strange buzzing and clicking sounds, and suddenly I was connected to the World Wide Web.

I had to learn to type, not with two fingers but using the entire keyboard. Symbols and buttons I had no idea how to use. It was a slow learning curve. A new world and a whole new way to find just about anything.

A "search engine." I liked the sound of the word. It didn't take long to find Dr. Barker and his website. Canadian Society for the Prevention of Cruelty to Children (CSPCC). It had a picture of Barker, old with grey hair. The site gave me the creeps right away.

I knew this man. I remembered his knee in my back pinning me to the floor while he injected me with exotic, mind-bending drugs. I remembered a lot of things he did to me and others.

Prevention of cruelty to children. Indeed.

Right there on the front page was the name Michael Mason, co-founder, and a little poem penned by Mason that began with the words, "A child's skull is easy to crush." I knew Mason had been a patient at Oak Ridge. Just like back in 1968, he was acting like a doctor rather than a mental patient.

I read every word on Barker's website, clicked every link. If you had asked what I thought Barker would be up to then, I would have said he would be working with kids. I knew how compassionate he was to children. I thought his website was dark and greasy. Something was wrong there. It had an email link. It was a scary thing to do, it felt like Russian roulette, but I clicked it.

All I said was I think we should talk. I was still trying to get some satisfaction from the College of Physicians and Surgeons. Surely he knew about it. I didn't think there was a chance he would reply, but he did.

Thus began a four-month email conversation. Barker told me he was still in contact with a few Oak Ridge patients. Some of them even came to visit from time to time, but Barker claimed to have never written so much to anyone. I most certainly had never done anything like it.

I learned to type much better during those months. Every morning I looked forward to his email. It felt as though we clicked on an intellectual level. We covered so many subjects, from philosophy to sailing and windsurfing, from our personal daily life to our mutual travel experience.

I enjoyed Barker's stories of visits to psychiatric hospitals in strange places, places that labeled political dissent a mental illness. Communist China way before it was opened to the West. East Germany. Burma. What information or techniques did he learn from behind the Iron Curtain? In the early 1960s, those countries were torture states. They were the enemies of the western world.

Dr. Boyd, the director of Oak Ridge, had already hired Barker before he went on these training expeditions. Whatever Barker had learned, he used it to set up the "therapeutic community" at Oak Ridge.

If not for the memory of Barker's knee in my back and the suffering he inflicted on me, we surely would have become friends. Something about psychopaths you must keep in mind: They are charming, and they will charm you.

From Linda McDonald, I had learned about CIA brainwashing LSD experiments. I was sure some of what went on in Oak Ridge was part of it. The use of LSD in clinical experiments funded in one way or another by intelligence agencies is well documented.

I called Barker out on it a few times. He always dodged the issue. He knew very well I was not paranoid. He knew my suspicions were based on well-documented case history.

At one point, Dr. Collin Ross was involved in our conversation. Dr. Ross is an expert it the field of covert government brainwashing experiments. He wasn't paranoid either.

Earlier in this story, I told you about the farm in Midland. Lots of hippie kids and no idea who owned the place. I discovered during our conversation that it was Barker's farm, the same farm where Matt Lamb and the other two amigos lived.

I asked Barker how it happened that Lamb lived with him. He told me the usual story of how a review board had decided Lamb was no longer considered dangerous. How many members of this "review board" were fellow mental patients? I wondered if Michael Mason was one of them.

Then Barker told me something extraordinary. He said Lamb wanted to go to Israel and join the Israel Defence Forced (IDF). Barker said Lamb needed the esprit de corps of a military environment.

"With his (Lamb's) Israeli bonds and my encouragement he went to Israel and fought in the Yom Kippur war. He returned to the farm discouraged by the IDF then went to Rhodesia, the only place a war was going on at the time."

Lamb was killed in 1976, apparently by "friendly fire." A *Globe and Mail* newspaper article about Lamb's death mentions another Canadian in Lamb's troop who was jailed for refusing to fight. So many questions about the life and death of Mathew Charles Lamb.

Lamb was released from a lieutenant governor's warrant, because he was no longer considered dangerous. But he wanted to join the army, where he could have guns again. Lamb should have been sent straight back to Oak Ridge, not to Israel for military training. As far as I knew, the only time Lamb had fired a gun was to murder two innocent people.

Also, how did he get a passport? And who was the "other Canadian" jailed for refusing to fight? Lamb was a mercenary, simple as that. He was not Rhodesian, but he was willing to fight and die for the white supremacist Rhodesian government. Mercenaries don't refuse to fight.

Much has been written about Matt Lamb, and some of those things have been re-written and altered. I know for certain that someone does not want the true story of Matt Lamb and Israel to be known. Barker is one of only a few people who know the truth.

What was the purpose of the CIA's brainwashing experiments if not to create mercenary fighters? Let's learn how to redirect the killer instinct of the psychopath. Make something useful out of them.

I didn't want to irritate Barker too much, so I didn't press the subject. I knew he was being incredibly stupid even talking to me. I was waiting for the College of Physicians and Surgeons to deal with my complaint, and Barker knew it. It was reckless of him to communicate with me, but he did anyway. I knew he would reveal something if I just kept him going. I was looking for information, and he was trying to manipulate me.

It almost worked. Near the end of our email correspondence, I asked pointed questions about the Oak Ridge program. Barker claimed he had just found out about my complaint, and his lawyer hit the roof when he learned we were communicating. He said we would have to wait until the OCPP finished with my complaint. Throughout the conversation, I thought Barker was hiding something.

I waited longer than I should for their decision. This time they had to admit the truth about the drugs and the treatment I had received at Oak Ridge. It was right there in my clinical record. But they took no action, because they called it "accepted standards of practice at the time." Convoluted, twisted verbal acrobatics. What was "standard" about LSD or scopolamine? Where was the standard for the "capsule"? There were no standards, no precedent. Everything in Barker's "therapeutic community" was experimental.

I gave up. No point trying to make anyone accountable. Forget about it and get on with building my business and enjoying life.

Then I got a phone call from a CBC reporter. I had talked to her more than a year before. The reporter, Paisley Woodward, had read all of the documents I had collected. She believed something about Oak Ridge was being concealed.

She had tried to pitch my story to CBC producers, but nothing had came of it. Now Paisley said CBC's *National Magazine* with Hana Gartner wanted to pick up the story. The *National Magazine* was a nightly, half-hour documentary broadcast that followed the CBC's national news. Millions of people watched it.

Paisley asked if I was willing to go to Ontario to film the documentary. She said we might even be allowed inside Oak Ridge. It was an opportunity to find accountability using a new approach. If I couldn't find satisfaction any other way, then I'd shout it from the mountaintop.

By that time my plastic fabricating business was becoming very successful. I had lots of clients and a storefront. I was worried about putting my face on national TV, but I had to do it.

52

IN JULY 1997, I FLEW TO TORONTO. BEFORE I LEFT VANCOUVER, I CONTACTED A FEW LAW FIRMS IN Toronto. I made an appointment with a junior partner at one firm. I won't identify him, because he would likely sue me. I'll just call him "JR."

When I arrived in Toronto, I went straight to JR's office and gave him copies of the documents I had collected. He looked mildly interested. When I told him I was there to film a documentary with the CBC about my experience, he became very interested.

We went for lunch to discuss my case. JR pointed to a table full of pinstriped, grey-haired suits at another table.

"I hope I don't wind up looking like them."

Sixteen years later, when I gave up on him and the idea of legal action, he had become one of those empty suits. I'll get to that later.

I gave JR everything I had collected about the Oak Ridge experiment. He told me there was a legal term for my kind of case. It was called a "slam dunk." He took on the case pro bono.

Business was good for my wife and me, but I didn't have money to pay a lawyer. I did give him a thousand dollars just to prove I was committed. It was a legal retainer.

JR knew the case would get publicity. A CBC documentary would be good for a young lawyer. He said he would send a draft statement of claim to me, and then we will see some action. He really was on my side. I was optimistic. I told him it wasn't about money. I didn't want to be compensated. I just wanted Barker, Oak Ridge, and the Ontario government held accountable. I was naïve about those things back then. I didn't realize it's always about money.

The next morning, we drove to Penetanguishene and on to Oak Ridge. This time, I had a TV producer and a camera crew with me. I walked up to the front door and pounded on it. I was there to kick some ass!

I wasn't a patient. They had no control over me, and they didn't like it. Oh, they were polite enough, but it was clear they didn't want publicity, not the sort of attention I was bringing to their front gate, anyway.

I noticed a few cosmetic changes, but the building was as oppressive as ever. Every door and gate made crashing metal on metal noise.

Smell is what triggers memories more than the environment. I can't say exactly what it was. Not a hospital smell. Floor cleaning solvent concealing something old and mouldy. The smell of a hundred years of fear. It was a subliminal smell. Wild animals would recognize it right away. And avoid it. Even so, the place didn't have the same effect if you were not in handcuffs.

I suppose I was too concerned with the camera crew and producer. I knew this was expensive, and I hoped I could give them what they paid for, but I didn't know what they wanted.

The crew was friendly with the staff. Somehow I was separated from the bon vivant. I was an object to be moved into place and filmed. We kept shooting the same things over and over. Walking from one room to another. They wanted me to be natural, like I was walking the halls of my old school.

The shower room. Pure evil cannot be washed away. It was exactly the same except for an attempt at a privacy screen between showerheads. George McCann, their deformed shower room ogre, was probably dead by then, but his evil presence was still there.

I sensed the producer wanted drama. So did I, but I had to hold myself in check. I thought if I let it out, even a little, there will be a confrontation, leaving me unable to continue.

I realized I was doing this for the CBC, not for me.

Then we went to "F" ward. The sun room. I talked about the drugs and the bugs and the demons. An entourage of Oak Ridge staff followed us around. They stood in the doorway watching.

Dr. Marnie Rice was there. I didn't know who she was at the time. On the way out, I thought I saw a tear in her eye. It was significant for me, because it was the first and only time I saw an appropriate emotional response from any staff at Oak Ridge. They always presented themselves as morally superior to their patients. Even when they were so wrong people died.

On to the main attraction: a sit-down meeting with Peter Woodcock. Of course, in 1997, Peter Woodcock no longer existed. He was George Kruger. A shiny, new German name not connected to a child killer. I still didn't understand how someone like Woodcock could change his name. Did his new name carry the weight of his old identity? The child killer? Was the Brotherhood involved? As far as I knew, Peter was not German, but now he had a German name.

They sat me in one of those heavy wooden chairs. Too heavy to pick it up and use as a battering ram.

Two burly guards stood behind me with arms crossed. Two more brought Woodcock into the room. I never would have recognized him. He looked like Mr. Magoo: short, fat, and nearly blind.

The guards walked him right up to my chair. I stood up before he got too close. I sensed the two guards beside me tense up. Did they expect this little creep to attack me?

We shook hands as he leaned in close to my face so he could see me, close enough that I could smell his breath. He smelled like chemicals. I took a step backward.

The entire CBC endeavor was focused on this moment. What did they want me to do? Woodcock was not my friend; he never was. He was a sycophant. No personality of his own, just a mimic of his circumstances.

I acted like I was at a class reunion. All I could do was be polite and make small talk. When he discovered I had been successful in life, he smiled.

"I'm so happy we were able to help you."

I wanted to reach over and punch him in the face! But I had learned my lesson a long time ago about not getting mad in a madhouse. Instead, I showed him the tattoo on my right arm, the same one he still had on his arm. Peter looked at it so closely I was afraid he might try to take a bite out of me.

Two versions of the CBC documentary were aired, one for British Columbia and one nationally. The national version did not include the tattoo scene. I don't know why.

I didn't understand a lot of things about Woodcock/Kruger. The last time I had seen him, he was a child killer. Now he was old, fat, and weak. And he had killed again. This time it was not a child but a fellow mental patient.

Much has been written about Woodcock, but there are huge holes in the narrative. For example, He was adopted by a wealthy family who sent him to private school. Who was the family? Was it Woodcock, Kruger, or something else? Was this wealthy family someone with the power to keep their name out of it?

Anyone who had ever met Woodcock knew he would keep killing as long as he was alive. I knew it, because he told me so, and I believed him.

How did it happen that he was released to Brockville Hospital, "greatly improved"? Whoever made the decision obviously didn't know him as well as I did.

He was released on his first day pass in thirty-four years. His escort took him to a movie. I think it might have been the only movie Woodcock had seen since the silver screen. What movie would be suitable for someone like Woodcock? *Silence of the Lambs,* of course. Hannibal Lecter would be a role model for Peter.

He left the movie, went out, and killed Dennis Kerr. A hatchet to the back of the head, I think it was, proving once again that the opinions and assessments of Oak Ridge were worse than useless.

My meeting with Woodcock came to an end. I sensed the producer's disappointment. They wanted some fireworks, but instead they got a class reunion. They had us surrounded with guards ready to pounce, but nothing happened.

The camera crew, producer, and the entire entourage left Peter and me alone in the visiting room. Were we being watched on hidden camera? Was I bait for another experiment?

I asked him about the Brotherhood and if he could tell me anything new.

"You disappointed my friends and got me in trouble," he said. "I wanted to kill you after that."

I laughed and told him I would twist him into a pretzel if he tried. He laughed, too, but there was no humour in it. I was sure if he thought he could do it; he would have given it a try.

What he didn't know was I had a mini cassette tape recorder in the pocket of my cargo pants. I sat as close to him as possible when he told me he killed more people than anyone would ever know.

"I did it for the Brotherhood. Dennis Kerr was the last hurrah."

The guards came back into the visiting room and took Woodcock to the hole where he spent the rest of his days.

He died on his birthday in 2010.

EPILOGUE

EIGHTEEN YEARS HAVE PASSED SINCE MY LAST ENCOUNTER WITH OAK RIDGE. THE BUILDING IS GONE, pounded into dust but not removed from the memory of those who survived. Burwash and Kingston Penitentiary are also long abandoned.

All my adult life, I thought I would go back to Burwash one day and look at the place. Maybe I could talk to the warden or something, tell him what it was like nearly fifty years ago. Recently, I discovered the place was abandoned a short time after I escaped. Now it's a haunted place, a hiker's destination. No roads lead to it. I found pictures of the window I cut the screen from and escaped out of into the forest. The building still stands, but the paint is peeling off the walls, and the glass from the windows is long gone. I really must go have a look for myself before I or Burwash crumble to dust.

I'm still here. I'm neither a victim or a survivor. I'm just a reminder for future generations. Canada has done things to its own citizens no better than tyrants in third world countries.

It would have been easy to fall into a life of crime and self-destruction. Thankfully, I never went down that path.

When Dr. Barker's knee was in my back holding me to the floor, I knew he was wrong, even if I was the only person in the world who knew it. I knew I was not a psychopath. Even if it took a lifetime, I was determined to prove myself. It made me strong.

Of course, they need to be sued and held accountable in a court of law. I tried, but the system does not work in favour of people like me. I didn't realize how extensive the Oak Ridge cover-up went until I looked closer. This is not a rant by a disgruntled client. Lawyers do what they do. I learned a lot about the process in sixteen years.

I want to talk about "conspiracy theories." Yes, that label will discredit anyone before they start. Let's define the term. "Conspiracy," two or more people get together in secrecy to plan or conceal something that might be illegal or immoral.

We know that never happens.

"Theory," an idea or thought or principle that has not yet been proven by empirical evidence.

Two perfectly reasonable words. One a legal term and the other a scientific term. Put them together, and it's an invective or pejorative accusation designed to discredit.

I have talked with serious journalists with a reputation who are afraid of the term. I'm not.

Was Peter Woodcock part of a mysterious German conspiracy? Were my brother and I targeted from a young age? All I can say for certain is Woodcock introduced me to his friends, and they, in turn, introduced me to others.

I heard about Operation Paperclip (the secret employment of German scientists, engineers and technicians following World War II) decades before it became a "conspiracy theory."

Hugh Morrison introduced me to a death squad truck driver in Guatemala.

Does an international human trafficking conspiracy exist? I can't prove it does, but there is a common thread that runs through my life.

I was injected with scopolamine in Burwash. That resulted in a pointless prison escape that led me straight back to Oak Ridge. Was that a conspiracy?

My apartment building was burned down on January 1, 1980. Let me take a moment to something this clear. The Angus apartment was a landmark building, but in my research for this book, I could not find one picture of the building or the five-alarm fire. All I could find was one reference to the "landmark" building in an obscure, digitized Prince George newspaper. Otherwise, I could not even prove the building ever existed. Was it a conspiracy?

Matt Lamb was a conspiracy. I'm sure of it. Wikipedia is unreliable at best, but it has an article about Lamb. Understand that Wikipedia can be and is altered and edited all the time. When I first read Lamb's biography I was surprised to find no mention of him going to Israel direct from Barker's farm. Barker himself told me in our email exchange, "With his (Lamb) Israeli bonds and my encouragement he went to Israel where he fought in the Yom Kippur war."

I emailed the author of this Wikipedia story. I asked, "So, Matt Lamb never joined the IDF?" He didn't reply, but shortly afterwards, the story was edited. Oddly enough, the exact phrase Barker used was added. The new version went on to say Lamb hitchhiked to the front line of the war, where he was rejected by the IDF because of his background. The good thing about Wikipedia is you can go back and read previous versions before it was revised.

One more thing. The author of this Wikipedia article, who calls himself "Cliftonian," also removed a photo of Lamb proudly wearing his IDF uniform. I can understand why the IDF does not want it to be known they were recruiting psychopathic ex-mental patients.

Just a few oddities. There's more but let's not delve too far into conspiracy theories lest I discredit myself.

Now, what about my "slam dunk" lawsuit?

A few months after the CBC documentary, I received a draft copy of a statement of claim naming Dr. Barker and the Ontario Government as defendants. We were suing for a total of twelve million dollars. The statement of claim also named the CIA as conducting similar experiments, a point already proven in another court settlement.

I wasn't moved by the thought of a multimillion dollar settlement. The dollars were not the point. Our plastic fabricating business was doing well. We were making our own way. I was just happy my story was being taken seriously. I wasn't a nutcase babbling about some conspiracy theory. I had a team of lawyers and well-documented evidence. What could go wrong? How could they deny it happened? A law court and a jury of my peers was not the same as the College of Physicians and Surgeons or the Health Professions Board. It would be over quickly.

A year went by, and nothing happened. My lawyer called and told me he had left his law firm and started his own practice. Did I want to go with him or stay with the original firm?

I went with him. Then I found out he had placed an advertisement in a Toronto newspaper soliciting other Oak Ridge patients for a class action suit. I thought his first obligation was to represent me.

He asked if I wanted to be the lead case in this class action suit. I did not want that, and I made my preferences clear. I was not part of a class of child murderers, rapists, and bad actors. I could just imagine what might happen with a big financial settlement in the hands of Oak Ridge patients. I was never part of that class and would not be associated with them. I should not have been in Oak Ridge in the first place. My case went forward independent of the class action suit.

The boardroom meetings that took place between lawyers in cases like this continued. We were up against Canada's biggest law firm, McCarthy Tetrault, which represents the Government of Ontario. To my understanding, they were prepared to settle out of court. But when they found out my lawyer had turned it into a class action suit, they hit the roof. Those are the exact words my lawyer told me. They let him know from the beginning they would not settle with me and they would do everything to delay and fight my case.

And they did exactly that. Every detail, every motion, every court procedure was resisted. Year after year, they tried to wear me down. It started to look like I was the defendant, not Barker or the Ontario government. How many times did I have to travel across Canada to attend some useless and unnecessary hearing? Three times over a period of more than ten years I had to be interviewed and assessed by a psychiatrist, twice by our expert witness and once by the opposition's expert witness. Barker, the defendant, was never assessed.

I must admit that although I don't like psychiatrists and don't much trust the profession, I did like our expert witness psychiatrist, Dr. Brian Hoffman. In our second meeting, separated from the first by almost ten years, I asked why Barker would do such things as he did to me. His reply was simple and to the point: "Because he's nuts." It wasn't how one psychiatrist usually talked about another.

We even discussed the CIA's brainwashing experiments in the 1950s and 1960s, known collectively as MK-Ultra. Dr. Hoffman made it clear in his written report that I was not paranoid that I was merely exploring the similarities with the Oak Ridge experiments.

The opposition's "expert witness" psychiatrist was another thing entirely. I don't understand why my lawyers would allow the opposition's psychiatrist to assess me without counsel. Again, I wasn't the one on trial, but she was belligerent, rude, and antagonistic, deliberately trying to elicit some sort of angry response. That's what she was paid to do. I knew better than to react to such transparent provocation.

Our interview took place inside the locked doors of the Queen Street Forensic Psychiatry unit, an intimidating place chosen to make me feel vulnerable without a lawyer by my side. I was required to do a battery of psychometric tests inside a locked room, just like in Oak Ridge.

The tests were pure bullshit, in my opinion. Over five hundred questions. The print was too small for someone my age, and the questions were almost entirely age-based. They were essentially "what I want to be when I grow up" and not at all relevant to a mature man, but I had to do it under threat from my own lawyers. If I refused, the case could be dismissed. I began to think my lawyers weren't representing me. Their real agenda was the class action case.

Even if I was a raving lunatic, what would that have to do with the reason for my lawsuit? Most of the others in the class action were still locked up in prisons or mental hospitals. Did they have to go through the same ordeal as me?

I learned something about "expert witnesses" during that experience. He who pays the piper calls the tune.

One example will suffice. Their psychiatrist asked if I had ever lost my driver's licence for DWI. In her report to the court she wrote, "He claims" to have not. You see, the facts were not the point. In her presentation, it was just my "claim." She found it so hard to be nice to me but so easy to mischaracterize everything I said.

When I left her office, she unlocked the door and said, "You're free to go," as if it were up to her to decide whether or not I was free.

More years went past, and nothing moved forward.

In 2009, we closed our business in Vancouver and bought a house in the country. For a while, we ran a bed and breakfast and went sailing. Soon, I realized I wasn't a B&B sort of guy. I needed a workshop. I needed to make things and sell them. I turned the B&B cottage into a shop and went back to being Plasticsmith Inc.

In 2010, my lawyer advised me that I should settle with the Ontario Government and concentrate on going after Barker. I was doubtful, because I thought Oak Ridge was the government's responsibility, and Barker worked for them. Against my own judgement, I went along with his advice. I signed the paper and agreed not to disclose the amount of the settlement. I can tell you this though: It was paltry and thin to say the least.

And then came the turning of the screws, something the lawyers called a "bifurcated hearing." My lawyers wanted the entire settlement I had received from the Ontario Government, every dime, or they would not represent me at that hearing. Without legal representation, I would surely lose whatever motion the opposition put forward. I would also become liable for Barker's legal costs, and the case would be dismissed. They had me in a corner.

After sixteen years of delays and manipulation, it was clear to me. I was done with it. I couldn't risk my life's work to keep the case going, and I was not going to hand over the settlement just to help with disbursements in their class action. I gave up. I dropped my claim against Barker and walked away from it.

Then came another poke in the eye with a sharp stick. The lawyers took more than half the settlement I had reached reluctantly with the government. Again, I can't tell you the dollar amount, but what was left was just enough to take a short vacation to Japan.

I'm not bitter about it. I know the difference between wrong and right. Everything turned out right for my wife and me. We have done well on our own, and we are happy.

I haven't followed the case, but I believe the class action was de-certified. I doubt it will ever make it to court.

I sleep well at night knowing my occupation as a small business owner is respected.

As for Barker, he's an old man with a sketchy professional reputation. And he has a lot to answer for.

I hope he can feel my knee in his back.

APPENDIX

CANADA

The Secretary of State for External Affairs of Canada requests, in the name of Her Majesty the Queen, all those whom it may concern to allow the bearer to pass freely without let or hindrance and to afford the bearer such assistance and protection as may be necessary.

Le Secrétaire d'État aux Affaires extérieures du Canada, au nom de Sa Majesté la Reine, prie les Autorités intéressées de bien vouloir accorder libre passage au titulaire de ce passeport, de même que les facilités et la protection dont il aurait besoin.

THIS PASSPORT IS THE PROPERTY OF THE GOVERNMENT OF CANADA

CE PASSEPORT APPARTIENT AU GOUVERNEMENT DU CANADA

PHOTOGRAPH OF BEARER
PHOTOGRAPHIE DU TITULAIRE

FOR OFFICIAL USE ONLY
RÉSERVÉ À L'ADMINISTRATION

(Signature of bearer · Signature du titulaire)

6 VISAS

It is the responsibility of the bearer to obtain necessary visas.

Il incombe au titulaire d'obtenir les visas requis.

CONSULADO GENERAL DE NICARAGUA
GUATEMALA

VISA No. A608
Buena para dirigirse a *Nicaragua*
Ron un solo Viaje
VALIDA POR 60 DIAS
Tlo *libre*
Guatemala, *3 de mayo de 1980*

DELEGACION MIGRACION GUASAULE
Permanencia por treinta dias como turista
Sin autorización para trabajar
5 ABR. 1980

7 VISAS

Visitors Permit To Belize
From 21/1/80
To 4/2/80
Prime Officer

BELIZE Immigration Dept
DATE 5.2.80
DEPARTURE
Belize Western Border Station

KETCHIKAN, Alaska (AP) — Only a light sheen of oil was left on the water's surface when the capsized ore carrier Lee Wang Zin plunged without warning Tuesday to a 300-metre-deep grave at the bottom of the Gulf of Alaska, officials said.

There still was no trace of 28 missing crew members when the 225-metre freighter, being towed to a spot 110 kilometres off the southern tip of Alaska, sank suddenly about 35 kilometres west of Dall Island. The cause of the sinking was not known.

The ship, which spilled 100,000 gallons of fuel when it overturned Christmas Day near the Queen Charlotte Islands in a violent storm, had been en route to Japan from Prince Rupert, B.C., with a load of iron.

The bodies of two of the ship's 30 Taiwanese crew members were found before the search for survivors was halted. Personnel aboard the Salvage Chief, which had the Lee Wang Zin in tow, and the accompanying U.S. Coast Guard cutter Munro said the ship went down in about a minute.

The coast guard had planned to take the freighter to a point west of Dall Island and use either shells from the Munro's five-inch gun or explosives to rip open the hull and send the ship plunging almost 2.5 kilometres to the floor of an ocean canyon.

Franklin said water currents carried much of the leaked oil into the rivers inside Alaska.

Landmark destroyed by fire

VANCOUVER (CP) — A downtown Vancouver landmark, the Angus Apartments adjacent to the mansion built by Rogers Sugar founder B. T. Rogers, was destroyed by fire Tuesday night.

All the occupants of the three-storey brick building in the city's West End were believed to have been safely evacuated but an elderly woman was reported treated at hospital for smoke inhalation.

The Angus was built in 1914 and the original Rogers' mansion, now designated a heritage site, dates from 1901. Dominion Construction owns both the Angus and the mansion, which is under lease to Hy Ainsenstat, founder of the Hy's restaurant chain.

Witnesses said firemen poured a steady stream of water on the apartment to keep the fire away from the mansion.

Cause of the fire was not immediately known.

Ontario

Ministry of the Attorney General

Office of the Public Trustee

416/362-1331

145 Queen Street West
Toronto, Ontario
M5H 2N8

May 20, 1980.

Administrator,
Penetang Mental Health Centre,
Penetanguishene, Ontario.

Re: Steven Herbert Smith, 078838-4

Dear Sir/Madam:

Our records indicate the above-named was discharged or transferred from the Penetang Mental Health Centre. If this information is correct, it would be most appreciated if a Discharge or Transfer Notice could be completed and forwarded to the Public Trustee for the completion of our file.

When forwarding the Discharge or Transfer Notice for this patient, would you kindly notate same "Special Project - Records Section".

Thank you for your assistance herein.

Yours very truly,

E. L. Cowan for

D. B. Stascu,
Records Department Supervisor.

my

DEPARTMENT OF HEALTH FOR ONTARIO
MENTAL HEALTH BRANCH

O.H. Penetang Psychiatric Hospital

CLINICAL RECORD

CASE No. 2094 N
HOSPITAL INSURANCE

NAME SMITH, Steven
(surname)   (Christian names)

CERTIFICATE No.

December 16, 1968 (D.E.Roszmann, M.S.W.--sw)   Progress Note
On December the 12th this person was seen by the Review Board, which body decided that he should be discharged back into the community. As a result of this, arrangements were made for Mr. Smith to call a friend (Mr. Karl Wielanb in Toronto--phone number area code 416-4659776) so as to make arrangements for rehabilitation. Apparently, Mr. Wieland is going to assist our patient in finding a place and employment.

It was the opinion of the staff of this hospital that Mr. Smith would benefit from further treatment then what he received. However, under the present circumstances Mr. Smith is being discharged (by the Review Board) and a friend is planning his rehabilitation. Nevertheless, it is the general feeling of staff that Mr. Smith will at some point be returning to this hospital as a patient.

DEPARTMENT OF HEALTH FOR ONTARIO
MENTAL HEALTH BRANCH

O.H. Penetang

CLINICAL RECORD

CASE No. 2094N
HOSPITAL INSURANCE
CERTIFICATE No.

NAME SMITH, (surname) Steven (Christian names)

July 8th, 1968. (B. Mason - hw)

This 19 year old male was admitted to H ward from the F ward "Training Unit" on June 26, 1968. His behaviour on F ward fluctuated from a hostile unco-operative to negativistic attitude to one of a warm, co-operative and positive nature. He was considered a good student who had much potential for dissruptive manipulations. Patient spoke his mind and communicated to others honestly and openly, but this was a consequence of his training program.

Since his transfer to H ward, patient has been quite co-operative and is motivated to partake of the ward's social therapy program. At present he is working in the Industrial Therapy Shop and is a member of the Clarification #1 Committee. Patient has established a quick and deep relationship with patient Peter Woodcock and they are rarely seen apart from one another. Because of their physical resemblance, much identification has taken place especially for patient Woodcock. Steve has spent some time in Yorkville and is reflecting the image that is part of the "hippy syndrome". Patient Woodcock has been fascinated with Steve's focade and is attempting to project the same.

Steve's behaviour on the ward has been satisfactory and he is adjusting to the ward program quite well. His present medication is Noziran 25mg. I.M. q 1 h. P.R.N.

B. Mason, Social Worker.

August 21, 1968. (W. Elrick, Surgery Attendant - dm) Surgery Note
Examination of chest for possible aspiration of ribs. This patient choked last evening with violent coughing resulting in left chest pain. Slight elevation of temperature. Examination of Symptomaloloty negative today. No Pyrexia.

Oct. 8, 1968 (Dr. E.T. Barker - e.l.)   RENEWAL NOTE
This patient's Involuntary Certificate was to-day renewed for a further 6 months.

DEPARTMENT OF HEALTH FOR ONTARIO
MENTAL HEALTH BRANCH

O.H. PENETANGUISHENE
PAGE
CASE No. 2094N
HOSPITAL INSURANCE

CLINICAL RECORD

NAME SMITH, Steven
(surname)   (Christian names)
CERTIFICATE No.

April 29, 1968. (W. Elrick, Surgery Attendant - Jm.)
Given Gravol 100 mgs. I.M. at 8:00 a.m. This patient to have extra juice today only, orders of Dr. MacVittie. Given physical examination. Blood taken for routine blood count and liver function test by Dr. MacVittie.

May 7, 1968. (W. Elrick, Surgery Attendant - Jm.)
Given Scopolomine grs. 1/75th intravenously at 9:30 a.m. and 10:00 a.m.

*Sun room
Compressed
Encounter
Therapy*

May 9, 1968. (W. Elrick, Surgery Attendant - Jm.)
Given Dexidrene Spansules 30 mgs. caps 2 at h.s.

May 10, 1968. (W. Elrick, Surgery Attendant - Jm.)
Given Dexidrene Spansules 15 mgs. caps 2 at h.s.

April 28, 1968. Excerpt from Daily Ward Report - Jm.
Had what appeared to be a weak spell and fell flat to the floor, striking his face and causing a nose bleed. Attended to by Dr. Mackay. During the afternoon he complained of having a headache and feeling nauseated and was observed vomiting after supper. T 98, P 90, R 20. Patient rested quietly during the evening and appeared to be sleeping all night.

May 14, 1968. (W. Elrick, Surgery Attendant - Jm.)
Given Methidrene 30 mgs. I.M. at 1:30 p.m.

May 16, 1968. (W. Elrick, Surgery Attendant - Jm.)
Given Scopolomine grs. 1/75th per hypo at 12:45 and 1:45 p.m. Given Methidrene 30 mgs. I.M. at 2:45 p.m.

May 17, 1968. (W. Elrick, Surgery Attendant - Jm.)
Given Hyacine Hydrobromide grs. 1/75th per hypo at 10:45 a.m. and 12:15 p.m. and 2:45 p.m. Given Prostigmine tabs 2 at 11:00 a.m. Given Methidrene 15 mgs. I.M. at 1:15 p.m.

May 19, 1968. (W. Elrick, Surgery Attendant - Jm.)
Given Dexidrene 30 mgs. caps 2 at h.s.

May 22, 1968. (W. Elrick, Surgery Attendant - Jm.)
Given Methidrene 30 mgs. I.M. at 1:00 p.m.

May 22, 1968. (W. Elrick, Surgery Attendant - Jm.)
Received Dexamyl Spansules #2, caps 2 at 9:00 p.m.

May 24, 1968. (W. Elrick, Surgery Attendant - Jm.)
Given Methidrene 30 mgs. intravenously by Dr. Barker at 12:45 p.m.

May 25, 1968. (W. Elrick, Surgery Attendant - Jm.)
Given Dexidrene Spansules caps 2, 30mgs, at 10:15 p.m.

May 26, 1968. (W. Elrick, Surgery Attendant - Jm.)
Given Dexidrene Spansules caps 2, 30 mgs., at 10:20 p.m.

Form 127
IBM 67-4707

I never told you, but then you never asked, but I was raised in and through the life and fellowship of the Church! I even spent a summer on the mission field for the United Church when I was 19 - possibly a better summer than you had at 19, but I'm not sure of that. Any way I had a circuit of 7 different preaching points in and around Hearst, north of Kapuskasing and south along the Algoma Central. The most memorable occasion was preaching the same sermon to the same congregation two weeks in a row, and getting the sickening realization of it about 2/3rds the way thru the 2nd time. They were very kind. Said they got much more out of it the 2nd time. More sobering was having to take charge of the burial of a small child.

Anyway, back to the Bible.

No, a brief digression. I became an atheist after that summer and fought with everybody about the existence of God. Then I mellowed into Humanism - was even asked to speak at a Conference run by the Humanist Association of Canada, and if you've studied my resume (ha) you'd see the Humanist in Canada (HIC) even published one of my articles. More recently I've become a Post Modern Deconstructionist and if you can explain that to me in plain English you're even smarter than I already think you are.

Back to the Bible as they say. I'm sure you must have heard of it. And the New Testament? Ring a bell? Maththew, Mark, Kuke, and John - right through to Revelations.

Well my trusty old bible just happened to fall open on the floor the other day and land open at the Book of Revelations, actually Chapter 23. And when I looked at it - God, who is dead, must have inspired me to - I read Verses 1 to 4 and thought immediately that they must be prophetic about you and I. Sort of like you thought Thoreau was talking right to you. So here are verses 1-4.

For in the days of my youth he didn't torment me
And cast me into the fires of hell
Wherin I smouldered and burned these 30 long years.

And then I cried out to him in my pain
Thou hast haunted me these 30 long years!
I can find no other way.
We must speak.

And verily verily I say unto you,
That as we spoke, the Devil himself
Came down from his mighty throne
And began to enter into my heart, and me in his
And the fires began to die down.

Six hundred and sixty-six days we talked
Him with me and me with him
And verily verily I say unto you
When we met, his face to mine, and my face to his
And he clasp my hand and I clasped his
And I looked in his eye and he in mine
The pain was no more.

As I used to say when I was 19:
Here endeth the lesson and may God add His blessing to this reading of His holy word. Amen, amen and amen.

No pictures yet. Did you actually send pictures of yourself or ones of someone with a physique to match your mind.

And have you gotten Psychopathy and Consumerism yet? Guess not, were still talking! Remember, you gotta plod through The Juvenile Justice System and the Helping Professions. it's right up your alley. And read it first, before the journal makes you so mad you can't see!

Cheers

Elliott